A Social History of Anthropology
in the United States

A Social History of Anthropology in the United States

Thomas C. Patterson

BERG

Oxford • New York

First published in 2001 by
Berg
Editorial offices:
150 Cowley Road, Oxford, OX4 1JJ, UK
838 Broadway, Third Floor, New York, NY 10003-4812, USA

Berg is an imprint of Oxford International Publishers Ltd.

Library of Congress Cataloging-in-Publication Data
A catalog record for this book is available from the Library of Congress.

British Library Cataloguing-in-Publication Data
A catalogue record for this book is available from the British Library.

ISBN 1 85973 489 8 (Cloth)
1 85973 494 4 (Paper)

Typeset by JS Typesetting, Wellingborough, Northants.
Printed in the United Kingdom by Biddles Ltd, Guildford and King's Lynn.

For Wendy and Antonio

Contents

Preface

This book had its origins in a series of conversations I had with Antonio Lauria-Perricelli that date back to the late 1980s. Both of us were teaching history of anthropology courses and were dissatisfied with the books we were using. In our view, they did not refer to the social and political contexts in which anthropology was born and nurtured in the United States, and they certainly did not address how anthropologists as active agents fit into and helped to shape those contexts. We planned to write a book together. We drafted an outline and divided tasks; however, the unforeseen exigencies of everyday life made it impossible for him to continue the project. As a result, preparing the manuscript and getting it ready for publication became my responsibility. Nonetheless, Antonio continued to provide encouragement and advice as I wrote, and many of his suggestions were incorporated into the manuscript. This book is dedicated in part to him.

My theoretical perspective was forged in the crucible of politics in the United States from the mid-1950s onward. I was appalled by the racism, xenophobia, and censorship rampant in the country; I was inspired by the civil rights movement at home and by anticolonial movements that gained renewed vigor and swept across the world in the wake of the Second World War. Fieldwork in Peru in the early 1960s exposed me to a wide range of writers whose works I had not read before. Like many of my contemporaries, I began to read Mao Zedong, Amílcar Cabral, Frantz Fanon and Jomo Kenyatta among others; European social critics such as Jean-Paul Sartre, Simone de Beauvoir or Herbert Marcuse as well as anthropological colleagues from Europe and Latin America. From the early 1960s onward, I also began to read social theorists from the past – John Locke, Jean-Jacques Rousseau, Karl Marx, Frederick Engels, Herbert Spencer, Charles Darwin, Max Weber, Émile Durkheim and Sigmund Freud to name only a few – whose views get recycled, reinterpreted and reused each generation.

One of the goals in writing this book was to examine how such diverse sources of inspiration were brought together and deployed by anthropologists in one country – the United States – which arguably has more professional anthropologists today than any other place in the world. While the particular form of U.S. anthropology is more or less unique for historical reasons, the building blocks on which it rests are not; the latter are also used by anthropologists in countries as diverse as England, the former Soviet Union, Peru, India or Senegal. Anthropologists – such as Franz Boas or Bronislaw Malinowski – are known professionally throughout the world, yet their reputations in different countries often rest on different aspects of their work. For example, Boas's ethnographic work among the Inuit (Eskimo) or the Kwakiutl is probably cited more frequently in Canada than his papers on racism and immigration which were centrally important in the United States. Malinowski's studies of culture are probably better known in the United States than his formulations of colonial policy which dominated anthropological and political discussions in England during the 1930s.

Another goal was a restorative one. The contributions of many anthropologists were downplayed or not mentioned at all because of government crackdowns on the Left, especially in the 1920s and again in the years following the Second World War when various investigative agencies hounded some political activists and kept files on many thousands of others. This goal was not hagiographic. It was not my aim to write an account of the lives of anthropologists who were persecuted for their political activism. Nor was it my aim to relate the actions of anthropologists who sought to drive colleagues and students from the profession. These are chapters in the history of U.S. anthropology that remain to be written.

A third goal was to show that the production of anthropological knowledge is a dialectical process. It is shaped by what the world is and who the anthropologists and the diverse peoples they study are. Anthropologists in the United States have never come from a single background and have never held a single position on important issues. They have argued and continue to argue about the significance of how people relate to one another, of what factors shape their lives and how they have made or not made their own histories. This has become complicated in recent years by virtue of the fact that the peoples they study also have thoughts about these questions which differ from those held by some anthropologists and that these peoples are now participating in and contributing to those discussions.

Over the years, I have benefited from conversations with a number of anthropological colleagues and friends, living and deceased: Stanley Diamond, Eric Wolf, Eleanor Leacock, Bill Roseberry, Connie Sutton, John Gledhill, Christine Gailey, Karen Brodkin, Faye Harrison, Gavin Smith, Ida Susser, Don Nonini, Peter Gran, Kathy Walker, Gordon Willey, Frank Spencer, John Stinson-Fernández, Judy Goode, Richard Lee, Lee Baker, Jeff Maskovsky, Michael Kearney, Carole Nagengast, Carole Crumley, Peter Schmidt, Bob Paynter, David Price, William Peace, Carlos Vélez Ibáñez, and Eugene Anderson. I thank all of them for their help, support, and inspiration. I also want to thank my students at Temple University; we talked and listened to one another, and I learned so much from them.

Kathryn Earle, my editor at Berg, continues to provide sound advice, encouragement, and support. She remains simply the best editor I have ever worked with.

I particularly want to acknowledge the steady encouragement, detailed comments and instantaneous feedback of Wendy Ashmore – my partner in life, my co-*bon-vivant,* who makes me smile. This book is also dedicated to her.

Introduction

This book is concerned with the historical development of anthropology in the United States. The roots of anthropology lie in the eye-witness accounts of travelers who have journeyed to lands on the margins of state-based societies and described their cultures and in the efforts of individuals who have analyzed the information collected. In the late 1960s and early 1970s, a number of anthropologists – e.g. Kathleen Gough (1968a, 1968b), Dell Hymes (1969), Talal Asad (1973) and Stanley Diamond (1969, 1974) among others – recognized that the practice of anthropology was intimately linked to commerce and colonial expansion. In their view, anthropology appears during episodes of class and state formation created by conquest abroad and repression at home. One anthropologist described it as the study of people in crisis by people in crisis. Both the anthropologists and the groups they studied are in crisis, but how they experience that crisis may differ because they occupy different places in the structures of power created by imperialist civilization (Diamond 1974:93).

The relationships between anthropologists and the communities they study have changed and will continue to do so because of the contradictions and problems inherent in development of society on an increasingly world scale. While anthropologists cannot prevent change from taking place, they have regularly chosen sides in the struggles that ensued. For myriad reasons, anthropologists have not always taken the same side. Not all anthropologists have related in the same way to civilization or to the processes of class and state formation linked with colonial expansion.

Some have been ardent boosters of the new social hierarchies forged by conquest and repression. They have claimed that the cultural practices of the ruling classes are civilized, refined, and superior, and that those of the less powerful classes at home and the uncivilized communities on the margins of the colonial state are crude and inferior. They have portrayed the rise of civilization in terms of a theory of history that depicts a series of progressive changes, the civilizing process, from an original, primitive condition to more advanced, diversified circumstances. They have identified the conquest of nature, material improvement, and increasing modernity as motors driving these changes. They have provided historical accounts of the development of stratified societies characterized by the rule of law and the demise of tradition. They have sought to explain how existing power relations came to be and why they are legitimate.

Other anthropologists have been critics of imperialist civilization. They have argued that the egalitarian relations and practices which exist in cultures on the margins exhibit what is essential to the human condition – an essence that was lost or deformed during the civilizing process. These critics have recognized that the civilizing process is fraught with contradictions. They have condemned the way civilizations have dealt with colonial subjects and the subordinated classes in their own countries. They have indicted the genocidal and ethnocidal practices of imperial states. They have surveyed the contradictions that accompany the development of imperialist civilization – growing inequities coupled with steadily increasing alienation, immiseration, and the repression of desire. They have also explored the differences between civilized and uncivilized peoples to show the barbarism of both the civilizing process and civilization itself.

From this perspective, the study of anthropology is a dialectical process. It is shaped by what the world is and who the anthropologists and the diverse peoples they study are. The three are joined together by structures and practices of domination and subordination whose appearances do not always convey the full extent of their reality. To understand the changing positions and interrelations of the anthropologists and the communities they study in the structures that organize the world, it is essential to know what those structures are, how they came to be, and how they are changing. It is also essential to realize that people and anthropologists who have different positions in these structures of power see the world differently. As a result, a knowledge of the whole is a precursor for a fuller understanding of the parts.

Anthropologists recognize that historically constituted cultural, social, linguistic, and occasionally physical differences are significant for understanding human groups. The discipline's discontinuous history in time and space accounts for the contradictory claims that situate its origins variously in Classical Greece, Renaissance Italy, 16th-century Spain, Europe in the Enlightenment (late 18th century) or the Age of Imperialism (1870–1914). The authors of anthropological reports and the compilers who organized the data they collected were state employees who provided information about subject populations that would facilitate political control; others collected or used this information to criticize state-based societies and their practices toward colonial subjects and their own subordinated classes.

The various perspectives on the origins of anthropology have two things in common. One is that each period was a time marked by geographical expansion when people came into contact with strangers. They asked questions about the activities, beliefs, and languages of these groups and sought material evidence that would shed light on their social and biological histories. The second was that they acknowledged the importance and significance of cultural and social differences.

This study of the historical development of anthropology in the United States examines (1) the circumstances that facilitated the formation of anthropology first as a set of questions and practices and then as a discipline; (2) the shifting social and political-economic conditions in which anthropological knowledge has been produced, shaped, and deployed; (3) the appearance of practices centered in particular regions or groups; (4) anthropology's place in structures of power; and (5) the profession's role in creating and perpetuating images of past and contemporary peoples.

Organization of the Book

Chapter 1 examines the development of anthropology in the New Republic from the time of the Revolutionary War to the end of Reconstruction. It argues that anthropological information was used to shed light on pressing issues – forging a national identity, territorial expansion, and justifying slavery. The ethnographic, linguistic, and antiquarian descriptions of travelers, missionaries, settlers, and officials in the Indian territories buttressed claims of American exceptionalism, and allegations of racial differences were used to justify slavery and the removal of native peoples from their homelands. Jefferson and others in the American Philosophical Society studied Indian languages to discover their interrelations and connections with Old World peoples. The complex nineteenth-century discourse about race involved a number of issues: Was humankind a single species? Was there a hierarchy of races? Should the races intermingle or be separated? Were culture and biology fixed and immutable? In the 1870s, anthropologists became increasingly concerned with the development of civilization in general and of American Indian societies in particular. Local and national organizations such as the American Ethnological Society and the Smithsonian Institution were founded and published the results of anthropological inquiries.

Chapter 2 explores American anthropology in the Liberal Age, 1879–1929. The discipline was professionalized in the late nineteenth century – a time of intense discrimination against people of color, immigrants, women, and the poor. The discipline's center of gravity shifted in the early 1900s from the federal government (the Bureau of Ethnology and the National Museum) which was concerned mainly with Indian tribes in the West, to universities (Columbia, Harvard, University of California Berkeley at first) that offered advanced degrees and controlled professional certification. Their graduates were employed by the federal government, new colleges, and museums established by philanthropists after *c.* 1880. A struggle over the identity and direction of the field developed in the early 1900s between cultural determinists, eugenicists, and those who emphasized the biological bases of human diversity; it was played out in the National Research Council's Committee on Anthropology and was partially resolved in the 1920s. A number of anthropologists from the time of James Mooney, Franz Boas, Ruth Benedict, and William Jones onward were either members of stigmatized groups (immigrants, women, and American Indians), critics of the class structure and policies of American society, or both.

Chapter 3 deals with the United States during the Depression and the Second World War, 1929–1945. Many anthropologists were employed by New Deal agencies during the Depression and by wartime agencies that valued their holistic understanding of other cultures. Archaeological projects provided employment for thousands of men and women during the Depression. National Research Council and Social Science Research Council (SSRC) initiatives fueled interdisciplinary studies of the psychological consequences of acculturation and assimilation from the late 1920s onwards. Anthropologists were prominent in the formation of area studies programs in the 1930s. As war approached, explorations of the intersection of culture and personality were replaced by the national-character studies later used by the military. During this period, anthropologists challenged dominant racialist and eugenicist discourses in American society, and Black anthropologists employed outside the profession confronted Myrdal's *American Dilemma*. New philanthropies – such as the SSRC – promoted the vision of an interdisciplinary social science that would solve the world's ills.

Chapter 4 examines the expansion and transformation of anthropology in the United States during the period of sustained economic growth following the Second World War. Anthropology was reorganized in the late 1940s to exploit federal research funding and opportunities created by the GI Bill of Rights and the expansion of higher education. Working-class individuals entered the profession in large numbers and participated in its internationalization. Optimistic assessments about American hegemony and the sustained growth of its industries rekindled interest in theories of cultural evolution. Ideologies of anticommunism at home and national liberation movements abroad fueled the development of modernization theory and the construction of a Cold War anthropology underwritten by the Ford and Rockefeller foundations and the Fulbright program. Anthropological inquiry shifted from the study of tribal to that of peasant communities, and even to that of whole nations. The political center of the profession split in the late 1960s over the involvement of U.S. anthropologists in Pentagon-funded counter-insurgency research in Southeast Asia and local-level politics in Latin America. For a time, a significant portion of U.S. society realized that other cultures were different and that it was no longer possible to pretend that human history could be understood exclusively from the perspective of the West. As anthropologists grappled with the concerns of decolonization and the Black civil rights and women's movements, Marxist perspectives reappeared after being forced underground in the 1950s.

Chapter 5 surveys the transformation of the profession since the mid-1970s. Economic restructuring, privatization, and declining support for higher education formed the backdrop for this change. U.S. anthropologists increasingly viewed the world in terms of a global system in which their own society was linked to those of their traditional subjects by an increasingly internationalized economy, immigration, tourism, consumption, and media. Foundations, think tanks, and the World Bank promoted neoliberal theory and projects through research support and fellowships. In the wake of the neoliberal assault on the social sciences, there was a hardening of theoretical divisions within the discipline. Some retreated from analyses of social class structures and organized resistance movements into self-reflexivity and idealist perspectives associated with postmodernism. Others gravitated toward cultural studies with its emphases on texts, styles, and discourse analysis. Still others embraced uncritically the idea that we live in a global post-industrial, capitalist society increasingly composed of individuals who no longer belong to communities that are capable of organized political action. In spite of this apparent fragmentation of approaches, American anthropologists continue to address issues of import to the wider society.

The study sheds light on the social history of anthropology in the United States. Unlike internalist accounts of the field, it situates that history in the changing social, cultural, and political-economic circumstances of U.S. society as a whole. It considers the historical conditions that have permitted the existence of the discipline as well as the circumstances in which anthropological knowledge has been produced. It shows that the contradictions in the knowledge produced by U.S. anthropologists refract divisions in the wider society.

–1–

Anthropology in the New Republic, 1776–1879

The anthropological tradition that developed in the United States in the wake of the Revolutionary War was shaped by three overriding concerns: creating a national identity, episodic westward expansion and settlement in the Indian territories, and consolidating a slave-based economy in the southern states. Since the American writers who produced this tradition were themselves products of a milieu shaped by colonial expansion and the rise of industrial capitalism, they were already quite familiar with the arguments of the European advocates and critics of those circumstances.

The Americans read the same books, were familiar with the same bodies of social thought, and participated in the same debates as their contemporaries in Europe. This meant that they variously drew inspiration from the Bible as a source of historical information, from writers who proclaimed the immaturity or degeneration of the New World and its inhabitants, and from Enlightenment writers who argued that human society had progressed through a succession of different modes of subsistence culminating in the commercialism of an emerging capitalist civilization. It also meant that the Americans held a range of opinions about the nature, diversity, and history of humanity. Like many of their contemporaries, they tended to see peoples or nations distinguished from one another by differences of language, custom, and physical condition.

The Early Republic, 1776–1838

In the wake of the Revolution, it was imperative for the Americans to assert not only their national identity but also their capacity to develop a civil and political society that was morally superior to those of the European countries. At the same time, they had to refute the arguments of eighteenth-century writers – such as the influential French naturalist, Georges Louis Leclerc, the Comte de Buffon (1707–88) – who asserted the inferiority of the New World, its inhabitants and their societies. Buffon and his followers raised a political question of vital importance. Would the American experiment fail because of the obstructions imposed by nature? It was essential for the American envoys – such as Benjamin Franklin (1706–90), James Madison (1751–1836) or Thomas Jefferson (1743–1826) – to refute Buffon and his followers in the 1770s and 1780s if they were to obtain sorely needed financial assistance and credit in Europe. They had to show that nature was neither hostile nor immutable in the Americas and that the United States was indeed a good risk (Chinard 1947; Gerbi 1973).

In *Natural History* (1749), Buffon had claimed that the main difference between the Old and New Worlds lay in their geological age. Since the American continents were younger, in his view, nature was simultaneously less active and more severe than it was in the Old World. Their mountains were higher; their environments wilder and more inaccessible; and their animals smaller. Even the domesticated animals transported from Europe became smaller with the passage of time. Only snakes and insects truly thrived in the New World. The inert condition of nature which favored the growth of lower creatures such as snakes and insects prevented the development of higher organisms. Thus, nature had also affected the American Indians who were relative newcomers, thinly scattered across these hostile lands. Buffon wrote that

> Even those which, from the kindly influence of another climate, have acquired their complete form and expansion, shrink and diminish under a niggardly sky and an unprolific land, thinly peopled with wandering savages, who, instead of using this territory as a master, had no property or empire; and having subjected neither the animals nor the elements, nor conquered the seas, nor directed the motions of the rivers, nor cultivated the earth, held only the first rank among animate beings, and existed as creatures of no consideration in Nature, a kind of weak automatons, incapable of improving or fecunding her intentions. She treated rather like a stepmother than a parent, by denying them the invigorating sentiment of life, and the strong desire of multiplying their species . . .
>
> It is easy to discover the cause of the scattered life of savages, and of their estrangement from society. They have been refused the most precious spark of Nature's fire. They have no ardour for women, and, of course, no love of mankind (Buffon quoted by Chinard 1947:31).

For Buffon, the American Indians failed to develop civil and political institutions – i.e., civilization – because of their own weakly developed nature and passive acceptance of their surroundings. However, the European settlers in the Americas had already begun to conquer and transform nature. Subsequent writers frequently misrepresented Buffon's views by focusing exclusively on the indifference and harshness of nature in the New World. It was their opinions as much as those of Buffon that scientists and natural philosophers in the United States sought to refute.

The more prominent critics of Buffon and his followers were affiliated with the American Philosophical Society, which had been founded at the urging of Benjamin Franklin in Philadelphia in 1743 to promote "useful knowledge among the British plantations in America" (Freeman 1967; van Doren 1943). While Franklin countered their arguments citing evidence of the rapid growth of the English population in North America in the eighteenth century and Madison commented on climatic changes brought about by clearing land in Virginia, Jefferson's (1785/1982) *Notes on the State of Virginia* was a lengthy, detailed response which brought to bear a wide range of evidence including the discovery of mammoth bones in Ohio as well as the ethnological, linguistic, and archaeological information that he and others had collected over the years to support his claims (Chinard 1947:40–52).

Jefferson argued that nature was equal in the Old and New Worlds. Since nature was bountiful in the Americas, both the English settlers and the Indians, who were essentially the same race or people in his eyes, were able to realize their potential. His response was based on a theory of nature that resembled those of Enlightenment writers, such as Claude Helvétius (1715–71) or Adam Smith (1723–90), in France and Scotland (Curti 1980:71–103; Meek 1976; Miller 1988:56–90; Weyant 1973). He believed that human beings possessed the same innate moral sense, capacity to reason, and biological needs: "all men were created equal," and human nature was "the same on every side of the Atlantic" (Jefferson 1785/1982:121). While human nature was the same everywhere, it was only realized in society. As a result, the differences that existed between societies resulted from their environmental circumstances and the stage they had achieved in the development of civilization.

The American Indians were not distinguished from Europeans by differences in morality, intelligence, and strength, and their skin color was only slightly different from that of Europeans who lived in the Mediterranean. What did distinguish the Indians from their English-speaking neighbors in Virginia was that they hunted while the latter farmed. In other words, their level of social development resembled that of Europeans living north of the Alps at the time of the Roman Empire. However, since human nature was also plastic, if the Indians adopted agriculture, then their cultures could meet, intermix, and blend together with the more highly developed culture of the European settlers. In 1784, legislation was proposed in Virginia that promised free education, tax relief, and monetary credits to promote marriage between the Americans of European descent and the indigenous population (Miller 1991:65).

While Jefferson believed that the differences between Indian and European were superficial – a matter of environment and history rather than of biology – he did not extend the same argument to either women or Blacks. He claimed – like St. Paul and the Puritans and unlike Helvétius or Mary Wollstonecraft – that women as a group possessed less reasoning power than men and therefore that they should be encouraged to refine their aesthetic and moral endowments (Curti 1980:81–2). Jefferson, the slave owner ever-fearful of slave revolt and condemning of the institution itself at least in his early years, recognized that the condition of slaves was miserable. He also suspected that Blacks, who he believed were the moral equals of Whites, lacked their powers of reason and imagination. Black slaves, he argued, were less creative and innovative than the Roman slaves who lived under even more odious circumstances. The only difference he could discern was that the slaves of

Rome were White. His conclusion, usually hedged with qualifications, was that the conditions of women and Blacks were innate, a consequence of their nature and biology rather than of the circumstances in which they lived (Jefferson 1785/ 1982:139–42, 63; Jordan 1968:429–81).

Thus, Jefferson's views on human nature contained contradictions. If human nature was portrayed as mutable in his discussions of American Indians, then it was fixed and immutable as far as women and Blacks were concerned. If he implied in his discussions of Indians and Whites, not to mention in his political declarations, that all human beings belonged to the same species, then his writings about Blacks implied that races of humanity existed and that they existed in a hierarchy if they were not actually separate species. If his discussions of the Indians and their accomplishments vindicated the American environment, then his remarks about Afro-Americans justified slavery and his comments about women condoned inequality by excluding them from political debate.

Jefferson and his contemporaries held a highly political view of language. In their view, language was a distinctively human attribute that made communication possible. Some linked the origin of language to the Old Testament and saw it as originating when Adam gave names to various animals (Genesis II, 19–20) and diversifying when God confounded the tongue spoken by the people who built the Tower of Babel and dispersed them across the face of the earth (Genesis XI, 1–9). For others – such as Jefferson himself and Noah Webster (1758–1843) who followed the views of John Locke (1632–1704) – languages were not God-given but merely assemblages of utterances that signified particular ideas for their speakers. More importantly, however, they reflected the unique social and intellectual experiences of those speakers. Thus, a nation's language reflected its history – and studying things pertaining to its words was a way of gaining insight into both the history of nations and the history of humanity itself (Aarsleff 1982:108–10; Gray 1999:87–111; Smith 1979).

Jefferson believed that a knowledge of American Indian languages would certainly provide evidence of their origins.

> How many ages have elapsed since the English, the Dutch, the Germans, the Swiss, the Norwegians, Danes and Swedes have separated from their common stock? Yet how many more must elapse before proofs of their common origin, which exist in their several languages, will disappear? It is to be lamented then . . . that we have suffered so many Indian tribes already to extinguish, without having previously collected and deposited in the records of literature, the rudiments at least of the languages they spoke. Were vocabularies formed of all the languages spoken in North and South America, preserving their appellations of the most common objects in nature, of those which must be present to every nation barbarous or civilized, with the inflection of their nouns and verbs, their principles of regimen and concord, . . . it would furnish opportunities for those skilled in the languages of the old world to compare them with these . . . and to construct the best evidence of the derivation of this part of the human race (Jefferson 1785/1982:101).

Jefferson had already collected enough information about American Indian languages to convince himself that they were more diverse than those of the Old World. In fact, he argued, the inhabitants of nearby villages in North America often spoke different languages; he took this to mean that their separation was quite ancient. Thus, by the late 1780s, Jefferson, Benjamin Smith Barton (1766–1815) and others began to collect vocabularies and other ethnological information from various American Indian groups (Gray 1999:112–38; Greene 1984:376–408).

In 1786, President George Washington (1732–99) asked government agents in Ohio to collect Indian vocabularies which could be added to those already collected by Peter Pallas and which would "throw light upon the original history of this country and . . . forward researches into the probably connections between the northern parts of America and those of Asia" (Washington letter to Richard Butler, 10 January 1788, quoted by Gray 1999:112). Such an "affinity of tongues," he believed, would show that human differences were superficial, that all nations ultimately had the same origin, and that they were subject in some fundamental way to the same laws of nature (Gray 1999:112–3).

Similar requests were made over the next thirty years by Jefferson and others, and vocabularies of a number of American Indian languages were published (Edgerton 1943). The most widely cited of the early compilations was Benjamin Smith Barton's (1798/1976) *New Views of the Origin of the Tribes and Nations of America*, in which he compared the languages of North and South American tribes with those of the Old World in order to show that they had a common origin. By 1811, vocabularies of eighty-three American Indian languages existed (Greene 1984:385). Much of the information recording Indian languages was assembled by Peter S. Du Ponceau's (1760–1844) Historical and Literary Committee of the American Philosophical Society which was established with Jefferson's support in 1815 (Haas 1969; Smith 1983). The main difficulties with much of this early work were that the authors could not indicate the sounds of vowels and consonants, and that they did not produce an adequate classification of the historical or genetic relationships of American Indian languages similar to the one constructed by William Jones for the Indo-European languages (Aarsleff 1983:115–61; Kejariwal 1995).

In 1819, former president John Adams (1735–1826) encouraged Du Ponceau to follow Jones in his study of American Indian languages (Gray 1999:118). Du Ponceau did so. In his view, the languages spoken from Greenland to Tierra del Fuego were remarkably similar to one another; they shared complex structures and grammatical forms that distinguished them from all of the Old World languages. He called this distinctive feature "polysynthesis." The polysynthetic languages, which existed only in the Americas, were a more effective system than their Old World counter-parts for combining the greatest number of ideas in the least number of words (Du Ponceau 1819:xiv; 1838).

According to Du Ponceau, this reflected the superior intellect of the inventors of the American Indian languages; it was also ample proof that these languages were neither degenerate nor primitive. In fact, the Old World languages that were structurally closest to them – Latin, Greek and Slavic – had been spoken by those Europeans who had given rise to civilization itself. Du Ponceau's classification of American Indian languages underpinned all subsequent efforts in the nineteenth century to investigate their historical and genetic connections. His portrayal of American Indian languages countered claims that culture could not flourish in the United States; he suggested instead that these languages, remnants of a past age, and American English were worthy of study in their own right; they could provide the foundations for a truly national literature.

Du Ponceau was not the only American writer with a political view of language and aesthetics. In 1780, John Adams proposed to the Continental Congress that it establish a national language academy in order to promote the achievements of the new nation. While this academy would encourage the study of all languages and literatures, it would promote, correct, and improve American English. It would refine the language in a way that the English were unable to do because of their diverse regional and class dialects. The elaboration of American English would not only manifest the political ideology of the United States but would also enhance its standing in the community of nations (Heath 1977:18–24; Baron 1982). Noah Webster (1789:179) summarized Adams's views nine years later when he wrote that

> Customs, habits, and *language* as well as government should be national. America should have her own distinct from all the world. Such is the policy of other nations, and such must be *our* policy, before the state can be either independent or respectable.

Adams and Webster were just two of the Americans clamoring for the development of a national language. Benjamin Franklin, focusing his attention on the relation between the spoken and written word, had long advocated uniform spelling and clear, easily read typefaces which would make learning the language easier and facilitate its spread in the world marketplace. He also saw the economic benefits of such reforms:

> The general use of the French language has likewise a very advantageous effect on the profits of the bookselling branch of commerce; it being well known, that the more copies can be sold that are struck off from one composition of types, the profits increase in a much greater proportion than they do in making a greater number of pieces in any other kind of manufacture (Franklin 1789/1848:204).

While Congress never established the national language academy favored by the Federalists of New England, Webster and others did launch institutes in Boston and New York devoted to the study of philology and belles-lettres. However, more important than these short-lived language academies for the formation of a national language and literature was the fact that American nationalism intensified and became more complex after the War of 1812. This was marked by the publication of dictionaries explicitly concerned with American English, by the appearance of the influential *North American Review* in 1815, and by the rapid development of a consciously American literature through the writings of James Fenimore Cooper, Washington Irving, Edgar Allan Poe, and other authors (Spiller 1967; Whalen 1999). Many of the defining works of this national literature dealt with the violence of settler expansion into the Indian homelands in upstate New York and in areas west of the Alleghenies.

Plans for expansion into the Indian territories west of the Appalachians began a week after the end of hostilities with England in April, 1783; however, the country had no Indian policy until the Constitution was ratified in 1789. Until then, it was largely a hope shaped by the need to have the European states view the Americans as a moral, just, and responsible people. Washington had initially wanted Revolutionary War veterans to settle in the western lands in order to protect the frontier. He presumed incorrectly that the tribes would cede or sell land to settlers. This was not the case. In 1801, Jefferson adopted the policies that encouraged Indians to become farmers in order to obtain new land for settlers; on numerous occasions, he advocated intermarriage to reduce friction between the two and to destroy the distinction between savage and civilized people. However, by 1809, this policy was actively opposed by Tecumseh (1768–1813) who argued for the common ownership of land by all tribes so that no one group could cede land, and by his brother – Tenskwatawa (1775–1836), the Shawnee Prophet – who advocated casting off white civilization altogether (Drinnon 1980:92–5; Horsman 1967:129, 52–65; Sheehan 1973).

As settlers moved into the Indian territories, tensions rose, and the tribes in both the South and the Old Northwest became increasingly hostile. While the Indians viewed the settlers as unwanted intruders, the frontiersmen increasingly saw the Indians as savages who impeded their quest for land. In the words of Lewis Cass (1782–1866), who would become one of the leading architects of federal Indian policy in the 1820s and 1830s, the Indians were unchangeable in their physical and moral habits, unable to appreciate their own condition, and resistant to education and other attempts to ameliorate their circumstances. In short, the Indians were warlike nomads incapable of achieving civilization on their own or of learning it from others (Cass 1827, 1840).

The westward expansion of the United States occurred in bursts, each of which led to a period of intensified interest in American Indian tribes. For example, after the Louisiana Purchase in 1803, Jefferson sent Meriwether Lewis and William Clark to explore the newly acquired territory. He requested that they obtain ethnological information from each of the tribes they encountered regarding their health, morals, religion, history, subsistence activities, warfare, amusements, clothing, and customs (Jefferson 1803a/1962, 1803b/1962; Barton 1803/1959).

In the early 1820s, Lewis Cass, then the territorial governor and superintendent of Indian affairs in Michigan, compiled several lengthy questionnaires concerned with ethnological and linguistic matters that he sent to traders, military commanders, and Indian agents (Bieder 1986:150–5; Hallowell 1960:40–2; Prucha 1967). In Cass's view, this "frontier ethnology" would provide a justification for the government's new Indian policies and a corrective to the theories of Du Ponceau. Henry R. Schoolcraft (1793–1864), an Indian agent in Sault Ste. Marie for many years, provided Cass with much information. He echoed his sentiments about the depravity of American Indians and defended the policy of removing Indian tribes from their homelands to the areas west of the Mississippi River (Bieder 1986:146–93).

As settlers and land speculators poured into the valleys of the Ohio River and its tributaries, towns were established, and local antiquarians, such as Caleb Atwater (1778–1867), surveyed the antiquities of the region and recorded the presence of numerous ancient mounds and earthworks. "Who built the mounds?" was a question they asked repeatedly (Silverberg 1968; Tax 1973:63–122). Atwater (1820:123–4) thought that the Ohio earthworks "owe their origin to a people far more civilized than our Indians, but far less so than Europeans." This conclusion was reiterated a few years later by William Henry Harrison (1773–1841) who became the first president from the west. This theory separated the contemporary Indian tribes from the deeds of their ancestors, and challenged their right as independent nations to possess the lands they occupied. Depictions of the Indians as hunters and foragers were also a threat to their land claims. Such arguments also resonated with John Locke's (1690/1980:18–30) arguments in the *Second Treatise of Government*. As you will recall, Locke vested the origin of landed property in the labor that persons invested in the land to provide for their own consumption. While farmers transformed the land through their labor, hunters and foragers did not; hence, the latter had no natural right to their unimproved lands.

Chief Justice of the Supreme Court John Marshall (1755–1835) wrote the brief in *Johnson and Graham's Lessee v. McIntosh* (1823), which denied that the Indians possessed an unqualified right to their lands and vested that right instead in the settlers who discovered those lands. This case provided the legal grounds for removing the eastern tribes from their lands, including groups, such as the Cherokee, that had altered their circumstances and become farmers (Washburn 1959:26–9). In 1830, the federal government removed the Cherokee from their lands in Georgia and sent them on a death march known as the Trail of Tears to Oklahoma. Newspaper editor and abolitionist John Greenleaf Whittier (1807–92), among others, immediately protested the government's policy; he wrote that

> The present policy of our government toward the unfortunate Cherokee is one of unparalleled cruelty. . . . The curse of slavery is enough to seal our eternal infamy; the unjust eviction of the Indians will be a crime which men may never forget, nor eternal justice forgive (quoted by Kerber 1975:273).

Americans were aware of the cultural and physical diversity of the peoples who lived in the New Republic. A number of them sought to identify who the Americans were and who they were becoming in ways that would enhance the nation's standing in the eyes of the European countries. These were questions about slavery, morality, and politics as much as they were about race and environment. Slavery had had a profound effect on political debate before, during, and after the Revolution. The calls of the Sons of Liberty for life, liberty and, the pursuit of happiness (property) were also heard by the slave populations in Virginia and the Carolinas. On the eve of the war, the slaveowners had feared a slave uprising; fuel was added to these fears in 1775 when the Royal Governor of Virginia issued a proclamation granting lifelong freedom to any slaves who could escape and would bear arms against the American rebels. Most of the escaped slaves fought for the British; the rest took shelter with Indian tribes in the mountains and beyond. Perhaps twenty percent of the American slaves gained their freedom during the war, many of whom emigrated to Nova Scotia in the 1780s because of the political climate that prevailed in the new country (Nash 1986:271–5).

In 1782, Hector de Crèvecoeur (1735–1813) claimed that the Americans were a "new race of men" partly because of the strange mixture of blood that existed in no other country and partly because of the new mode of life they embraced (Crèvecoeur 1782/1904:46). In 1787, Samuel Stanhope Smith (1751–1819), moral philosopher and president of Princeton University, wrote that the new race or nation was not so much a product of intermixing as it was of Negroes and Indians being transformed into Whites because of the new habits of living they were adopting (Smith 1810/1965:100). In his view, the descendants of the Europeans, the Indians, and the Negroes belonged to the same species; the variability in their appearance resulted from the influence of climate and differences in their state of society or habits of living. Given the plasticity of the human species, the climate and culture of America would make the members of all of the races of the new nation, including the descendants of European workers and peasants, whiter. Thus, the state of society would augment or correct the influence of climate; however, his views would not overcome the inequalities brought on by slavery and laws.

Not everyone, however, accepted the views that America was or should become a nation of mixed bloods. Benjamin Rush (1745–1813) – Philadelphia physician, signer of the Declaration, and abolitionist – took a slightly different view from that of Smith. He too had recognized the racial diversity of America on the eve of the Revolutionary War. Whites, Indians, and Negroes had distinctive racial characteristics. Indians, for example, exhibited no madness or melancholy and lacked envy because of the equality of power and property in their society; however, he believed that they had no future because of their intemperance with alcohol. Rush further argued that "All the vices which are charged upon negroes in the southern colonies . . . such as Idleness, Treachery, Theft, and the like, are the genuine offspring of slavery" (quoted by Takaki 1990:29). The black color of their skin, he asserted, should not qualify them for slavery. Like some of his contemporaries, Rush was concerned with the cause of black skin color and believed it resulted from a disease. If this was true, then it could be cured. He identified the disease as leprosy for which there was no cure at the time; consequently, he advocated the separation of races to prevent the spread of the disease.

In 1792, Jonathan Edwards suggested to the Abolition Society of Connecticut that the sins of slavery would necessitate a compensation ". . . inconceivably more mortifying than the loss of all their real estates, . . . the mixture of their blood with that of the Negroes into one common posterity" (quoted by Jordan 1968:544). No one, except Smith, thought that intermarriage was a solution to the problems of inequality and prejudice. Marriages between individuals of African and European heritage, which had not been uncommon in the late seventeenth century, had been banned in a number of colonies by 1700 (Goldfield 1997:39–45). The White-Indian marriages called for by Jefferson and others in the 1780s actually took place in frontier areas; however, by the 1820s, the children of these unions faced growing discrimination as tensions mounted along the frontier and as settlers and their political agents increasingly portrayed them as savages incapable of being civilized and clamored for the implementation of Indian removal policies (Bieder 1980). Such views would soon spawn a large literature on the hereditary and social nature of hybrids.

Others followed Edward Long, whose *History of Jamaica* and views on the racial inferiority of African slaves were serialized in *The Columbian Magazine* in 1788. He and the English physician Charles White claimed that the different races actually represented regular gradations of humanity. In their view, Europeans were the highest, most advanced grade, while Africans were the lowest and least developed. In White's view, anatomical differences, as well as differences in morality and intelligence, distinguished the European from the more "ape-like" Negro (Greene 1954; 1984:320–42). Still others flirted with Lord Kames's vague suggestion that the various races were actually separate species.

Such views, combined with the anti-miscegenation laws, buttressed the views of James Madison (1751–1836) who believed that the removal of freed slaves from Virginia was necessary, because "The repugnance of the White to their continuance among them is founded on prejudices themselves founded on physical distinctions, which are not likely soon if ever to be eradicated" (quoted by Jordan 1968:553). The idea of Negro removal was widespread in Virginia in the 1790s. By 1805, any freedman or woman who did not leave the state within one year faced re-enslavement. Neighboring states – such as Ohio, Kentucky, Maryland, and Delaware – soon enacted legislation that banned African Americans from entering to take up permanent residence. From the perspective of these legislators, the new republic would be a white nation. Former slaves could return to Africa, which many of them did when Liberia was established in 1847.

Race and Manifest Destiny in Industrializing America, 1838–1879

The idea of white racial superiority became an increasingly prominent feature of everyday discourse in America during the 1830s and 1840s. It gained momentum after the citizens of Georgia seized Indian lands, displaced their residents and extended the institution of slavery into the new territory, thereby linking Indians and African slaves in the same discourse. John Quincy Adams (1767–1848) and others believed events like this were bound to happen, because the two races were inexorably fixed at lower stages of social development – savagery in the case of the Indians and "somewhere between pastoralism and primitive agriculture" for the Africans (Saxton 1990:87). They were signs of their inferior, subordinate status and position in a racial hierarchy topped by native-born, Anglo-Saxon Protestants. At the same time, they buttressed the ideology of Manifest Destiny, which viewed American expansion "as evidence of the innate superiority of the American Anglo-Saxon branch of the Caucasian race . . . [which was] a separate, innately superior people who were destined to bring good government, commercial prosperity, and Christianity to the American continents and the rest of the world" (Horsman 1981:1–2). These sentiments were fueled by rising resentment against the torrent of Irish Catholic immigrants coming to America and by the war looming on the horizon with Mexico over land claims west of the Mississippi.

By 1840, many politicians and social commentators had come to believe that the cultural differences exhibited by Indians and Africans on the one hand and Anglo-Saxon Americans on the other were rooted in biology (Stanton 1960). In their view, the different races of humanity formed a natural hierarchy topped by native-born, white Protestants. They argued that the different races possessed varying degrees of intellect. For Charles Caldwell (1799–1851), America's leading phrenologist in the 1830s, these differences were manifested in the shape and size of their crania and brains. The brain, for phrenologists,

> was composed of individual faculties that controlled personality, thought, and moral action; that the strength of these faculties could be determined by protuberances on the skull; and that each race manifested its cultural traits through the shape of the cranium (Bieder 1986:59).

Caldwell (1830) had earlier criticized Samuel Stanhope Smith's claims that all human beings belong to the same species, and that differences in skin color resulted from the interaction of bile with high heat and humidity. For Caldwell, the four races of humanity – Caucasians, Mongolians, Indians, and Africans – were actually separate species distinguished from one another by the quality of their intellects and minds (Erickson 1997a, b) which could, of course, be determined by inspecting the size and shape of their skulls. The Anglo-Saxons were, for Caldwell, "the most endowed variety of the Caucasian race," and that "inhabitants of the United States, being also of the best Caucasian stock . . . promise to be even more [productive] than the Britons of the future ages" (quoted by Horsman 1981:128).

While Caldwell was a minor, relatively unimportant figure in the history of American science, his fascination with race and intellect inspired Samuel G. Morton (1799–1851), Philadelphia physician and corresponding secretary of the Academy of Natural Sciences, whose investigations were at the center of American ethnological research in the late 1830s and early 1840s, to amass one of the world's largest collections of human crania, many of which were purchased from grave robbers and collectors on the frontier. His goal was to make an objective, scientific assessment of the racial differences in skull size and shape which he believed underpinned behavioral differences. While more cautious than Caldwell, he also believed that phrenology provided an excellent indication of "national traits" (Bieder 1986:66–7, 73; Stanton 1960:25–44).

Morton accepted Johann Blumenbach's (1752–1840) earlier racial classification which was based on differences in skull form and skin color. For Blumenbach (1795/ 1865), there were five races: Caucasian, Ethiopian, Mongolian, American Indian, and African. However, Morton rejected Blumenbach's claim that racial diversity resulted from the degeneration of the original Caucasian racial type as peoples migrated into new environments, ate new foods and coped with their new circumstances. The problem for Morton was that he accepted a biblical chronology which placed the age of the earth at less than 6000 years; both Caucasians and Africans were represented on Egyptian monuments that were sculpted more than three thousand years ago. In his view, there simply was too little time in human history for one race to have evolved from the other (Morton 1839:1–3). This meant that racial differences – such as intellect or color – were permanent.

Morton's (1839) pathbreaking *Crania Americana* was more than an attempt to explain the differences between the levels of development of the "demi-civilized" Indians of Mexico and Peru and the Moundbuilders, all of whom farmed, and the remaining "barbarous" tribes in North and South America, whose members subsisted by hunting and foraging. He made thirteen different measurements on each of the 256 skulls he had accumulated to show that there was a gradation in the average brain size of the five races. He argued that Caucasians had the largest cranial capacities followed by Mongolians, Malays, American Indians, and Ethiopians in descending order (Morton 1839:220; Gould 1981). In his view, the behavioral differences between the various races were primordial, not acquired. The American Indians, for example, had not adopted a civilized manner of life from their Caucasian neighbors because of the limited mental capacities manifested by their smaller brain sizes. His measurements showed that, excepting the Eskimo, the American Indians were indeed a distinct race composed of two families: the "demi-civilized"

Toltecan whose tribes farmed and the American whose tribes hunted; this implied that the Moundbuilders belonged to a different family from that of the tribes that had historically occupied the Ohio River Valley.

In *Crania Aegyptiaca*, Morton extended his investigations with measurements on more than 100 skulls removed from tombs in Egypt and sent to him by George Gliddon, the American consul in Cairo. He concluded from this study that the differences between Caucasian and Negro cranial capacities had existed for more than three thousand years. This supported, he believed, his claims about the permanency of certain racial characteristics. Furthermore, he asserted that the inhabitants of ancient Egypt, the cradle of civilization, were neither Caucasian nor Negro. They were instead a mixture of "several distinct branches of the human family" – the Caucasian, the Semitic, the Austral-Egyptian, and the Negro. Furthermore, since the ancient Egyptians enslaved peoples they conquered, the Negroes must have been slaves (Morton 1844:1, 59). Southern politicians and slave owners delighted in this conclusion and saw it as a vindication of their own social practices (Stanton 1960:51–3).

Morton raised questions about the status of race. If the races were, in fact, separate species as some had already claimed, then why were the offspring of Indian-White and Negro-White matings fertile and able to produce children of their own? Morton's answer was that morphological differences were ancient and fixed. Josiah Clark Nott (1804-65), a Philadelphia- trained physician from Alabama, took a different tack. He dropped the criterion of fertility, arguing that Caucasians and Negroes were morphologically distinct species that possessed different susceptibilities to disease (Erickson 1997c). He produced evidence purportedly showing that individuals with mixed racial heritages, such as mulattos, experienced higher mortality and shorter life expectancies than individuals of either parent race (Nott 1843). This echoed a claim made a year earlier by Edward Jarvis (1842), a Southern physician who argued that the incidence of insanity was ten times greater among the Free Negroes in the North than among slave populations in the South; from this, Jarvis "deduced that slavery must have had a wonderful influence upon the development of the moral faculties and intellectual powers of the individual [Negro]" (Stanton 1960:58). In other words, both Nott and Jarvis claimed that there was a direct linkage between race and health.

As American expansion westward proceeded during the 1840s, American travelers increasingly portrayed the peoples of Mexico's northern provinces as a mixed or "mongrel" race with considerable Indian blood. In California, this mixed race was "unfit to control the destinies of that beautiful country," since its members were "scarcely a visible grade, in the scale of intelligence, above the barbarous tribes by whom they were surrounded" (quoted by Horsman 1981:210–11). Stereotypes such as these were ruthlessly exploited by President James Buchanan (1791–1868) and others in their depictions of Mexicans during the 1840s as they justified a war with Mexico in order to seize new land west of the Mississippi. The Mexicans, in their view, had failed to make the land bountiful. When the hostilities finally ended in 1848, the United States, which had already annexed Texas, now added New Mexico, Arizona, Utah, Nevada, and Alta California to its national territory.

If scientific racism had its roots in the educational and cultural institutions of Philadelphia, then the cultural entrepreneurs of New England and Harvard College were the hotbed of the ideology of Anglo-Saxon superiority. Edward Everett (1794–1865) – Harvard professor, classical archaeologist, ambassador to England, Secretary of State, and editor of *The North American Review* – claimed that "the Anglo-Saxon race, from which we Americans trace our descent is surpassed by none other that ever existed" (quoted by Horsman 1981:226). These sentiments were shared by many of his Harvard colleagues including the eminent naturalist, Louis Agassiz (1807–73), who argued that the various races were indeed separate species and that they were arranged hierarchically with Blacks at the bottom and Whites at the top. (Agassiz 1850). After writing the introduction to Nott and Gliddon's widely reviewed *Types of Mankind* published in 1854, Agassiz described the threat that the health and physical disabilities of mixed races posed to civilization and morality (Agassiz 1854; Gould 1981:48).

The views of Morton, Nott, and Agassiz – the American polygenists – regarding the existence of a racial hierarchy did not go unchallenged. African-American abolitionist Frederick Douglass (1817–95) disputed them (Douglass 1854/1950). He argued that they had misappropriated the peoples of ancient Egypt when they claimed them to be Europeans and their civilization as a European rather than an African accomplishment. Douglass focused on the circumstances that underpinned their biological determinism. A racial hierarchy did exist in the United States; however, it was rooted in social and economic circumstances rather than physical or biological ones. Discrimination against Blacks, Douglass argued, existed both legally and in the public mind, because their skin color was linked with "the degradation of slavery and servitude" (quoted by Goldfield 1997:92). He also pointed to the similarities between the Negroes and the Irish who had begun to enter the United States in large numbers in the 1830s. Many of the Irish immigrants were unskilled laborers and servants who lived in urban slums. At the time, they were often called "white niggers," because they occupied the lowest rung of a labor force that was increasingly stratified by ethnicity, race, and gender. They dug canals, mined coal, and toiled at various tasks that were deemed too dangerous for expensive slaves to undertake.

During the Civil War, Agassiz advised the United States Sanitary Commission which, together with the Provost Marshal-General's Bureau, made anthropometric measurements of nearly 24,000 soldiers, sailors, Indians, mulattos, and Negroes between 1863 and 1865 in order to refine their understanding of racial types and their differences (Haller 1971:19–21). The Sanitary Commission was a semi-official organization composed of "predominantly upper-class . . . patrician elements which had been vainly seeking a function in American society" during the war (Fredrickson 1965:100). Its expenses were underwritten in substantial part by insurance companies. Along with other medical and anthropometric studies made in the nineteenth century, they were quickly used by insurance company statisticians to establish the empirical foundations for differential premium and rate structures based on race and to verify their necessity (Haller 1971:60–8).

Morton, Nott, and other polygenists of the new American school of anthropology, such as Ephraim G. Squier (1821–1888), were confident that anthropometric studies would yield a scientific understanding of human history. They had little confidence in historical reconstructions based on language comparisons. In their view, linguistics and philology were not exact sciences, because the language spoken by any given people was likely to have been influenced by diverse circumstances. Morton liked to point out that the Mongols, Hindus, and Negroes who inhabited Madagascar spoke the same language (Stanton 1960:98). The other reason why they shunned philological studies was that scholars who based their historical reconstructions on language also believed that humanity was a single species, that the physical attributes of a group were not causative, and that human behavior, or culture, was shaped by social and historical circumstances and, consequently, was mutable rather than fixed.

Albert Gallatin (1761–1849) – Jefferson's Secretary of the Treasury, diplomat and one of the founders of the American Ethnological Society – was the most articulate spokesman and defender of Enlightenment views in the 1840s (Bieder 1986:16–54; Bieder and Tax 1976). Gallatin (1836/1973:142–59) accepted as fact that humanity was indeed a single species; that the Indians of North and South America were a single people as the similarity of the structural and grammatical forms of their languages showed; and that nations in Mexico, Central America, and Peru had progressed from savagery toward civilization because they adopted agriculture and lived in environments that resembled Old World centers of civilization. He also did not believe that the contemporary American Indians of the Ohio and Mississippi river valleys had degenerated from an earlier stage of social development in which they farmed, as many antiquarians concerned with the ancient moundbuilders of the region had suggested. In his view, the mental abilities and moral feelings of the Indians were products of their environment rather than of physical characteristics such as skin color.

Gallatin's (1836/1973) "Synopsis of the Indian Tribes within the United States" was the first systematic comparison of North American Indian languages. He made use of Du Ponceau's studies as well as information gleaned from a questionnaire concerned with vocabulary and grammar that the Secretary of War sent to Indian agents, travelers, and missionaries in 1826. He also mapped tribal locations and language distributions. Unlike Du Ponceau, however, who believed that the polysynthetic languages of the American Indians were advanced, Gallatin argued that they were more primitive than ancient Greek – that is, they represented an earlier and, hence, older stage in the historical development of language itself; as a result, the American Indian languages also held clues not only about the origins of language but also about the development of human reason itself (Gallatin 1836/1973:202).

Gallatin began his ethnological and philological studies in the 1820s at the same time as Lewis Cass and others were clamoring for the adoption of policies that would allow them to remove Indians from their homelands east of the Mississippi River. Unlike Cass, Gallatin believed that "the Indians need not be exterminated to facilitate the advance of American civilization" (Bieder 1986:42), While he advocated buying Indian lands, he also recommended that the federal government create conditions on the new reservations that would compel the Indians to adopt agriculture. Moreover, the government should also promote education programs for their children in order to advance the cause of civilization (Gallatin 1836/1973:154–6).

During the 1840s, when he was already in his eighties, Gallatin confronted an intellectual milieu that was increasingly sympathetic to theories of degeneration and polygenism; these theories were based on a belief in the inferiority of the non-Caucasian races (Bieder 1986:52). Gallatin addressed these theories indirectly in his last works, which considered whether civilization had developed independently in the Americas or was a consequence of diffusion. He believed that adoption of agriculture was the motor leading to the development of cities, arts, and the sciences. In his mind, the different traditions of mathematics and astronomy in Central America and Peru confirmed the independent development of civilization in those regions (Gallatin 1845:181–5). He was also intrigued by reports describing the agricultural societies of the American Southwest, and wondered whether they resulted from contact with or diffusion from the peoples further south or were again examples of independent development (Gallatin 1848).

By the 1850s, scholars who studied American Indian languages found it increasingly difficult to publish the results of their inquiries, and *The North American Review*, which had been a major outlet earlier in the century, stopped publishing articles on Indian languages after 1860 (Andresen 1990:127–8). Nevertheless, a society concerned with study of language and languages had been formed in 1842 by classical and biblical scholars. It was the American Oriental Society, whose goals were to inquire into the history and literature of the civilized nations of the Orient and to cultivate the learning of Asian, African, and Polynesian languages. Its first president was John Pickering (1777–1846) who had produced an important survey of American Indian languages in 1830. However, in his opening address, Pickering scarcely mentioned their existence and focused instead on the need to compile materials for a "general ethnography of the globe" (Pickering 1849:5).[1] For the Harvard-educated Pickering who viewed language as a distinctly human form of behavior, this meant studying language apart from the social contexts in which it occurred (Andresen 1990:106).

William Dwight Whitney (1827–94), Professor of Sanskrit and Comparative Philology at Yale, made several significant contributions to the study of language and anthropology after the Civil War (1860–65), as the publication of information about American Indian languages reached its nadir. A language such as English, in his view, was "the immense aggregate of articulated signs for thought accepted by, and current among, a certain vast community . . ." whose members speak its myriad local and class varieties (Whitney 1867/1971:16). While new dialects appeared among common peoples and the speech of elites and lettered classes adhered to tradition, the same processes of change – combination and adaptation – were actually occurring in both. The appearance of new forms and meanings depended on forgetting established historical connections, on the one hand, and on the other making new linkages between the thing signified and its spoken sign. The processes of combination and adaptation remained the same as the form of the language changed; consequently, the prevailing analogies of composition used by its speakers to select new items were also transformed.

Whitney was acutely aware of the social and political contexts in which language change occurred. He pointed out that the sphere in which English was spoken was expanding rapidly precisely because of the social and political conditions that existed in the nineteenth century. In the United States, the spread of American English was displacing American Indian languages and reducing the linguistic diversity of the continent. He described this in the following way:

> As, here in America, a single cultivated nation, of homogeneous speech, is taking the place of a congeries of wild tribes, with their host of discordant tongues, so, on a smaller scale, is it everywhere else: civilization and the conditions it makes are gaining upon barbarism and its isolating influences (quoted by Andresen 1990:151).

The implication of this was clear to Whitney (1867/1971:91): "no individual's speech directly and necessarily marks his descent; it only shows in what community he grew up. Language is no infallible sign of race." Like any other element of acquired civilization, it was transmitted from generation to generation, from community to community, and from race to race. In the United States, Indians, Africans brought from their native homes, and Irish immigrants had by necessity learned American English and been incorporated into that speech community. Thus, the fusion and replacement of languages was made possible when individuals who spoke different tongues were brought together in the same community.

Like his contemporaries, Whitney was not particularly concerned with the study of American Indian languages. He believed that they were locked in a death struggle with the speakers of American English for territory. As a Sanskrit scholar, he believed that the Indo-European languages were most developed in the sense of having undergone the processes of combination and adaptation for the longest time;

furthermore, since written texts have survived from earlier stages in their development, it was possible to trace their history with higher degrees of certainty.

While the interest in American Indian languages ebbed rapidly in the 1850s, concern with the American Indians continued unabated because of westward expansion and settlement after the War with Mexico (1845–8). The identity of the Moundbuilders continued to be the question asked most frequently. Were they a race of semi-civilized farmers that had disappeared, as Morton and William Henry Harrison claimed, or were they merely the ancestors of the contemporary Indian inhabitants of the region as James McCulloh (1829) and Schoolcraft implied? The fact that the newly established Smithsonian Institution chose to publish E. G. Squier and Edwin H. Davis's (1811–88) lavishly illustrated *Ancient Monuments of the Mississippi Valley* (1848) as the first volume in its publication series, Smithsonian Contributions to Knowledge, attested to the importance of that question.

With the encouragement of Joseph Henry (1797–1878), renowned physicist and first secretary of the Smithsonian Institution, Squier and Davis attempted to bring science to bear in order to resolve the question of the Moundbuilders's identity. "At the outset," they wrote,

> all preconceived notions were abandoned, and the work of research commenced, as if no speculations had been indulged in, nor anything before known, respecting the singular remains of antiquity scattered so profusely around us. It was concluded that, either the field should be entirely abandoned to the poet and the romancer, or, if these monuments were capable of reflecting any certain light upon the grand archaeological questions connected with the primitive history of the American continent, the origin, migration, and early state of the American race, that then they should be carefully and minutely, and above all, systematically investigated (Squier and Davis 1848:139).

As a result of their investigations, Squier and Davis felt that the contemporary American Indian tribes and their ancestors were incapable of constructing the mounds. They were erected instead by an ancient race that subsequently migrated to Mexico and that was replaced in the Mississippi Valley by the contemporary Indian tribes. In effect, Squier and Davis separated the contemporary inhabitants, who were portrayed as hunters and foragers, from the agriculturalists who built the mounds and who had transformed the soil into a means of production. Thus, Squier and Davis provided a purportedly scientific argument to support claims based ultimately on John Locke's *Second Treatise*, which vested the origin of landed property in labor: any land cultivated by persons for their subsistence was part of their property as were the fruits they harvested from it for their own consumption.

In 1849, Squier made the connection between property and race more clearly after President Zachary Taylor had sent him as chargé d'affaires to Central America, where he nearly precipitated a war with England. Squier argued that the Moskito Indians of the Caribbean coast, whom the British supported, were a mixed race:

The Mosquitos have none of the conditions essential to nationality, according to the standards of common sense and the requirements of the laws of nations. An insignificant handful in respect to numbers, they wander along the parks and bays of the coast, obtaining a precarious subsistence from fishing and the natural products of the earth. They are without fixed habitations, without a written language, without laws, the institution of marriage, or even a distinct idea of God. They have no conception of the responsibilities of government, nor are they capable of discharging its duties (quoted by Olien 1985:118).

This mixed race, he claimed, "were inferior to the Indians of the United States in personal appearance, and definitely below them in the mental scale" (quoted by Olien 1985:118). Consequently, in his view, the Moskito certainly had no legitimate claim to landed property in that country.

Squier's arguments echoed comments made earlier by John Lloyd Stephens (1805–52), the renowned author of travel accounts and President Martin van Buren's representative to the crumbling Central American Federation in 1839 (Hinsley 1985a). When he saw the Maya ruins at Copán, Stephens (1841, vol. 1:102) wrote that its monuments

> put at rest to once and forever, in our minds, all uncertainty in regard to the character of American antiquities, and gave us the assurance that the objects we were in search of were interesting, not only as the remains of an unknown people, but as works of art, that the people who once occupied the Continent of America were not savages.

In his view, the ruins at Copán reflected the artistic imagination of civilized men (Stephens 1841, vol. 1:158–9). Since the contemporary inhabitants of the region had no recollection of the ruins, he argued, the buildings must have been erected by an ancient civilization. This perspective added fuel to the idea of the Moundbuilder race, even though Stephens himself thought that they were built by the ancestors of the present-day Indians whose culture had degenerated through time (Stephens 1841, vol. 2:356, 442, 55–7).

Stephens suggested to Frederick Catherwood, his traveling companion and the artist whose etchings would make ancient Maya ruins famous, that they should

> buy Copán! remove the monuments of a by-gone people from the desolate region in which they were buried, set them up in the "great commercial emporium," and found an institution to be the nucleus of a great national museum of American antiquities (Stephens 1841, vol. 1:115).

Stephens and Catherwood bought Copán for $50. Subsequently, they tried unsuccessfully to buy the ruins at Quiriguá and Palenque. Stephens's aim was to take the ruins to New York to establish a museum of American antiquities.[2] When an associate attempted to remove plaster casts of the monuments at Palenque, the residents insisted that he pay them $4,000 or $5,000 for the right to make duplicates of their monuments; he refused and the casts were broken. When they returned to the United States, both Stephens and Catherwood hoped to profit financially from their travels. Catherwood opened a panorama to display Maya antiquities as well as his engravings and water colors; unfortunately, everything was destroyed when the exhibit burned to the ground. Stephens's books were best-sellers in their day and he profited immensely from their sale. Stephens and Catherwood were certainly not the first to see and exploit the commercial value of American antiquities; Squier had also attempted to sell the collection of Moundbuilder artifacts he amassed in the 1840s (Brunhouse 1973:101–6; Silverberg 1968:132; Tax 1973:149–72).

New voices were heard in the Moundbuilder controversy in the 1850s. Schoolcraft (1851–7, vol. 4:135–6) decided that "the mounds need not have been built by peoples with an advanced civilization but could have been constructed by peoples at a barbarian level of culture" (Willey and Sabloff 1993:44). Samuel Haven (1806–81), secretary of the American Antiquarian Society which had been founded in 1812, echoed Schoolcraft's sentiments regarding the identity of the Moundbuilders, pointing out that the mound contained "no tokens of civil institutions, of mechanical employments, and the cultivation of science and literature" (Haven 1855:155–6). In a word, he challenged the idea of the Moundbuilder race.

Haven (1855:153) also agreed with Schoolcraft's remarks about the absence of earthworks, mounds and antiquities west of the Mississippi. At a time when rights to landed property were being argued in the courts in terms of a history of prior occupation, Haven and Schoolcraft were in effect denying that the American Indian tribes had any history of occupation in the region. To avoid muddying the waters even further on this issue, Haven did not mention the ruined pueblos that travelers were discovering in the American Southwest or the contemporary inhabitants of the Pueblos who farmed and hence had transformed the soil from an object of production to a means of production.

News of the "village Indians" of the Pueblos also came to the attention of Lewis Henry Morgan (1818–1881) by the late 1850s. Morgan, a Rochester lawyer who had represented the Seneca Indians in a land dispute with the Ogden Land Company, wrote his famous *League of the Ho-de-no-sau-nee, or Iroquois* (1851) at a time when the stability of the union was threatened by the growing rift between the North and the South over slavery and capitalism. He was firmly committed to the political union of the two regions; he also believed that progress toward civilization was led by "a stable middle class that meliorated the social system by the expansion of trade, industry, and education" (Resek 1960:10).

Morgan's interest was drawn to the major issue of the day: the unity of the human species. Were human beings the members of a single, racially diverse species as some suggested, or were the various races different species as Morton and others claimed? He set about resolving this debate in an ingenious way. In 1858, Morgan discovered that the Iroquois and Ojibwa, who spoke distinct languages, had kinship systems that "were identical in their fundamental characteristics" (Morgan 1871:3). Over the next few years, he studied the kinship systems of other North American Indian tribes and eventually concluded that the systems of kinship terminology were essentially the same across the continent; this led him to conclude "that the North American Indians had a common origin" (Kuper 1985:10). Following Schoolcraft and Haven, he thought that the American Indians ultimately came from Asia and that their origins might lay among the Turanian speakers of that continent. To test the hypothesis, he asked an American missionary to prepare schedules of the kin terms used by the Tamil peoples and Dravidian tribes of South India. When he finally compared these schedules with those of the Iroquois, he concluded that the kinship structures were the same (White 1957). This was conclusive proof, in Morgan's eyes, of the Asiatic origin of the American Indians. He would later write in his *Systems of Consanguinity and Affinity of the Human Family* that

> When the discoverers of the New World bestowed upon its inhabitants the name of Indians, under the impression that they had reached the Indies, they little suspected that children of the same original family, although upon a different continent, stood before them (Morgan 1871:508).

In other words, there was a single, diverse human species. Morgan further believed that the classificatory kinship systems shared by the peoples of South Asia and the Americas were an indication of their biological affinity. That is, culture and heredity were linked.

In an unpublished paper on animal psychology written in 1859, he argued not only for the unity of the human race but also the unity of the human mind. He wrote that

> Man, indeed, progresses in knowledge from generation to generation, but yet the limits of human understanding have not been advanced one hair's breadth within man's historical period. All the capacities of the entire race of man existed potentially in the first human pair . . . Notwithstanding portions of the human race have thus risen to the heights of civilization, other portions, as the Bushman and the Hotentot, still sit in the darkness of ignorance and intellectual imbecility. The Bushman, however, is of the human genus; and logically, the point of comparison between man and the species next below him, commences with the Bushman just as legitimately as with the European (quoted by Trautmann 1987:28–9).

What distinguished Bushmen from Europeans, in Morgan's view, was more their respective levels of social development than their physical appearance or race. The hunting and foraging mode of subsistence of the Bushmen was characteristic of savagery – the early or primitive stage of humanity. The Europeans were civilized – that is, they had attained a higher stage of social development in which their subsistence needs were satisfied by farming, animal husbandry, and fishing, and they wrote and kept records. For most of human history, however, people remained at the stage of savagery. While our savage ancestors provided the foundations for human progress by stabilizing subsistence needs and developing language, they nevertheless remained undeveloped and inferior when compared to civilized people.

Morgan believed that progress, the movement from one stage to the next, resulted from technological innovations that transformed the modes of subsistence and the kinds of social institutions that were inextricably linked with them. In a letter to Joseph Henry of the Smithsonian Institution, he wrote that "the real epochs of progress are connected with the arts of subsistence which includes the Darwinian idea of the 'struggle for existence'" (quoted by Resek 1960:136–7). In his view, the dietary improvements that ensued fueled both the physical expansion of the brain and improvements in beliefs and social institutions. In *Ancient Society*, Morgan referred to this as "the growth of intelligence through invention and discovery." He described the process in more detail:

> Without enlarging the basis of subsistence, mankind could not have propagated themselves into other areas not possessing the same kinds of food, and ultimately over the whole surface of the earth . . . [W]ithout obtaining an absolute control over both its variety and amount, they could not have multiplied into populous nations. It is accordingly probably that the great epochs of human progress have been identified, more or less directly, with the enlargement of the sources of subsistence (Morgan 1877/1963:19).

Furthermore, such progress, he argued

> was substantially the same in kind in tribes and nations inhabiting different and even disconnected continents, while in the same status [i.e. stage of social development], with deviations from uniformity in particular instances produced by special causes. The argument when extended tends to establish the unity of origin of mankind (Morgan 1877/1963:18).

This was certainly a different argument from those of polygenists, like Morton or Squier, for example, who claimed (1) that the inequalities in technological development found among different peoples were a consequence of differences in their innate abilities, and (2) that these abilities were immutable.

Morgan used an evolutionary theory of change to describe human progress – the movement from savagery through barbarism to civilization (Kuper 1985). He used both archaeological and ethnological information to construct and describe the movement of human society from one stage of development, or ethnical period as he called them, to the next. Each stage was marked by the appearance of particular inventions – such as pottery, plant and animal domestication for barbarism, and writing and records for civilization. Other institutions, such as monogamous marriage or private property, he believed appeared only after civilization had already been achieved. While he used the idea of stages of development to organize his argument, Morgan was actually more concerned with the processes underlying the shift from savagery through barbarism to civilization than with the sequence in which those changes actually occurred (Leacock 1963:Ixv). He was also acutely aware that institutions would continue to change in the future as society itself changed (Morgan 1877/1963:499).

The rise of civilization, in Morgan's view, was ultimately the product of a series of fortuitous circumstances.

> Its attainment at some time was certain; but that it should have been accomplished when it was, is still an extraordinary fact. . . . It may well serve to remind us that we owe our present condition, with its multiple means of safety and of happiness, to the struggles, the sufferings, the heroic exertions and the patient toil of our barbarous, and more remotely, of our savage ancestors. Their labors, their trials and their successes were a part of the plan of the Supreme Intelligence to develop a barbarian out of a savage, and a civilized man out of this barbarian (Morgan 1877/1963:563).

Morgan also employed a concept of uneven social development. He thought that, at any given moment in time, some peoples were more advanced than others and that tribes either advanced by borrowing from the more developed culture or they were held back by their geographical isolation and circumstances. Like many of his time, he also believed that the Indo-European and the Semitic speakers of Europe and the Mediterranean were the most advanced peoples of the time:

> by the commingling of diverse stocks, superiority of subsistence or advantage of position and possibly from all together, [they] were the first to emerge from barbarism. They were substantially the founders of civilization. But their existence as distinct families was undoubtedly, in a comparative sense, a late event. Their progenitors are lost in the undistinguishable mass of earlier barbarians . . .
>
> The most advanced portion of the human race were halted, so to express it, at certain stages of progress, until some great invention or discovery, such as the domestication of animals or the smelting of iron ore, gave a new and powerful impulse forward. While thus restrained, the ruder tribes, continually advancing, approached in different degrees of nearness to the same status; for wherever a continental connection existed, all the tribes must have shared in some measure in each other's progress. All great inventions and dis- coveries propagate themselves; but the inferior tribes must have appreciated their value before they could appropriate them. In the continental areas certain tribes would lead; but the leadership would be apt to shift a number of times in the course of an ethnical period [i.e., stage of development] (Morgan 1877/1963:38–9).

Morgan further believed that there was a functional relation between the economy and the form of the political organization. The transformation from a social to a political organization occurred when agriculture and herding had become productive enough to allow people to live in cities and to acquire private property. Using Classical Greece as a case, he argued that the civil powers gradually withdrawn from the kin-based units such as clans were re-invested in institutions – such as military commanders or municipal magistrates – associated with the new territorially based constituencies. In his words, "the city brought with it new demands in the art of government by creating a changed condition in society" (Morgan 1877/1963:264).

Morgan argued that the early forms of political organization were based on personal rather than political ties (Leacock 1963:Iii–IIxx). It was only after societies became territorially based, a process that began with the advent of agriculture, that the first steps toward political organization occurred: clans that restricted the number of possible marriage partners were followed by chiefs and tribal councils, by tribal confederacies, then by nations with divisions between a council of chiefs and assemblies of the people, and finally, "out of military necessities of the united tribes came the general military commander" (Morgan 1877/1963:330).

Two other changes were also linked functionally with the shift from a socially to a territorially based political organization and the development of property. They were the increasing importance of the monogamous patrilineal family and the diminished status of women. The centrality and dominance of men in the patriarchal family – the complete control they had over the household and their ability to isolate its members from the larger society – placed severe restrictions on the participation of women in decision-making (Leacock 1963:Iixv–xvi).

Morgan discussed the growth of private property in the final part of *Ancient Society*. On the one hand, he believed that social classes were disappearing in the United States. On the other, he suggested that "It was left to the then distant period of civilization to develop into full vitality that 'greed of gain' (*studium lucri*), which is now such a commanding force in the human mind" (Morgan 1877/1963:537). While he thought progress was ultimately both inevitable and beneficial, Morgan also believed that the rise of civilization had, in fact, destroyed something valuable: the values of those past and present-day peoples who knew neither private property nor the profit motive. He wrote that

> Since the advent of civilization, the outgrowth of property has been so immense, its forms so diversified, its uses so expanding and its management so intelligent in the interests of its owners, that it has become, on the part of the people, an unmanageable power. The human mind stands bewildered in the presence of its own creation. The time will come, nevertheless, when human intelligence will rise to the mastery over property, and define the relations of the state to the property it protects, as well as the obligations and the

limits of the rights of its owners. The interests of society are paramount to individual interests, and the two must be brought into just and harmonious relations. A mere property career is not the final destiny of mankind, if progress is to be the law of the future as it has been of the past. The time which has passed away since civilization began is but a fragment of the past duration of man's existence; and but a fragment of the ages yet to come. The dissolution of society bids fair to become the termination of a career of which property is the end and aim; because such a career contains the elements of self-destruction. Democracy in government, brotherhood in society, equality in rights and privileges, and universal education, foreshadow the next higher plan of society to which experience, intelligence and knowledge are steadily tending. It will be a revival, in a higher form, of the liberty, equality and fraternity of the ancient gentes (Morgan 1877/1963:561–2).[3]

In 1878, Morgan traveled to the Southwest where he visited existing Pueblos and studied the ruins of several abandoned ones. The trip had importance consequences. First, the Pueblos demonstrated, in his view, the existence of primitive communism: that is, societies in which the nuclear family survives only because it was part of a larger unit that was held together by the equitable sharing of resources. He also thought that the archaeological remains found by Stephens and others in Guatemala and the Yucatan also showed the existence of primitive communism (1880a, 1881). Second, convinced of the importance of the American Southwest as a laboratory and potential window on the development of ancient society, Morgan and Frederick Ward Putnam (1839–1915), the Director of Harvard's Peabody Museum of American Archaeology and Ethnology, attempted to persuade Charles Eliot Norton (1827–1908), chairman of the newly founded Archaeological Institute of America, to commit funds to study Indian architecture from the Pueblos to the Isthmus of Darien (Morgan 1880b). After lengthy discussions the Institute agreed to hire Adolf Bandelier (1840–1913) to conduct archaeological and historical investigations in the American Southwest. Third, at the suggestion of Henry Adams, Morgan urged John Wesley Powell (1834–1902), Director of the newly established U.S. Geological Survey and Bureau of American Ethnology, to initiate ethnological studies of the Indian tribes of the western United States.

Morgan had been concerned with the plight of American Indians since his legal work for the Seneca in the 1840s. As the western frontier began to close, he again turned his attention to their circumstances in the western territories. In 1862, he urged President Abraham Lincoln to no avail to set aside lands for two Indians territories west of the Mississippi River After Custer's defeat at the Little Big Horn, Morgan reiterated his views in *The Nation*. He described the failure of the country's Indian policy since the Jacksonian era and criticized the government's genocidal war against the Dakota tribes.

Who shall blame the Sioux for defending themselves, their wives and their children, when attacked in their own encampment and threatened with destruction? . . . Before the summer is over we may expect to hear of the destruction of a great body of these unreasoning and unreasonable Indians, who refuse to treat for the surrender of their lands upon terms they do not approve, and whose extermination may be regarded by some as a merited punishment. The good name of the country cannot bear many wars of this description (Morgan 1876:41).

In 1877, he renewed his request to President Rutherford B. Hayes to establish Indian territories west of the Mississippi River – again to no avail.

Eight years earlier in 1869, civil rights advocate Cora Daniels Tappan had described the thrust of the government's policies more tersely and perceptively in the *Boston Gazette*. She wrote

A government that has for nearly a century enslaved one race (African), that proscribes another (Chinese), proposes to exterminate another (Indian), and persistently refuses to recognize the rights of one-half of its citizens (women) cannot justly be called perfect (quoted by Kerber 1975:295).

Tappan described the social circumstances in which anthropology was born and nurtured in the United States.

Discussion

American anthropology developed from the eighteenth century onwards, not as an activity divorced from the concerns of everyday life but rather as one that shed light on the pressing issues of the day: forging a national identity, territorial expansion, and justifying a slave-based economy in the southern states. The initial focus was to explain the origins of the American Indians who were simultaneously portrayed as symbols of the new nation, people whose political organization should be emulated and then, increasingly, as obstacles to expansion and progress. Patriots dressed as Mohawks dumped tea into Boston harbor on the eve of the Revolution; Indians appeared in songs, slogans, and Paul Revere's engravings; and an Indian woman became the nation's first symbol long before either the Eagle or Uncle Sam appeared on the scene. The American Indians were exemplars of democracy in the new republic, and the plan for the new government described in the Articles of Confederation resembled the political structure of the Iroquois Confederacy (Grinde and Johansen 1991:111–2, 62). After the War of 1812, American Indians were increasingly seen, especially in the old Northwest Territory, as warlike nomads who stood in the way of progress which the American settlers of the area defined as opening new lands to agriculture and commerce.

As you will recall, Jefferson, Du Ponceau, and others studied American Indian vocabularies and languages as a means to discover their origins and relations with each other and with peoples of the Old World. By the 1820s, antiquarians increasingly employed studies of the objects and buildings made and used by the ancient inhabitants of the Americas as a means to discern their identity and connections with one another and with Old World peoples. The findings of both language studies and archaeology fueled debates about national identity, comparisons with peoples of the Old World, and the superiority or inferiority of the Americas as an intellectual and cultural milieu.

The other early concern was to explain the relations between Indians, Blacks, and Whites in a society that was already viewed as tri-racial by the time of the Revolution. The discourse that emerged was complex. It pitted those who believed that humankind was a single species against those who saw each race as distinct species. It pitted those who believed in the separation of the races against those who advocated that America, or at least Indians and Whites, should intermingle and become a mixed race. It pitted those who believed in the equality of humankind against those who argued that there was a natural hierarchy of races with Whites at the top and peoples of color, including the Irish, or racial hybrids at the bottom. It pitted Rush and others who argued that discrimination was a consequence of social and economic circumstances against those – such as Morton or Agassiz – who saw the differences between peoples determined by heredity. It pitted those who believed that culture of a people or class could be changed by altering their circumstances against those who argued that culture and biology were fixed and immutable. Legislators and courts have incorporated aspects of this discourse in the laws they have enacted and upheld since the colonial period and the first days of the new republic.

American anthropology added a new concern to its repertoire in the 1870s: the historical development of human society from earliest times to the present. This was a product of the insights of Lewis Henry Morgan and the achievements of archaeologists in Europe. They thought that improvements in technology bespoke social and moral improvements as well. This was an ideology that echoed the sentiments of men of an emerging middle class who, as Bruce Trigger (1989:109) has noted, "were pleased to view themselves as a wave of progress that was inherent in human nature and perhaps even in the constitution of the universe." Unfortunately, this view was not extended to American Indians, ex-slaves, immigrants, and women, all of whom they viewed as mentally, physically, and morally inferior to themselves. This perspective was becoming hegemonic at precisely the time anthropology was professionalized in the United States. We shall examine this connection in more detail in the next chapter.

Notes

1. Pickering's call for a "general ethnography of the globe" was underpinned by The Wilkes Exploring Expedition, 1838–1842, which made stops in South America, Australia, New Zealand, Samoa, Fiji, Tonga, Tahiti, and the Pacific Coast of North America. The organization and accomplishments of the expedition are discussed in Barry A. Joyce's (2001) *The Shaping of American Ethnography*.

2. In the 1850s, Stephens's effort to purchase Palenque and remove it to the United States raised interest in London. "The British Museum through the British government stirred the British consul in Guatemala. Something had to be done about purchasing a great Maya city for the British Museum," and the consul sent two German scientists to report on the ruins at Quiriguá (Blom 1936:1).

3. Morgan's *Ancient Society* attracted the attention of Karl Marx and Frederick Engels. Marx (1880–2/1974:95–242) took copious notes on the book between 1880 and 1882. Engels (1884/1972:236–7) concluded his *Origin of the Family, Private Property, and State* with Morgan's judgment of civilization found in the quotation cited above. While Marx and Engels viewed Morgan as an authority on the ethnology of primitive peoples, other features of Morgan's work attracted their attention as well: his emphasis on the relation between technological innovations and new economic relations, his discussion of communal or collective relations in primitive societies, his analysis of the emergence of private property and the state, his notion of dialectical return found in the last sentence of the quotation, and his awareness of how primitive social relations are dissolved and reconstituted in civilized societies (e.g. Krader 1974).

–2–

Anthropology in the Liberal Age, 1879–1929

A dominant image of nineteenth-century America was that it had been forged by westward expansion through the Alleghenies, across the Mississippi Valley, over the high plains and Rocky Mountains to the Pacific. The advance of white settlement from the Atlantic coast was said to have tamed the savagery of this wilderness and its inhabitants, as farmers and then merchants moved into almost empty lands. In the process, the wilderness of the Ohio and Mississippi Valleys, which was unfit for civilized peoples, was transformed into the "garden of the world." However, this "agrarian utopia was destroyed, or rather aborted," as Henry Nash Smith (1950:191) perceptively noted, "by the land speculator and the railroad monopolist. These were in turn but expressions of the larger forces at work in American society after the Civil War – the machine, the devices of corporate finance, and the power of big business over Congress." By the 1870s, more than a dozen cities from Pittsburgh and Chicago to Kansas City were industrial centers that belonged to the new age of steam and steel rather than to the agrarian past. The wilderness beyond the agricultural frontier, which had receded steadily earlier in the century, was closed. Westward expansion, which ultimately caused the disappearance of free land, also eliminated the safety valve that relieved poverty in the East and that promoted equality and democracy as members of the urban poor and middling classes became Midwestern farmers. As the frontier closed, the farmers were transformed into agrarian capitalists whose fate hinged on distant markets, shipping costs, and fluctuations in commodity prices (Smith 1950:159, 257–8).

However, after the Indian wars of the 1880s, just when it seemed that civilization had finally triumphed over savagery in this story, calls for further imperial expansion reappeared as big business sought access to and control over foreign markets, first in the Caribbean and Latin America and then in the Pacific and the Far East. In the 1890s, America annexed Western Samoa, acquired Hawaii and conquered Puerto Rico, the Philippines, and Cuba. This brought millions of dark-skinned people into America's political orbit. At the same time, the industrialization of the American homeland and the exclusion of African-Americans from its workplaces attracted tens of millions of immigrants from southern and eastern Europe – Italians, Slavs, Greeks, and Jews – who sought jobs in the racially and ethnically stratified labor markets of the industrial cities in the Northeast and the Great Lakes states.

The classism, racism, sexism, and xenophobia associated with these events were recorded in a national mass media whose development after the Civil War was buttressed by cheaper printing costs, by the half-literacy that large segments of the population had gained in free public schools, and by the growth of a national market for books and magazines that was facilitated by the expansion of the railroads (Patterson 1995:39–53; Smith 1967:v–vi). These were subsequently expressed in the various Jim Crow laws of the 1890s and in the anti-immigration legislation and Palmer raids of the 1920s, which targeted Blacks and working-class immigrants and political radicals.

The late nineteenth and early twentieth centuries were also marked by the creation and expansion of the federal bureaucracy, by an increase in the number of colleges, by new curricula, and by the appearance of new professions. Anthropology as a profession developed in this context. Between 1879 and 1900, most of the individuals who earned their livelihood from anthropology were employed by one of three government agencies with intertwined histories: the Smithsonian Institution, the National Museum and the Bureau of Ethnology, which was renamed the Bureau of American Ethnology in 1894. However, by 1910, the profession's center of gravity had shifted away from the federal government toward museums and universities.

The Beginnings of Professional Anthropology

Collectors and explorers insured that a steady stream of ethnographic and archaeological specimens from the western territories, as well as vocabulary lists from extant Indian peoples in the region, flowed eastward in the 1850s and 1860s (Goetzmann 1959, 1966). In 1868, the Secretary of the Smithsonian Institution noted that twenty percent of new materials accessed each year were anthropological, and that donors often spent their winters residing in the institution's living quarters as they organized their collections (Hinsley 1981:69–71). The volume increased in the 1870s as survey parties from four exploring expeditions in the West brought back photographs and reports of ancient ruins and cultures as well as information about contemporary native peoples. Nevertheless, the acquisition of anthropological information was still for the most part incidental to the primary goals of these expeditions, which were to explore and map the lands beyond the 100th meridian and to note their natural resources.

Two events in the 1870s altered the organization of these surveys. One was a congressional investigation in 1874, instigated by the War Department, that queried the cost and duplication of effort of the surveys. Four years later, the House Appropriations Committee refused to provide further funding until the surveys were consolidated and their budgets were trimmed. The Army's influence over congressional appropriations waned after General Ulysses S. Grant left the presidency and James Garfield, Grant's successor, recommended that the exploration of the West as well as its exploitation and settlement be placed under the control of the Secretary of the Interior rather than under the War Department (Goetzmann 1966:479–88).

The other pivotal event had occurred earlier, in 1873, when the Commissioner of Indian Affairs and the Secretary of the Interior asked Major John Wesley Powell (1834–1902), the leader of the Colorado River survey, to report on the conditions of the Indians in Utah and Nevada and the circumstances that brought about their plight (Darrah 1951:194–204; Goetzmann 1966:569–71). Powell had crisscrossed the region many times without military escort since his first expedition in 1867. He had met Indians, recorded their languages and made collections of their arts and crafts. He spoke to many in their own language, and his honesty and integrity earned him their respect. After meeting with a tribal council in 1873, Powell returned to Washington to report on the illegal activities of various Indian agents and to make recommendations to Congress. The Army should discontinue its military campaigns against the Indians, he argued, and the various tribes and wandering bands should be placed on reservations with sufficient arable soil, water, game, and other resources. In his view, the reservations should be schools where the Indians could farm and learn about private property, practical crafts and the ways of the white man (Powell and Ingalls 1874:23–5). In a word, they should be centers of acculturation where the Indians could become Americanized and self-reliant.

By 1877, the acquisition of ethnological and linguistic information had become a major priority for Powell. He had already collected more than 200 vocabulary lists, and – after consulting with Yale's eminent philologist, William D. Whitney, who had participated briefly with his brother in one of the western surveys – he published a guide describing how Indian vocabularies should be collected (Powell 1877). Powell was also lobbying various congressmen and close friends, such as U.S. Grant and James Garfield, about the value of anthropological research in the West (Noelke 1974:viii). In addition, he wrote popular accounts for the mass media, which publicized various aspects of Indian life in the West. In a report to the Secretary of the Interior, Powell (1878:15-16) provided a detailed explanation of the "Indian problem" and restated the urgent need for immediate inquiry:

> The work is of great magnitude; more than four hundred languages belonging to about sixty different stocks having been found within the territory of the United States. Little of value can be accomplished in making investigations in other branches in the field without a thorough knowledge of the languages. Their sociology, mythology, arts, etc. are not properly known until the people themselves are understood, with their own conceptions, opinions, and motives . . .
>
> The field of research is speedily narrowing because of the rapid change in the Indian population now in progress; all habits, customs, and opinions are fading away; even languages are disappearing; and in a very few years it will be impossible to study our North American Indians in their primitive condition except from recorded history.

. . . The rapid spread of civilization since 1849 has placed the white man and the Indian in direct conflict throughout the whole area, and the "Indian problem" is thus thrust upon us and it *must* be solved wisely, or unwisely. Many of the difficulties are inherent . . . but an equal number are unnecessary and caused by the lack of our knowledge relating to the Indians themselves. Savagery is not inchoate civilization; it is a distinct status of society with its own institutions, customs, philosophy, and religion . . .

Among all North American Indians, when in the primitive condition, personal property was almost unknown, ornaments and clothing only were recognized as the property of the individuals, and these to only a limited extent. The right to soil as landed property, the rights to the products of the chase, etc. was inherent in . . . a group of relatives . . .

We have usually attempted to treat with the tribes through their chiefs, as if they wielded absolute power; but an Indian tribe is a pure democracy; their chieftaincy is not hereditary, and the chief is but the representative, the speaker of the tribe, and can do no act by which his tribe is bound without being instructed thus to act in due and established form. The blunders we have made and the wrongs we have inflicted upon the Indians because of a failure to recognized this fact have been cruel and inexcusable, except on the ground of our own ignorance.

Following the recommendations of the Secretary of the Smithsonian Institution and of the National Academy of Science, Congress created the Bureau of Ethnology in 1879 to complete and publish materials relating to the Indians of North America. It also named Powell as director of the new bureau. The bill also directed other agencies, notably the Smithsonian Institution, to turn over vocabulary lists and other relevant materials so the work could be completed (Darrah 1951:254–69).

To complete the work mandated by Congress, Powell recruited a group of men and women, many of whom, like himself, had been born or raised in the Midwest. They included native Protestants, two Irish immigrants, and a part-Tuscarora Indian. Their previous work experience was diverse: surveyor, artist, army surgeon, army officer, farmer, newspaper reporter, blacksmith, schoolteacher, missionary, lawyer, and naturalist to name only some of the jobs they had before coming to the Bureau (Darnell 1969:2–3; Noelke 1974).

The most important long-term goal Powell set for the Bureau's personnel was a compilation of North American Indian languages and a classification of their genetic relationships. This was intended to update and extend the earlier studies of Albert Gallatin and George Gibbs. Specifically, Powell wanted to (1) standardize linguistic terminology, (2) determine the first names given particular languages, (3) classify the languages in families or stocks, and (4) determine where in the United States various languages were spoken when they were first recorded. At one time or another, the project involved virtually everyone affiliated with the Bureau (Henshaw and Mooney 1885). It was also supported by General Francis A. Walker (1840–97), Director of the 1880 Census and former Commissioner of Indian Affairs, who requested that Powell make a census of the Indian tribes and classify their linguistic affiliations. Walker believed that the study of Indian languages had a practical value:

it was essential for administering Indian tribes. In his view, tribes whose members spoke closely related languages should be settled on the same reservations (Darrah 1951:268–9; Noelke 1974:72–93).

Powell's (1891) own influential classification appeared in 1891. It was based on the study of vocabularies and divided the Indian languages north of Mexico into fifty-eight families. It provided a basis for organizing the chaotic ethnographic material that had been collected earlier in the century, and for organizing the tribal synonymy that had also been one of Powell's research priorities in the 1880s. These particular, long-term lines of inquiry came to fruition with the appearance of the *Handbook of American Indians North of Mexico* (Hodge 1907–10) and the *Handbook of American Indian Languages* (Boas 1911). In the twentieth century, anthropologists who adopted Powell's view concerning the close relationship between language and culture used his classification as a framework for tackling problems in comparative ethnology and culture history (Hymes 1963:82–3).

Unbeknownst to Powell, a group of antiquarians lobbied Congress in 1881 and persuaded its members to attach a rider to the Bureau's $25,000 appropriation for continuing ethnological research among North American Indians: "*Five thousand dollars of which shall be expended in continuing archaeological investigation relating to mound-builders and prehistoric mounds*" (Powell 1894:xli). Displeased with this turn of events and interference with his research agenda, Powell nevertheless acquiesced and quickly organized a Division of Mound Exploration, eventually appointing Cyrus Thomas (1825–1910) to direct investigations of mounds and other archaeological sites east of the Rocky Mountains (Darnell 1969:36–40). A year later, Congress directed Powell to allocate $10,000 for research on the mounds in the Mississippi Valley and another $10,000 for archaeological investigations in the Southwest. This left him with less than $5000 for ethnological and linguistic studies he considered more urgent and important (Judd 1967:18–9).

In Powell's view, the prehistoric mounds of the Midwest had been built by various groups; consequently, the idea of a single moundbuilder race should be discarded. Thomas, however, initially believed they "were the vestiges of a dense and extinct population whose advance in civilization was much superior to that of the known American Indians" (Henshaw 1883:xxxi). During 1880s, he gathered information on two thousand mounds, and, although his final report did not appear until 1894, his conclusions were already evident a decade earlier. The mounds, in his view, were built either by the tribes that resided in those regions when the Europeans arrived or by their ancestors; there was no evidence of any Moundbuilder race that had migrated from either the American tropics or the Old World; and the level of cultural development of the tribes that built the mounds was comparable to that of contemporary Indians who hunted and foraged to gain their livelihood. Thomas's conclusions had a familiar echo given that he was carrying out his investigations at the same time as the federal government was actively dispossessing Indians from their homelands in the Mississippi Valley, arguing that they had no claims on these lands since they were wanderers who had not improved the land by investing their labor in the soil in order to reap its harvests.

Powell, like his contemporaries, was influenced by the ethnological writings and social evolutionary theory of Lewis Henry Morgan as well as by the evolutionism of Herbert Spencer and Charles Darwin. He incorporated many of their conclusions in his own writings about American Indians and about the evolution of human society from savagery through barbarism to civilization and finally to enlightenment where individuals will cooperate rather than compete and law will rest on their equality with one another (Powell 1882, 1883, 1885, 1888). His ethnological papers as well as his theories of progressive development of humankind were published in the *Annual Reports of the Bureau of Ethnology*, in the *Transactions of the Anthropological Society of Washington* – an organization that he and the staff members of Bureau and the Smithsonian Institution formed in 1879 – and in the *American Anthropologist*, which was originally owned by the Anthropological Society of Washington and replaced its *Transactions* in 1888.

Powell played a central role in the foundation of professional anthropology in the United States. He supported and ensured the publication of the field investigations of a score of researchers who came from diverse backgrounds. One of the most innovative and original of Powell's researchers at the Bureau was James Mooney (1861–1920), an Irish-American newspaper reporter originally from the Midwest (Colby 1977; Moses 1984). Mooney was concerned with peoples, mostly American Indian tribes, whose members had been displaced, sold into slavery, and generally abused by the spread of civilization and its agents. In the 1880s, he worked with poor whites and Cherokees in North Carolina. In 1890, he traveled to the West, shortly after the US Army had massacred more than 200 men, women, and children at the Pine Ridge reservation in South Dakota, because of their mistaken belief that the dancing associated with the Ghost Dance religion signaled an imminent uprising.

For three years, Mooney talked with Paiute, Arapaho, Sioux, and Kiowa to gain first-hand knowledge. He learned that the Ghost Dance was a religious movement adopted by a number of western tribes, whose members were experiencing the dissolution of their own tribal cultures in the wake of the deliberate destruction of the great buffalo herds in the 1870s and the influx of settlers into their homelands. He wrote that:

> When the race lies crushed and groaning beneath an alien yoke, how natural is the dream of a redeemer, an Arthur, who shall return from exile or awake from some long sleep to drive out the usurper and win back for his people what they have lost. The hope becomes a faith and the faith becomes the creed of priests and prophets, until the hero is a god and the dream a religion. The doctrines of the Hindu avatar, the Hebrew Messiah, the Christian God, and the Hesûnanin of the Indian Ghost Dance are essentially the same, and have their origin in a hope and longing common to all humanity (Mooney 1896:657).

When Mooney compared the Ghost Dance to other religious developments described in the Bible or linked with the growth of Christianity, Powell (1896:lx), fearing public and congressional backlash, wrote that the Ghost Dance was a fantasy belonging to a pre-Scriptural stage of culture. Nevertheless, he published Mooney's work without change, and Mooney persisted in his comparisons of the Ghost Dance with other movements that erupted suddenly in times of rapid social and cultural change, when people were forced to seek solace from the wretchedness of their lives in a heartless world.

Powell's fears over a political backlash were not without merit. In the late 1880s, he had made powerful enemies in Congress as well as the scientific and business worlds because of his assertion, as Director of the U.S. Geological Survey, that the federal government should own water in the West. "Fix it in your constitution," he told the Senate Select Committee on Irrigation in 1889, "that no corporation – no body of men – no capital can get possession of the right of your waters. Hold the waters in the hands of the people" (quoted by Darrah 1951:304). Western congressmen and land speculators denounced Powell's conclusions. A few months later, Edward D. Cope (1840–97), a Philadelphia paleontologist whom Powell had refused to employ earlier, wrote to the *New York Herald* accusing him and Othniel C. Marsh (1831–99), a Survey paleontologist who was the president of the National Academy of Sciences, of attempting to control all of the government's scientific work. While Powell weathered Cope's attack, it was used by congressmen, mostly from the West, in an effort to control both the size and the direction of federally supported science. In 1892, his congressional opponents cut thirty percent from the Survey's appropriation and asserted control over how and where the funds allocated should be spent. Powell resigned as Director of the Geological Survey in 1894 and devoted the last eight years of his life to the Bureau of Ethnology (Darrah 1951:336–49).

Powell's organizational skills were matched by those of Frederick Ward Putnam (1839-1915) who until his death in 1915 was the driving force behind the growth and success of the Peabody Museum of American Archaeology and Ethnology at Harvard University. Putnam also developed anthropology programs at the Field Museum in Chicago, the American Museum of Natural History, and the University of California in the 1890s (Mark 1980:14–61). The Peabody Museum was established in 1866, when Othniel C. Marsh convinced his uncle, George Peabody, to found an anthropology museum at Harvard. The first curator was Jeffries Wyman (1814–74), a student of Agassiz's who had made anthropometric studies for the U.S. Sanitary Commission during the Civil War and who had subsequently turned his attention to shell middens along the New England coast (Hinsley 1985b). When Wyman died, Putnam, a naturalist at the Peabody Academy of Science in Salem and the publisher of *The American Naturalist*, was selected as his replacement.

Putnam's goals were to expand the museum's research collections, to construct a building to house them, and to launch a publication series that would publicize the museum, its holdings, and its work. He continued Wyman's archaeological investigations of coastal shell middens and began to explore mounds in the Ohio Valley, ruins in the Southwest, and glacial deposits for traces of the Ice Age inhabitants of the Americas. The first section of the museum building was completed in 1878; the last in 1915. The first of the *Papers of the Peabody Museum of American Archaeology and Ethnology* appeared in 1876, and a series of *Memoirs* launched two decades later described the archaeological investigations of individuals affiliated with the museum in Central America and the Yucatan Peninsula. When the Department of American Archaeology and Ethnology was created by Harvard in 1890, teaching provided another outlet for Putnam's abilities (Dexter 1980).

For the next four years, however, Putnam's energies were devoted to planning and raising money for a permanent museum in Chicago that would ultimately house the archaeological and ethnological collections made for the upcoming World's Columbian Exposition. In 1891, Putnam was asked to chair the fair's Department of Archaeology and Ethnology, and he took a three-year leave of absence from Harvard to collaborate with anthropologists from the Bureau of Ethnology and the Smithsonian Institution's National Museum. In the process, he employed more than fifty students and associates to collect specimens and anthropological data. However, Putnam, the fair's directors, and the Smithsonian scientists had different ideas about the nature of the ethnological exhibits and where they should be located on the fairground.[1] He proposed an "out-of-doors exhibit of the native peoples of America, in their own houses, dressed in their native costumes, and surrounded by their own utensils, implements, and weapons and the result of their own handiwork" (quoted in Hinsley 1991:347). The natives would work quietly in their homes on a wooded island far from the bustle of the midway and the industrial exhibitions. The Smithsonian scientists wanted to portray Indians living and working in particular environments as well as in terms of the environment and of a racial hierarchy capped by White civilized communities which, as Otis T. Mason (1838–1908) remarked, were defined by their reverence for government, their patriotism, and their love of their native land (Rydell 1984:58–65; Hinsley 1981:108; Dexter 1970). The directors of the fair demanded that the native peoples live on the midway, a mile-long strip set aside for sideshows and amusements (Dexter 1966). The political intrigues were intense. Putnam was marginalized by those who preferred the Smithsonian's natural history mode of exhibition and midway location for the living ethnological exhibits, and he eventually resigned in 1893.

In 1894, Putnam was asked by Morris K. Jesup, president of the American Museum of Natural History, to develop a Department of Archaeology and Ethnology at the New York institution. Putnam accepted a part-time position as curator and spent the next decade seeking money to pay staff members, to launch expeditions, and to purchase specimens. In 1903, he accepted an invitation from Phoebe Apperson Hearst and Benjamin Ide Wheeler to establish an anthropology department and museum of anthropology at the University of California. Hearst's gift to the university included money for ethnological and linguistic research among California Indians, for archaeological investigations in Peru and Egypt, and for research in gravel formations to determine the time when people first arrived in California. However, a downturn in the financial markets in 1904 diminished the flow of Hearst's money, and this led to the curtailment of the field expedition in Peru and to cutbacks in the archaeological and ethnological surveys in California. Once again, Putnam was forced to find money to keep the operation going. He finally retired from California in 1909 and returned to Cambridge, where he died a few years later (Mark 1980:43, 47). Putnam's intellectual legacy from during his career, according to an assistant in Chicago, was "to show the advancement of evolution of man" (quoted by Baker 1998:52).

Daniel G. Brinton (1837–99), a physician and Professor of Ethnology and Archaeology at the Academy of Natural Sciences in Philadelphia, also witnessed the professionalization of anthropology in the late nineteenth century (Darnell 1976, 1988). Brinton lectured and published regularly on American Indian linguistics and ethnology from the 1860s onward.[2] In 1880s and 1890s, he began to lecture and write about racial differences and the hierarchy of races he discerned. Brinton's writings were contradictory. On the one hand, he wrote about the psychic unity of mankind which implied that there were no fundamental differences in mental capacities of peoples from different cultures, since their natural endowments were modified by their circumstances; hence, a Fuegian who received an education in Europe could be redeemed for civilization (Darnell 1988:94).

On the other hand, Brinton (1896:68) claimed in his 1895 presidential address to the American Association for the Advancement of Science that "the black, brown and the red races differ anatomically so much from the white . . . that even with equal cerebral capacity they never could rival its results by equal efforts." That there were higher and lower races (sub-species) – identified by language, religion, and physical criteria – was a reaffirmation of the polygenic views espoused by Samuel Morton and other Philadelphia-trained physicians earlier in the century (Brinton 1890:47–50, 96–107). Brinton's description of races combined physical traits with observations about language, religion, and culture. The five races he identified – white Eurafricans, black Austroafricans, coppery Americans, brownish Asians, and dark Insular peoples – legitimated the common-sense categories that had already been used in political debates for two decades and that provided a justification for the Jim Crow legislation and anti-immigrationist sentiments of the 1890s (Baker 1998:36–7).

Brinton further claimed that the races, or sub-species, were arranged hierarchically, and that "the leading race in all history had been the White Race" (Brinton 1890:102), which was divided into two branches – the South Mediterranean whose Semitic-Hamitic members lived from Spain across North Africa to the Middle East, and the

North Mediterranean whose members lived in Europe and were further divided into three ancient stocks: the Euskarics who lived in remote areas south of the Alps, the Caucasians of Eastern Europe, and the widespread Aryacs or Anglo-Saxons who originated in northern Europe. In Brinton's view the Anglo-Saxons stood at the top of the racial hierarchy, while the darker-skinned ones were at the bottom. They were separated by a series of not-quite-white buffer races – i.e., the Caucasian, Euskaric, and South Mediterranean stocks that had already sent more than ten million immigrant workers for the stratified labor markets of America's industrial heartland (Patterson and Spencer 1994).

Powell and Putnam, influenced by the ethnological and theoretical writings of Lewis Henry Morgan in particular and by the theoretical writings of Herbert Spencer in a more general way, were social evolutionists who believed in the progressive development of humanity. Powell, Putnam, and Brinton were also influenced by Spencer's Social Darwinism which, in the simplified versions that were popular in the United States, saw and portrayed the development of the human species and society in terms of competition and "survival of the fittest" (Hofstatter 1955).[3] However, not every anthropologist at the turn of the century shared the views of Powell, Putnam, and Brinton concerning the existence of racial hierarchies or the superiority of civilization as a social type, or even that there was a necessarily fixed relation between race, language, and culture. We shall examine these anthropologists and their critiques in the next section.

Professionalization, Certification and Political Commitment

Just as important as the expansion of industrial production and the closing of the western frontier in shaping everyday life and popular culture during the Progressive Era were the genocidal and ethnocidal attacks on American Indians and the rising tide of discrimination against African Americans and immigrants. The Black Codes – a series of state laws enacted in the South from 1865 onward – limited the economic options available to freedmen and freedwomen outside of plantation work, and the Compromise of 1877 effectively blocked Blacks from industrial jobs in the North (Foner 1988:198–200). These were filled in part after 1880 by some of the 23 million immigrants who arrived from Southern and Eastern Europe "with neither a promise of employment nor the ability to speak English. Additionally, labor violence associated with the Haymarket Riot of 1886 made native Americans anxious" (Hyatt 1990:103).

As a result, foreigners faced unrelenting discrimination and persistent efforts to restrict their entry into the United States. For example, Chinese immigration was restricted after 1882, and the American Protective Association formed in 1887 sought to ban the further immigration of Catholics so that time-honored American policies and traditions would not be disrupted. Anti-Semitism was already so rampant by the late 1870s that Joseph Seligman, a wealthy New York banker and close friend of both Abraham Lincoln and Ulysses S. Grant, was not permitted to register as a guest at the Grant Union Hotel in Sarasota Springs, and Bernard Baruch was denied membership in a fraternity, in both cases simply because they were Jews. Anti-immigrant sentiments were further heightened in 1894, when the Immigration Restriction League was organized by Harvard graduates who sought to maintain "America's Anglo-Saxon heritage and traditions" and had the support of Henry Cabot Lodge, U.S. Senator from Massachusetts, who thought there were "ineradicable differences between the races of men" (Dinnerstein 1994:44).

This was the social milieu in which American anthropology was professionalized, and the profession's center of gravity slowly shifted from the federal government and the private museum to the university, thus providing credentials and certification to the next generation of anthropologists. Franz Boas (1858-1942), who played an important role in this transformation, worked in this milieu, and it had a profound and immeasurable impact on both his life and his career, since he was a political radical, a foreigner, and a Jew.[4] In 1887, Boas gave up a position at the Berlin Ethnographic Museum because of Bismarck's antiliberal policies and rising anti-Semitism in Germany to accept an assistant editorship at *Science*, the publication of the American Association for the Advancement of Science. Boas's most perceptive biographer noted that political commitments shaped his vision of anthropology, and that

> these commitments were more fundamental than the professionalization of anthropology, although professionalism was sometimes strong enough to clash successfully with Boas's politics. Professionalism acted as a brake on Boas's political activism, at least until his later years. On the other hand, professionalism was often an apolitical mask for deeper political convictions. The intensity of Boas's politics and its influence on his scholarship are shown by his admission (to F. von Luschan 12/20/1919) that the "only relief" was to "explode periodically in print" and then he felt "a little better for a while!" (Willis 1975:309).

As a university student, Boas took courses in the sciences, languages, geography, psychophysics (which came to be called experimental psychology), and philosophy. He was also influenced by neo-Kantian thinkers who gave expression to liberal and socialist ideals in the oppressive political climate of Bismarck's Germany during the 1870s and 1880s (Köhnke 1991; Willey 1978). Their views and those of his family underwrote Boas's lifelong commitment to freedom of thought. He believed that individuals had the right to challenge "the authority of tradition" in ways that "free us from the errors of the past" and that "prevent individualism from outgrowing its legitimate limits and becoming intolerable egotism" (Boas 1938:201–3).

The neo-Kantians also maintained that there was a tension between natural and human sciences. Natural scientists, they argued, seek to explain the relationship of objects, whereas those concerned with the human sciences have to deal with the fact that people think and have some control over their actions. The goal of the human scientists was to understand the forms people construct to explain their experiences (Boas 1887a). The fact that knowledge was always produced from particular points of view raised questions for Boas regarding "the role of subjective mental activity in the perception of the external world" (Lesser 1968:102), and it put the problem he investigated in his doctoral dissertation – perceptions of the color of water – in new light. A year-long sojourn with an Inuit (Eskimo) community in Baffinland in 1883 taught Boas that the color of water, which could be measured precisely with scientific instruments, was not perceived in the same way by Germans and Inuit; he would conclude that the differences could not be explained solely by reference to the natural environments in which they lived (Boas 1887/1974, 1888/1964).

Boas was concerned with the relationship of the objective and subjective worlds – the connection between the physical and the psychic. In order to understand their interconnection, it was necessary to look behind appearances to get at the "genius of a people," its culture – i.e., the fundamental elements that constituted the character of its members and gave meaning to their lives, elements that were modified by geography and history, that incorporated foreign materials, and that were transmitted from one generation to the next. Culture, for Boas and the neo-Kantians, was a relatively autonomous totality with interrelated parts. In the 1880s, Boas saw culture embodied in the folklore and sentiments of people, which manifested what its members considered good and bad, commendable and objectionable, beautiful and otherwise (Stocking 1968:133-61, 195-233). Their mythology embraced their "whole concept of the world," their "individuality" and their "genius," and gave "a clear insight into the passions that move" them (Boas quoted by Stocking 1968:223–4). Since cultures could be compared, an understanding of one culture would provide insights into and questions about other cultures.

Boas's ideas built on the legacy of Johann Herder – an eighteenth-century supporter of the French Revolution and the Declaration of the Rights of Man as well as a critic of the German nobility. Herder had distinguished civilization from culture (Patterson 1997:72–3; Bunzl 1996). Civilization was, in his view, mechanical and associated with the state; it erased people's knowledge, their shared patterns of thought, and their understanding of everyday life. That is, civilization destroyed the spontaneity and creativity of authentic culture which was rooted in the thoughts and language of people who lived in remote, relatively unstratified communities.

The residues of Boas's views that persist to the present are his recognition of a plurality of cultures and his cultural relativism. He believed that anthropologists gained understanding of "a culture through first-hand experience with living peoples and how they understood their conditions of existence" (Cove 1999:110; Boas 1901:2–3). He also argued that indigenous understandings were not the same as a systematic ethnology, even though they brought to the fore those things that interested the people themselves (Boas 1916:393). In his view, the anthropologists' reason for understanding a culture ultimately had different foundations from the motives of the members of that group. Boas's cultural relativism was complex.[5] As a methodology, it assumed that anthropologists were able to suspend, at least temporarily, the values and viewpoints of their own culture and to assume those of the cultures they were studying. However, the study of different cultures was not, in his view, an invitation to promote relativistic attitudes in which nothing was stable or relativistic attitudes toward ethical standards. The comparative study of cultures provided Boas with "the materials and incentives to transcend the limitations of both cultural relativism and ethnocentrism" (Bidney 1968). It led him to write that

> [his] ideals have developed because I am what I am and have lived where I have lived; and it is my purpose to work for these ideals, because I am by nature active and because the conditions of our culture that run counter to my ideals stimulate me to action (Boas 1938:204).

Shortly after Boas arrived in the United States in 1887, he launched a critique of cultural evolutionary thought which viewed human history as the end-product of a universal, unilinear process that began with savagery and progressed through barbarism to civilization. While he accepted the idea that evolution was historical development, he rejected claims that all societies necessarily followed the same course of development or that all societies necessarily moved from simple to more complex conditions (Boas 1887b, 1887c). The focus of his critique was the way that Otis T. Mason, the Curator of Ethnology at the National Museum, had organized its exhibits. Each exhibit was an orthogenetic arrangement of a particular class of objects – such as cooking pots, masks, or woodworking tools – that purportedly represented their development from earlier, simpler forms to more recent, more complex ones. Boas argued that Mason's classifications did not constitute explanations of the historical development of those objects, because the objects themselves were not related. They had been wrenched from the social contexts of the groups in which they were made and used and had meaning. Boas stressed the importance of explaining ethnological collections in terms of the histories of the cultural groups to whom they belonged.

Boas's views about the theoretical underpinnings of Mason's museum exhibits as well as an earlier critique of environmental determinism were already major sources of annoyance to the Washington anthropologists by the time of the World's Columbian Exposition in Chicago where he worked as Putnam's assistant. Like Putnam, Boas was also marginalized by the fair's trustees, and he resigned shortly after William H. Holmes (1846–1933) was named Director of the Department of Anthropology at the Field Museum in 1894.[6] For the next two years, Boas was only sporadically employed; during this period, he worked a few months for Putnam at the American Museum of Natural History. However, in the winter of 1895/96, Putnam succeeded in getting Boas an appointment as a special assistant at the museum and another as a lecturer at Columbia University for the 1896/97 academic year (Dexter 1976).

In spite of his precarious financial position during this period, Boas still continued his critique of the theory and practice of American anthropology. This time, he focused his attention on the correlation between race and culture that Brinton and others presumed.[7] At the 1894 meeting of the American Association for the Advancement of Science, he questioned whether there was a correlation between racial type and level of cultural development, whether there was a hierarchy of racial types, and whether the white race had a greater aptitude for producing civilization than did other racial types (Boas 1894/1974). In a word, he challenged their racialist theories and the racist attitudes they buttressed in the wider society (Haller 1971). When he pointed out that "the variations inside any single race are such that they overlap the variations in another race so that a number of characteristics may be common to individuals of both races," he came close to challenging the utility of the race-concept itself as an analytical category (Boas 1894/1974:227). An examination of the historical development of early civilizations in the Old World led him to conclude that they were not the product of a particular race but rather the amalgamation of ideas that were derived from and shared by diverse races; in other words, "historical events appear to have been much more potent in leading races to civilization than their faculty, and it follows that achievements of races do not warrant us to assume that one race is more highly gifted than the other" (Boas 1894/1974:227). Boas also pointed out that, while there was no relation between racial type and cultural development, racism supported by racialist theories presented "a formidable obstacle" to the advance and progress of African Americans in the United States.

Two years later, Boas (1896/1940) extended his critique of the hegemonic cultural evolutionary theories in the United States. He pointed out that, when Brinton and others sought to discover the laws that governed the development of society, they assumed that particular traits were characteristic of certain stages of development, and that societies exhibiting those traits had necessarily experienced the same processes of growth and had consequently followed the same developmental pathway. In contrast to their efforts "to construct a uniform systematic history of the evolution of culture," Boas advocated comparative studies of the historical circumstances in which various peoples emerged and the growth processes that were actually involved in the development of these cultures (Boas 1896/1940:280).

In 1891, while he was teaching in the Psychology Department at Clark University, Boas launched the first of his studies of human growth and development

(Darnell 1982; Herskovits 1943; Tanner 1959). Unlike his contemporaries who were mainly concerned with establishing "standard" growth curves, Boas showed that children in fact grew at different rates, that the growth of a typical individual might be accelerated relative to those standard growth curves at one period and retarded at another, and that variations in the tempo of growth were characteristic of both mental development and physical growth (Boas 1895). Like some of his contemporaries, Boas knew that the growth and development of children were affected by their social circumstances – e.g., upper-class boys and girls were larger than children of the same age raised in less affluent circumstances. During the next two decades he would extend these studies to children in Oakland, Toronto, Atlanta, Puerto Rico, and the Hebrew Orphan Home in New York, and undertake longitudinal growth study of children enrolled in a private school near New York.

In 1907, Boas was one of the experts employed by the U.S. Immigration Commission that was established by President Theodore Roosevelt. Boas and his assistants were charged with investigating the effects of the American environment on immigrants and their children. They measured 17,821 subjects and concluded that head form was not stable, as most students of race believed, but rather that it changed relatively quickly in response to environmental factors. He wrote that

> the adaptability of the immigrant seems to be very much greater than we had a right to suppose before our investigations were instituted. . . .
>
> Not even those characteristics of a race which have proved to be most permanent in their old home remain the same under the new surroundings; and we are compelled to conclude that when these features of the body change, the whole bodily and mental make-up of the immigrants may change.
>
> These results are so definite that, while heretofore we had a right to assume that human types are stable, all the evidence is now in favor of a great plasticity of human types, and permanence of types in new surroundings appears rather as the exception to the rule (Boas 1911/1912:2, 5).

Once again, Boas challenged established views both in the wider society and in the emerging profession. The U.S. Immigration Commission dismissed Boas's claims, arguing that there was no corroborating evidence. Boas was understandably outraged in 1924 when Congress passed the Immigration Restriction Act, whose nationalism, xenophobia, and racism he deplored as "nordic nonsense" (Boas 1925; Hawes 1968).

Boas's views on racism and his studies of child growth ultimately led to an invitation from W. E. B. Du Bois (1868–1963) to measure African-American children in Atlanta and to participate in a conference on the Negro physique at Atlanta University in 1906. Boas agreed and gave the commencement address that year. His acceptance of the invitation placed him in the middle of the struggle for racial equality; it allied him with the vindicationist wing led by Du Bois which argued for integration and put him in opposition to the faction led by Booker T. Washington at the Carnegie-supported Tuskegee Institute which stressed the acquisition of skills and property as well as the maintenance of the existing social order (Baker 1998:120–5; Drake 1980; Williams 1989, 1996). When the National Association for the Advancement of Colored People was founded in 1910, Boas (1910) was a charter member and wrote about the race problem for its magazine, *The Crisis*.

Boas's participation in the struggles for social justice and racial equality was not confined to lecturing, joining organizations, and writing articles. In the fall of 1906, he attempted to establish an African American Museum in New York to counteract racism. He solicited funds from Andrew Carnegie, John D. Rockefeller, and two supporters of Negro education, George Peabody and Robert Ogden. All of them declined to provide financial support for the project. He then turned to the Bureau of American Ethnology, which also declined to support it, because it might arouse "race feeling" in Congress and jeopardize the Bureau's appropriations. Boas also sought and finally got some financial support from Carter J. Woodson, Elsie Clews Parsons, and George Peabody to support and train African American students at Columbia (Beardsley 1973; Willis 1975).

Boas's participation in civil rights' struggles was not confined to immigrants and African Americans. In 1915, he wrote to a U.S. Senator arguing that women should be granted the same privileges enjoyed by men. Two years later, he took up the cause of the Kwakiutl Indians when the federal government threatened to enact legislation that would prohibit the potlatch. He informed the government that this would cause great hardship and that it should "not restrict Indian practices simply because a particular custom was alien to American culture" (Hyatt 1990:118).

The profession of anthropology was restructured at the turn of the twentieth century. This reorganization had two major dimensions. The first was the formation of a national professional organization, the American Anthropological Association, with its own journal, the *American Anthropologist*. It was established in the context of local anthropological societies that included professionals who gained their livelihoods from anthropological inquiries as well as amateurs. The Washington anthropologists wanted an inclusive membership policy for the new organization, while Boas preferred one that limited membership to professionals. McGee and the other members of the Washington group prevailed until the organization created an Executive Committee in 1912, which marked the beginning of a shift in the balance of power in the profession from individuals employed by the government and museums to those with academic credentials and university affiliations (Stocking 1968:283–5).

The second dimension of the reorganization involved the emergence of graduate training programs in anthropology at Harvard, Columbia, Chicago, the University of Pennsylvania, and the University of California at Berkeley (Thomas 1955). By 1912, these institutions had awarded doctorates in anthropology to twenty men.

During the next two decades, there was a more than fourfold increase. By 1928, a total of fifty-three men and nine women had received Ph.D. degrees in anthropology. Harvard and Columbia granted the largest number of degrees. Twenty-four men received doctorates from Harvard, and Boas had supervised the dissertations of fifteen men and seven women at Columbia.

In spite of the rapidly growing number of anthropologists with university certification, the profession was still small, and the processes of reorganization and centralization proceeded slowly in the early decades of the twentieth century. One reason for this was the continued existence or formation of local or regional anthropological societies whose members could effectively challenge the hegemony of Washington anthropologists and Boas's intellectual leadership. The career of Edgar Lee Hewett (1865–1946) is a case in point (Fowler 1999; Hinsley 1986). Hewett was a Midwestern schoolteacher who became interested in Southwestern Archaeology in the 1890s. With friends, he founded the Archaeological Society of New Mexico in 1898 and, within a few years, became the recognized spokesman for archaeology in the West. Hewett gained national prominence with the passage of the Antiquities Act of 1906. From 1904 onward, Congress debated the merits of several alternative bills – one backed by the Smithsonian, the American Anthropological Association, and the Archaeological Institute of America; and another proposed by Hewett who enlisted the aid of the politically powerful Charles Lummis of Los Angeles. The Westerners argued that the bill supported by the Easterners gave the Smithsonian too much control over local archaeological sites. The Hewett-Lummis version became law. Hewett's tactics particularly annoyed Boas and Putnam but apparently not W. H. Holmes and Jesse Fewkes (1850–1930) at the Smithsonian Institution, with whom he had close personal relations.

At the same time, Hewett successfully lobbied the Archaeological Institute of America to establish a School of American Archaeology in Santa Fe with himself as director and his salary paid by the institute. In 1907, he launched an archaeological field school which was attended by two Harvard students, Alfred V. Kidder (1885–1963) and Sylvanus Morley (1883–1948), both of whom would soon become prominent archaeologists in the United States. Two years later, the politically well-connected Hewett convinced the state legislature to establish the Museum of New Mexico. In the process, Hewett cemented his reputation in the Midwest and the West as a leader in the emerging profession.

Hewett had consolidated his position and influence by 1910 and was able to beat back criticism of his research and administration of the School in Santa Fe. For example, in 1909, Putnam, Boas, and Charles Bowditch, who were critical of Hewett's research and opportunism, took their criticisms to the annual meeting of the Archaeological Institute of America and lost; Hewett's school and activities took money and other resources that Putnam, Boas, and Bowditch wanted to use to support the International School of American Archaeology and Ethnology in Mexico (Godoy 1970).

In 1910, Hewett allegedly made statements impugning Boas's integrity; Boas responded publicly and, once again, criticized Hewett's administration of the School in Santa Fe. Hewett's friend, William H. Holmes, who by this time had succeeded Powell as Director of the Bureau of Ethnology and had his own axe to grind, came to his aid and cut off the Bureau's financial support for Boas's ongoing linguistic research. As a result of his political connections and tactics, Hewett had a shaping effect on the development of American anthropology from 1904 through the mid-1920s. His influence and prominence, especially in the Midwest and West, were virtually unchallenged until he tangled with John D. Rockefeller, Jr. over the fate of Santa Fe in the mid-1920s (Stocking 1985).

Hewett's stature and political connections were such that any anthropologist seeking to work in the American Southwest, particularly in New Mexico, from 1910 onward had to get his approval before beginning his or her studies (Givens 1992:42). This included the pioneering archaeological investigations of Nels C. Nelson (1875–1964) and A. V. Kidder in the years immediately preceding the First World War – the first stratigraphic excavations and dating of artifacts in the area and among the first uses of stratigraphy in the United States – which were carried out with his consent (Kidder 1924; Nelson 1916). Stratigraphic excavations and the recognition of cultural stratigraphy marked the beginning of a methodological revolution in American archaeology (Willey and Sabloff 1993:97–108).[8] By the 1920s, Kidder was emerging as the major figure in American archaeology. This was partly because of the high quality of his investigations at Pecos; more importantly, however, it was the result of his administrative skills, the annual conferences he organized at Pecos, and the field experience and research opportunities that he provided for students and younger scholars. Kidder collaborated with, trained, or influenced most of the next generation of archaeologists who worked in the American Southwest or for the Carnegie Institution of Washington in southern Mexico and Central America (Woodbury 1973, 1993:3–77).

In 1901, Andrew Carnegie used ten million dollars of United States Steel Corporation bonds to establish the Carnegie Institution of Washington to promote original research and "to discover the exceptional man in every department of study whenever and wherever found, inside or outside of schools, and enable him to make the work for which he seems specially designed his life work" (quoted by Reingold 1979:318). In the first years of its existence, the Carnegie provided minor grants for W. H. Holmes's studies of early man in the Americas, and Robert S. Woodward, its president, consulted with Boas and other former colleagues at Columbia about the possibility of moving into new fields of inquiry. By 1911, he was convinced that a department of anthropology should be formed; however, William Barclay Parsons, an engineer and one of the Carnegie trustees, pushed for Central American archaeology and got the enthusiastic support of other trustees (Reingold 1979:329–31). A long search was launched; the lobbying was intense. Sylvanus Morley, who proposed to conduct archaeological investigations at Chichén Itzá in southern Mexico, was finally selected in 1914; Holmes and Frederick W. Hodge (1864-1956) at the Smithsonian supported his candidacy over that of Alfred Tozzer, who had the support of Putnam, Bowditch, and perhaps Boas; Hewett apparently tried to derail Morley's candidacy by criticizing the project his employee had proposed. The Mexican government, which had recently enacted a strict antiquities' act to control the movement of antiquities from the country, approved the Carnegie's project at Chichén Itzá with the proviso that no artifacts would be permanently removed from the Yucatan Peninsula (Givens 1992:79–87; Woodbury 1973:53–4).

Morley began his archaeological investigations almost immediately. The program flourished and grew; however, in 1925, Thomas Gann, a physician affiliated with the project and a close personal friend of Morley's, purchased a pre-Columbian jade object and smuggled it out of the country. The Mexican authorities – i.e. Manuel Gamio, a former student of Boas's – learned that the jade had been exported illegally by a member of Morley's staff and complained to John C. Merriam (1869–1945), the Carnegie's president, who contacted his friend A. V. Kidder for advice. The jade was returned and presented to the Mexican government as a gift. However, the reputation of the Carnegie was tarnished. An advisory committee was formed to reorganize the project and to expand the scope of its investigations to include ethnology, ethnohistory, geology, geography, climatology, botany, zoology, physical anthropology, and linguistics. In 1929, Merriam asked Kidder to become director of the Carnegie's new Division of Historical Research and of its Middle American research program (Givens 1992:89–119; Woodbury 1973:52–87).

Shortly after the Armistice ending the First World War, Boas was outraged by information he acquired regarding Morley and three other American archaeologists associated with the Carnegie or with the International School of American Arch-aeology and Ethnology in Mexico. They were spies who used anthropology as a front for their espionage activities in Central America and Mexico during the First World War (Sullivan 1989:132–7). Boas had already angered people with strong patriotic sentiments when he denounced patriotism on the pages of *The New York Times* (January 3, 1915), opposed the United States' entry into the First World War which he considered a clash between imperialist states (*The New York Times*, February 9, 1917), and publicly announced his membership in the Socialist Party in 1918. That anthropologists whom he knew or supported – Morley, H. E. Mechling who attended the International School in Mexico City, Herbert Spinden (1879–1967) of the American Museum of Natural History, and J. Alden Mason (1885–1967) of the University of Pennsylvania – were spies was seen by Boas as more than a personal betrayal; without naming them, he told the readers of *The Nation* (December 20, 1919) that they "had prostituted science by using it as a cover for their activities as spies" (Boas 1919/1974:336). They were not the only anthro-pologists to serve with Army or Navy Intelligence during the First World War;

Kidder, William C. Farabee (1865–1925) of the University of Pennsylvania, Marshall Saville (1867–1935) who was Boas's erstwhile colleague at Columbia, and Samuel Lothrop (1892–1965), who purchased collections in Nicaragua and Costa Rica for George Heye, also served in military intelligence units (Price 2000).

Boas's article in *The Nation* incensed a majority of the anthropological community in the United States. On December 30, 1919, the American Anthropological Association adopted in Cambridge by a vote of twenty-one to ten a censure motion prepared by W. H. Holmes, which read

> RESOLVED: That the expression of opinion by Dr. Franz Boas contained in an open letter to the Editor of "The Nation" under date of October 16, 1919, and published in the issue of that weekly for December 20, 1919, is unjustified and does not represent the opinion of the American Anthropological Association. Be it further
>
> RESOLVED: That a copy of this resolution be forward to the Executive Board of the National Research Council and such other scientific associations as may have taken action on this matter.
>
> It is further respectfully asked, in the name of Americanism as against un-Americanism, that Dr. Franz Boas and also the ten members of the American Anthropological Association, who by voting against the latter resolution thus supporting him in his disloyalty, be excluded from participation in any service respecting which any question of loyalty to the United States Government may properly be raised.
>
> To question the honor of The President of the United States is a disloyal act. To criticize and make public the secret measures of the military service before peace is signed and with apparent intent to embarrass scientific researches on the part of certain students in foreign countries is a doubly disloyal act. To support disloyalty as it was actively supported in Cambridge by certain members of the American Anthropological Association is a distinctly disloyal act and should be recognized as such.
>
> Boas and his followers have sought to gain control of and direct anthropological researches in this country, especially those undertaken on behalf of the nation. There appears no danger that the [National] Research Council may give this group control of researches and measures affecting the most intimate and vital interests of the nation – interests which should be entrusted those, and only those, whose standard of citizenship is wholly above criticism (Holmes quoted by Spencer 1979:792–3).

In the days immediately following the adoption of the resolution, Holmes urged patriot-scientist Charles D. Walcott, his former colleague in the Geological Survey who had become Secretary of the Smithsonian Institution, to use his influence to get Boas expelled from the National Academy of Sciences. Holmes also supplied Walcott with hearsay evidence that Boas was a German spy. Walcott apparently forwarded this information to A. Mitchell Palmer, the U.S. Attorney General, who conducted a "thorough investigation" of Boas's activities and found nothing implicating him in "pernicious radical activities" (Spencer 1979:720–1, 87–8). However, within the next few months, Boas was forced to withdraw his candidacy for a seat on the National Research Council which was presided over by John C. Merriam, who would soon become president of the Carnegie Institution of Washington.

Within a few years, at least one of Boas's supporters – Robert H. Lowie (1883–1957), who was at the American Museum of Natural History – felt sufficiently pressured by the conditions in which he worked either to revise his political views or at least to stop expressing them publicly in the period before Attorney General Palmer began to disrupt radical political and labor organizations by arresting and deporting their members (William Peace, personal communication). The Palmer raids, as they were called, were led by J. Edgar Hoover – an ambitious patriot, racist, and xenophobe – who used the attacks to establish himself as the first director of the Federal Bureau of Investigation.

While patriotism precipitated Boas's censure, the latter also involved old divisions and antagonisms (Darnell 1969:476–83; 1998:261–9; Stocking 1968:270–90). Of the twenty-one individuals who supported the censure, fifteen identified themselves as archaeologists, ten of whom worked in Mexico or Central America. Three others described themselves as physical anthropologists. Twelve were trained at Harvard, and three were employed by the federal government. At the time, Harvard Mayanist A. M. Tozzer called them the "Maya-Washington crowd." Six of the ten individuals who supported Boas, by opposing the censure motion, identified themselves as ethnologists. They included six former students and two close associates, several of whom were politically radical Jews whose parents had emigrated earlier from Central Europe (Stocking 1968:276–90).

Struggles over the Future of Anthropology, 1916–1932

Three distinct conceptions of anthropology existed during and after the First World War. Briefly, the one crafted by Franz Boas and his students argued that culture rather than race determined behavior and stressed the interconnections of ethnology, linguistics, folklore, archaeology, and physical anthropology. The second one, crafted by Aleš Hrdlička (1869–1943) of the National Museum, asserted the primacy of the biology and attempted to establish physical anthropology as an autonomous academic discipline.[9] The third was that of Charles B. Davenport (1866–1944) and other spokesmen of the eugenics movement, who were the direct heirs of late nineteenth-century Social Darwinism; they saw eugenics as a practical science and viewed all human differences in terms of heredity and a rank-ordered racial hierarchy with White Anglo-Saxon Protestants at the top and other groups arranged below them in terms of decreasing whiteness (Allen 1976, 1983).[10] The National Research Council was an important arena of struggle for the proponents of these views as the war ended and peace reappeared.

The National Research Council (NRC) was established in 1916 as a means of mobilizing science and research for the war effort. The NRC would acquire a permanent status in 1918 as a result of an Executive Order (Number 2859) signed by President Woodrow Wilson; the Executive Order was engineered by Elihu Root (1845–1937) and George E. Hale (1868–1938), both of whom were affiliated with the Carnegie Corporation, the umbrella organization which linked together Andrew Carnegie's various philanthropies, and whose board of trustees had publicly "acknowledged its wish to preserve Anglo-Saxon prerogatives, customs, and genes" (Lagemann 1989:30, 33–50). The formation of the NRC coincided with the heyday of the eugenics movement in the United States, whose proponents claimed that the Anglo-Saxon race was being swamped by all of the babies that were being born to the members of inferior races – e.g. Mediterraneans, East Europeans, Jews, American Indians, Asians, Blacks, and poor people. At a practical level, the eugenicists argued for sterilization, selective breeding, and restricting the immigration of peoples from Eastern and Southern Europe and of individuals with dark skins.[11] The formation of the NRC also coincided with radical union organizing and labor agitation by workers who were drawn largely from the races deemed inferior by the eugenicists and by the wealthy capitalists who supported them – e.g. Carnegie, Mary Harriman, John D. Rockefeller, the Kellogg family which made breakfast cereal, and Henry Fairfield Osborn (1857-1935) who was president of the American Museum of Natural History (Allen 1976, 1986, 1987).

In the fall of 1916, George E. Hale, the Director of the NRC, turned to W. H. Holmes, rather than to Boas, to organize its Committee on Anthropology. Holmes immediately discussed this with Aleš Hrdlička, his long-time associate and ally at the National Museum, whom he wanted on the committee. Holmes and Hrdlička faced a dilemma. They were not anxious to have Boas, the recognized leader of American anthropology, or any of his allies in the profession on the committee. They feared that Boas would seize control of the committee's research agenda and that this would give him and his students unprecedented control over the direction of American anthropology. Moreover, Boas's conception of anthropology as practical and composed of ethnology, linguistics, folklore, archaeology, and physical anthropology was distinctly at odds with that of Hrdlička who had long campaigned to establish physical anthropology as an independent discipline.

In his recommendations of January 15, 1917 to Hale, Holmes followed Hrdlička and proposed that the investigations of the Committee on Anthropology would

> have in view the betterment of the people of the nation [and] are concerned almost exclusively with the practical side – with the man that is to be: with his physique, his functions and mentality, his heredity and eugenics, his sociology, hygiene and pathology (quoted by Spencer 1979:638).

The names Holmes proposed for membership on the committee were those of Hrdlička, Boas and Davenport; the list also included a number of physicians whose main qualification was that they controlled facilities where the investigations Hrdlička proposed could be carried out (Spencer 1979:638–9).

Hale balked when he saw Holmes's proposal. He was disturbed by the biomedical thrust of the inquiries, by Holmes's disregard for the selection procedures established by the NRC that mandated cooperation with the American Anthropological Association which Boas and his allies controlled, and perhaps by Holmes's reluctance to nominate his friend, James H. Breasted (1865–1935) – the Egyptologist at the University of Chicago – for the Committee on Anthropology. Holmes gained a temporary edge when President Wilson broke diplomatic relations with Germany and the other Central Powers on February 3, 1917 – a move that Boas denounced as a declaration of war in *The New York Times* (February 9, 1917). Because of the letter, Hale recommended to Holmes that Boas be dropped from the committee. Holmes agreed, but he dropped both Boas and Davenport (Spencer 1979:639–47).

In April 1917, Holmes told Hrdlička that Madison Grant (1865–1938), whose best-selling *Passage of the Great Race* (1916) had been published a year earlier, offered to provide financial assistance for the committee's work in exchange for membership on it. Grant was a wealthy New York lawyer, racist propagandist, and virulent antisemite who had presumably learned of Holmes's problems from his friend Henry Fairfield Osborn at the American Museum, who was also a friend and confidant of Hale. In spite of reservations about Grant's book and the value of eugenics research in general, Hrdlička followed Holmes's advice. He readily took Grant's money and, with less enthusiasm, accepted his membership on the committee. Boas expressed his outrage over Grant's inclusion in the Committee on Anthropology in a letter to Hale who forwarded it to Holmes. When Hrdlička saw the letter he asked Holmes to fill the remaining slot on the committee with Davenport. Holmes did so, and that turned out to be a mistake (Spencer 1979:650–7).

By December 1917, Grant and Davenport were disgruntled. Grant perceived correctly that Hrdlička only wanted his money, and Davenport realized that Hrdlička had no interest in his eugenic investigations. Grant complained to Hale that the committee was unable to implement the survey because it could not agree on the design of the anthropometric form that should be used. In Grant's opinion, the committee had become pre-occupied with establishing Hrdlička's physical anthropology journal. Holmes and Hrdlička met with Hale on January 4, 1918 in order to clarify and resolve the issues. Hale supported Davenport's proposals and told them to use the anthropometric schedule Davenport employed at the Eugenics Record Office, because it would give "scientifically comparable results". Holmes attempted to resign, pointing out that he had been appointed "Chairman of the Committee on Anthropology not of the Committee on Anthropology and Eugenics" (Spencer 1979:672–3); Hrdlička also threatened to resign, but Hale asked him to explain in detail his objections to Davenport's research project. Hale did not accept their resignations immediately in order to forestall embarrassing questions.

In February 1918, Hale chose Davenport – not Holmes or Hrdlička – to represent the interests of the Committee on Anthropology to the Division of Medicine and Related Sciences of the NRC. Holmes resubmitted his resignation a month later, and Hrdlička responded by requesting that Clark Wissler (1870–1947), a student of Boas who was employed at the American Museum of Natural History, be added to the committee and by adding Boas and two of his allies, Alfred Kroeber (1876–1960) and Bertold Laufer (1874–1934), to the editorial board of his *American Journal of Physical Anthropology*.

In March, Davenport and Grant attempted to consolidate their position on the Committee on Anthropology and to eliminate possible interference from Boas and the American Anthropological Association. With the backing of Henry F. Osborn, they established a rival anthropological society, the Galton Society for the Study of the Origin and Evolution of Man, which was centered in New York City at the American Museum of Natural History. Grant wrote that the membership of the new society would be "self elected and self perpetuating, and very limited in members, and also confined to native Americans, who are anthropologically, socially, and politically sound, no Bolsheviks need apply" (quoted by Spencer 1979:680). Davenport chaired the new society which included prominent eugenicists on the NRC, at the American Museum of Natural History, and in universities; its membership was soon expanded to include Clark Wissler of the American Museum of Natural History and Harvard physical anthropologist Earnest A. Hooton (1887–1954) (Spencer 1979:680–1).

In April, Davenport reported that the NRC's Committee on Anthropology would be reorganized as a section in the Division of Medicine and Related Sciences. It would consist of four subcommittees that would investigate the anthropometry of men who had inducted into the army, race in relation to disease, the races of Europe, and race in relation to psychology. Hrdlička was not satisfied, however. In a memo to Hale, Hrdlička complained that

> The Committee which once had such great prospects and in which there was so much of my own, is now divided into a number of no further related, small bodies, and I am to fill a pro-forma secretaryship in a little body the prospects of success of which have become such that its head has practically thrown in the sponge (quoted by Spencer 1979:684).

From Hrdlička's vantage, it must have seemed that fate intervened once again, for John C. Merriam – paleontologist, Galton Society member, and future President of the Carnegie Institution of Washington – was named in May 1918 to oversee the NRC's peacetime conversion. One of Merriam's first acts was to ship Hrdlička to New York to work on a confidential report being prepared under the direction of Isaiah Bowman at the American Geographical Society. For the next six months, Hrdlička wrote about the ethnology of Eastern Europe (Spencer 1979:672–85).

Merriam, who had also taught anthropology for a number of years at Berkeley earlier in his career, was concerned with the problem of organization in anthropology. He quickly decided that it should have a close relation with psychology. His intentions became clearer, however, in a lecture he delivered to the members of the Galton Society in December 1918. The problem with anthropology, he argued, was that anthropologists had focused too narrowly on problems associated with American Indians and that they had failed to convince university administrators that the problems they investigated were, in fact, of universal concern. This, of course, was mainly an attack on Boas and his students. Later that month, he addressed a joint meeting of the American Anthropological Association (AAA) and Section H of the American Association for the Advancement of Science (AAAS), indicating that each group should appoint a single representative to what would become the NRC Division of Anthropology and Psychology (Spencer 1979:686–90).

Boas responded that the responsibility for organizing and directing anthropology should not come from individuals but rather from representatives of the three main subfields selected by the members of the AAA and the AAAS. Boas agreed with Merriam that the scope of anthropology should be expanded, but he also recognized the difficulties he had experienced throughout his career in attempting to fund overseas research. Hrdlička was displeased because Boas had not paid enough attention to physical anthropology, and wanted more work on human paleontology and racial anthropology among the white and negro populations in the United States (Spencer 1979:690–4).

In July 1919, Merriam announced the organization of the Division of Anthropology and Psychology. There would be nine anthropologists and nine psychologists. The AAA would select six members and the NRC Executive Committee would appoint three. Hrdlička, who was still a member of the NRC's Committee on Anthropology, approached Clark Wissler, the AAA president, to select six delegates; a list of nominees drawn up by the AAA Executive Committee was sent to the members. Boas, Wissler, Kroeber, Laufer, Jesse Fewkes (1850–1930), and Roland B. Dixon (1875–1935) were elected. Holmes was outraged, because Hrdlička had not been elected to the new NRC committee. Boas's remedy – place Hrdlička on the committee and stagger the terms of the members – was accepted; Boas, Hrdlička, and Wissler were appointed for one year, while the other members had two- or three-year terms (Spencer 1979:700–23).

Boas was forced to resign from the Division of Anthropology and Psychology after his letter exposing the four anonymous anthropologists who had spied in Latin America during the war appeared in *The Nation*. He was replaced by F. W. Hodge (1864–1956) of the Bureau of American Ethnology. Hrdlička was not re-elected and was replaced by James H. Breasted whom the NRC Executive Committee appointed. Wissler, who was elected chair of the Division, recommended six projects to the NRC: (1) a study of racial groups and populations in the United States;

(2) intelligence testing of college students; (3) the stimulation of graduate work; (4) an anthropometric survey of college students; (5) archaeological surveys; and (6) a study of race mixture in Hawaii.

In 1926 Hrdlička, who had been reappointed to the committee two years earlier, proposed that the NRC establish a committee to undertake anthropological and psychological studies of American Negroes. A committee that included Boas, Hrdlička, Davenport, Hooton, and Kidder was elected to oversee this research. Hrdlička wanted a research institute in Washington; the other members agreed with Boas's suggestion to carve up "the work among individuals or institutions whose work could then be efficiently managed by the committee" (Spencer 1979:744).

By the mid-1920s, the terrain of the struggle between the forces led by Boas, Hrdlička, and Davenport had changed significantly. Congressional testimony provided by Davenport and funded indirectly by the Carnegie Institution of Washington was used as an ideological justification for the Johnson Act of 1924 which established immigration quotas based on the 1890 census; since the vast majority of the immigrants were from Eastern and Southern Europe after 1890, this meant that only a relatively few individuals from that region would be accepted each year. The eugenicists also provided an ideological justification for the enactment of sterilization and miscegenation laws in numerous states during the 1920s and 1930s.

At the same time, however, geneticists such as L. C. Dunn (1893–1964) and H. J. Muller (1890–1967) in the United States and J. B. Haldane (1892–1964) in England were raising serious objections to eugenics as a field of inquiry; their critiques merged with those of individuals who opposed the eugenicists' political activities. By 1929, Merriam, who was now president of the Carnegie Institution of Washington, began to examine what the Institution had received in return for the nearly $3,000,000 it had invested in Davenport's eugenics research programs since 1904. He appointed a committee that included L. C. Dunn, Kidder, and Wissler to evaluate the data. The committee concluded that Davenport's data relied on the subjective assessments of fieldworkers and that his claims about individual traits needed to be tested with more precise quantitative. Merriam convened a second panel in 1936 that included Dunn, Hooton, Adolph Schultz (1891–1976), and Robert Redfield (1897–1958); this committee concluded that Davenport's data were virtually worthless. Three years later, Vannevar Bush, Merriam's successor, ended its support for Davenport's projects. The eugenics movement was transformed with Rockefeller support as its focus shifted from heredity to population control and to birth-control experiments on an international scale (Allen 1986:253-4).

While Hrdlička was unable to convince either the directors of the Smithsonian Institution or the NRC's Department of Anthropology and Psychology to convert his division at the National Museum into a full-fledged research and teaching institute, he did succeed in making the National Museum a major research and training center. He also used the *American Journal of Physical Anthropology*, which first appeared in 1918, to establish a small network of researchers, many of whom were anatomists in medical schools. Realizing that many of the subscribers were also members of Section H of the American Association for the Advancement of Science, he began to garner support among them for an independent association of physical anthropology. During the next year, the organizing committee of the new American Association of Physical Anthropologists (AAPA) recruited eighty-three members: forty-seven anatomists, two physicians, eighteen zoologists and eighteen anthropologists, only eight of whom were full-time physical anthropologists (Spencer 1997). One goal of the new association was to further teaching and research in human phylogeny, ontogeny, variation, and differentiation (Spencer 1979:746–7).

During the 1920s, cultural determinists – Boas and younger anthropologists, notably Ralph Linton (1893–1953), Melville J. Herskovits (1895–1963), and Margaret Mead (1901–78) – reasserted the hegemony of their views within the profession and challenged the hegemony of the eugenicists' views in the wider society when they attacked the methodology of racial intelligence testing used by psychologists. Linton (1924:71) concluded that the intelligence tests used by the U.S. Army "were more dependent on education and social opportunity than race, and that the differences revealed cannot be adduced as proof of racial inequality." Mead (1926:659) pointed out that the existing studies of racial mental differences failed to control for either social status (class) differences or the effects of language-use patterns (e.g. did the subjects use one language in public and another one at home). Herskovits (1926) was critical of studies that purportedly showed a correlation between the degree of racial admixture (defined mostly by skin color) and intelligence; his examination of a diverse group of Howard University freshmen with similar educational backgrounds showed no correlation between purportedly Negro physical traits and test scores.

At the end of the decade, Boas restated his views about the linkage between race and culture:

I do not believe that any convincing proof has ever been given of a direct relation between race and culture. It is true enough that human cultures and racial types are so distributed that every area has its own type and its own culture, but this does not prove that one determines the form of the other . . . The error of modern theories is due largely to a faulty extension of the concept of individual heredity to that of racial heredity. Heredity acts only in lines of direct descent. There is no unity of descent in any of the existing races, and we have no right to assume that the mental characteristics of a few selected family lines are shared by all members of a race. On the contrary, all large races are so variable and the functional characteristics of the component hereditary lines are so diverse that similar family lines may be found in all races, particularly in all closely related local types, divisions of the same race. Hereditary characteristics when *socially* significant *have* a cultural value as in all cases of race discrimination or in those cultural conditions in which a specially gifted line is given the opportunity to impress itself upon the general culture (Boas 1930:91–2).

This concept of culture was different from the one that Boas had deployed at the beginning of the twentieth century (Stocking 1968:195–233). His earlier concept of culture had emerged from the coalescence of two independent lines of inquiry – one concerned with folklore and the other with the purported racial mental differences. Following neo-Kantian writers, Boas believed that the "genius of a people" – i.e. its culture – was found its language, knowledge, skills, arts, and mythology; in other words, the folklore of a tribe, which could be collected relatively easily, embodied the ethical prescriptions of its members and described what constituted ethical behavior (Boas 1904/1940). His studies of the folklore of the Northwest Coast tribes showed, however, that many of the elements of their mythologies had been borrowed from neighboring peoples, reworked and reinterpreted to make them conform to ethical beliefs and values of the borrowers (Boas 1902). These stories – i.e. their culture – were transmitted from one generation to the next and, more importantly, children learned them in the context of the present rather than in terms of how the various elements were added to the whole (Boas 1899/1974:95–7). In other words, he viewed the Northwest Coast tribes as a set of historically conditioned, interacting totalities rather than in terms of a sequence of developmental stages. He further argued that, while the history of industrial development showed evidence of Spencerian progress, other "human activities that do not depend on reasoning do not show a similar type of evolution" (Boas 1904:517).

Boas's views about the purported mental differences of races developed along different lines. He disagreed with studies which linked racial and cultural evolutionary hierarchies and proclaimed that the mental abilities of dark-skinned primitive peoples were inferior to those of the civilized white peoples of Northern Europe. When he discussed the issue in the 1890s, he typically found alternative explanations for the differences that were rooted in the cultural or social realms rather than in race or cranial capacity. By 1901, he had turned to studies in experimental psychology – such as the one carried out by British anthropologists Alfred C. Haddon (1855–1940) and W. H. R. Rivers (1864–1923) in the Torres Straits – which showed that there were no significant differences between the sensory abilities of primitive peoples off the coast of New Guinea and those of civilized men in Europe (Haddon 1901). In Boas's (1901) view, this meant that all peoples had the same basic mental organization governing the same fundamental psychological processes. Thus, the behavioral differences between primitive and civilized peoples were not rooted in racial mental differences but rather in culture – the body of tradition that the members of a tribe passed from one generation to the next. This meant that the civilized peoples of Europe were as bound by tradition as were the tribesmen of the Torres Straits. It also meant that culture was not reducible to inherited traits of a biological or psychological nature.

In a response to the claims of the eugenics movements, Alfred Kroeber distinguished the organic and cultural realms of people and referred to culture as the "superorganic." In his view, culture was an emergent phenomenon that existed outside of the people who bore it. He wrote that culture "is not mental action itself; it is carried by men, without being in them. But its relation to mind, its absolute rooting in human faculty, is obvious" (Kroeber 1917/1952:38). He proceeded to look at the interrelations of culture, the individual and the group. In his view,

> The accomplishment of the individual measured against other individuals depends, if not wholly then mainly, on his organic composition as compounded by his heredity. The accomplishments of a group, relative to other groups, are little or not influenced by heredity because sufficiently large groups average much alike in organic makeup (Kroeber 1917/1952:47).

Edward Sapir (1884–1939), another of Boas's students whose interests ranged broadly from linguistics and philology to psychiatry, agreed with Kroeber that culture, the "genius of a people," could not be reduced to inherited traits of a biological or psychological nature (Sapir 1924/1949:311); Darnell 1990:143–50); however, he felt that Kroeber's reification of culture eliminated individuals from history and obscured the relationship between culture and the psychic in the process (Sapir 1917). Sapir focused instead on the place of the individual in a theory of culture – the relation of the cultured individual to the cultural group. He pointed out that there was "no real opposition, at last analysis, between the concept of the culture of a group and the concept of an individual culture," because they were interdependent (Sapir 1924/1949:321).

Sapir had a dialectical understanding of the connection between the individual and culture of a group. In his view, individuals seek to master and transform the group's culture at the same time that they seek to reconcile their strivings with the general life of the community (Sapir 1924/1949:321–7). They were torn between the desire to create and the desire to conform. Culture, for Sapir, was not located above people, as it was for Kroeber, but rather between individuals. Culture, in his view, provided them with "traditional givens – linguistic, aesthetic, social – out of which they will construct their lives" and which "as creative personalities" they bend "to their own purposes, reshaping culture in the process" (Handler 1986:147). In Sapir's (1924/1949:326) words,

> The self seeks instinctively for mastery. In the process of acquiring a sense of mastery that is not crude but proportioned to the degree of sophistication proper to our time, the self is compelled to suffer an abridgment and to undergo a molding. The extreme differentiation of function which the progress of man has forced upon the individual menaces the spirit; we have no recourse but to submit with good grace to this abridgment of our activity, but it must not be allowed to clip the wings of the spirit unduly. This is the first and most important reconciliation – the findings of a full world of spiritual satisfactions within the straight limits of an unwontedly confined economic activity. The self must

set itself a point where it can, if not embrace the whose spiritual life of a group, at least catch enough of its rays to burst into light and flame. Moreover the self must learn to reconcile its own strivings, its own imperious activities, with the general spiritual life of the community.

Sapir's efforts in the mid-1920s to develop a theory of culture that drew inspiration from ethnology, linguistics, and personality studies were well-suited to a milieu in which both the NRC and the newly formed Social Science Research Council were encouraging social scientists to break down the barriers separating their work and to do a better job at pointing out to the public the relevance of their work. As you will recall, in 1918, the President of the National Research Council urged anthropologists and psychologists to forge closer links with one another and admonished anthropologists for being too narrow in their research concerns and for not convincing university administrators that their research problems were universal concerns. When Sapir took a position at the University of Chicago in 1925, he was arriving at an institution that already supported an interdisciplinary program in the social sciences and had recently been the birthplace of the Social Science Research Council which, in its early years, sought to transcend the "excessive overspecialization" of individual researchers and "to enhance the public image of the social sciences" (Darnell 1990:298). Sapir's broad interests and ability to develop meaningful working relationships with individuals in diverse disciplines thrived in these circumstances, and he was quickly recognized and acknowledged as a leading figure in the field, a truly public intellectual.

Discussion

Anthropology was professionalized in the waning years of the nineteenth century and the beginning of the twentieth century. The first professional anthropologists were employed by the federal government in the surveys of the Western states, the National Museum, and the Bureau of Ethnology. By the time of the First World War, the profession's center of gravity had already shifted from the federal government to universities and museums. As a result, anthropologists in the universities controlled both the certification and reproduction of the discipline. By 1932, seventy men and twenty women had received doctorates in anthropology, nearly two-thirds of which were awarded by Columbia and Harvard. More than half wrote dissertations that dealt with ethnological topics (47); twenty with archaeology, fifteen with physical anthropology, and eight with linguistics.

Because of their location or the composition of their boards of trustees, the universities with graduate programs in anthropology also developed regional geographical interests. For example, Kroeber's and Lowie's students at the University of California at Berkeley tended to focus their attention on the native peoples of the Western states; a number of Harvard's students wrote dissertations on the Maya of southern Mexico and northern Central America; and the University of Pennsylvania had an early interest in the Caribbean which articulated well with the Scientific Survey of Puerto Rico that was sponsored by the New York Academy of Sciences before the First World War.

Specializations, reflecting perhaps the neo-Kantian distinction between the natural and human sciences, were already apparent on the eve of the First World War. The linguists were the first to create a separate professional organization: the Linguistics Society of America was established in 1925 and had both philologists and anthropologists as members. The American Association of Physical Anthropologists was created four years later in 1929 and brought together eighteen anthropologists and nearly fifty human anatomists. The Society for American Archaeology was created in 1934 when twenty-five men and six women signed the constitution of the new organization to promote scientific research in the archaeology of the New World.

Anthropology was professionalized during a period characterized by intense discrimination against people of color, immigrants, women, and poor folks. These groups were often lumped together and portrayed as savages or the members of inferior races regardless of the class backgrounds of the individuals involved. By 1932, Boas had trained a number of individuals from these stigmatized groups – e.g. East European Jews, women, and American Indians. These anthropologists were representatives of those social categories that provided the objects of anthropological inquiry. In a sense, they were simultaneously the object of inquiry and the subject who conducted the investigation. Boas, Mooney, and others established collaborative relationships with the members of stigmatized groups in the early days of the discipline, and Boas himself had long-term working relationships with the African-American historical sociologist and civil rights activist, W. E. B. Du Bois (1868–1963) and with Elsie Clews Parsons (1874–1941), comparative sociologist and feminist activist. In addition, Boas, Kroeber, and Lowie trained eight of the nine women who received Ph.D. degrees from American universities before 1929. The result of this was that a significant number of the first-generation anthropologists were not only members of stigmatized groups but also critics of the class structure and practices of American society.

Notes

1. This was not the only source of tension between Putnam and the Washington scientists. Thomas C. Chamberlin (1843–1928), former Survey geologist, was partly responsible for the marginalization of Putnam at the Columbian Exposition. Chamberlin argued that his former colleagues at the Survey – Charles D. Walcott (1850–1927) in geology and William Henry Holmes (1846–1933) in anthropology – were ideally suited to lead a scientific complex centered around the museum that was being planned and the University of Chicago (Hinsley and Holm 1976:311; McVicker 1990, 1999). A second source of tension resulted from an attack on the views of Putnam's friend and amateur archaeologist, Reverend George F. Wright (1838–1921). Putnam and Wright believed that people had lived in the Americas during the Ice Age. In 1892, Bureau anthropologist William J. McGee (1853–1912), Holmes at the National Museum, and Chamberlin used professionalization and the language of science to attack Wright's (1892) *Man and the Glacial Period*, which claimed that the Geological Survey had misinterpreted the geological evidence for glaciation in North America and that the stone implements found in glacial gravels in Ohio and New Jersey were conclusive evidence for the existence of glacial man in North America (Hinsley 1976:46–51).

2. Brinton was only marginally involved in the development of anthropology at the University of Pennsylvania's Museum of Archaeology and Paleontology which was established in 1889 (Darnell 1970, 1976). The driving forces behind the Museum in the 1890s were William Pepper (1843–98), paleontologist and provost of the university, and Sara Stevenson (1847–1921), curator of the Egyptian and Mediterranean archaeology section. The other curators and staff members of the museum were Edward Cope, the paleontologist; Charles C. Abbott (1843–1919) who claimed to have found traces of Ice Age man in the Trenton Gravels; Babylonian archaeologist Hermann Hilprecht (1859–1925); Near Eastern philologist Morris Jastrow (1861–1921); and ethnologist Stewart Culin (1858–1929). With the financial support of Phoebe Hearst and others, Pepper and Stevenson organized and sent archaeological expeditions to Nippur, Egypt, and Peru in the decade following its incorporation. When the term paleontology was dropped from the museum's name in 1899, it signaled a "shift away from studying human beings in the context of natural history and toward developing a new 'natural history of civilization'" (Conn 1998:85, 82–95).

3. Powell, Putnam, and Brinton did not read Frederick Engels's (1820–95) *The Origin of the Family, Private Property and the State: In Light of the Researches of Lewis H. Morgan* (1884/1972). Engels focused on the differences between primitive society and civilization with its social class-structures and political organization. He argued that private possession of the means of production

was absent in the early stages of human society and that production relations were "essentially collective," that "consumption proceeded by direct distribution of the products within larger or smaller communistic communities," and that the division of labor was based on gender. Engels further argued that the kinship systems studied by Morgan revealed systems of obligations between individuals – i.e. economic relationships. Finally, he argued that the collectivities which organized life in primitive society were dissolved when class structures and private property appeared, and when families and women were removed from the safety of the clan and were forced to fend for themselves (Engels 1884/1972:95, 137–45, 233; Leacock 1972).

4. Boas was born in the wake of the liberal revolution that spread across Europe after the French king was overthrown in 1848. His home was a place "where the ideals of the revolution of 1848 were a living force" (Boas 1938:201; Frank 1997; Hyatt 1990:3–16; Lesser 1968, 1981). His mother, Sophie Meyer Boas, was a left-liberal who organized and taught at a Froebel kindergarten in Minden. She also knew of a number of individuals who were imprisoned or exiled by the Prussian government in the wake of the Revolutions of 1848–9. They included Carl Schurz who fled to the United States with a price on his head and who, after a political career, introduced Boas to museum directors in New York; Ernst Krackowizer, a leader of the Austrian revolt of 1848 whose daughter, Marie, Boas married in 1887; and Abraham Jacobi (1830–1919) who had married Sophie Boas's younger sister, was jailed for treason, and escaped to the United States in 1853. Jacobi, who became a prominent physician, later married Mary Corinna Putnam who was the daughter of George Palmer Putnam, the publisher, and the cousin of Frederick Ward Putnam who was Boas's patron during the early part of his career.

5. John Cove (1999:112–3) has pointed out how indigenous communities have successfully used arguments rooted in cultural relativism to achieve political ends in the late twentieth century.

6. Holmes emigrated from his native Ohio in 1871 to study art in Washington; a year later, he became the official painter for the Hayden survey of the western United States. He became Honorary Curator of Aboriginal American Ceramics at the National Museum in 1882 before moving to the Field Museum in Chicago in 1893. He returned to Washington in October, 1897 to head the Department of Anthropology at the National Museum. Following Powell's death in 1902, he became Chief of the Bureau of American Ethnology, a position he held for seven years before returning full-time to the National Museum. In 1920, he resigned from the National Museum to direct the National Gallery of Art. Holmes's position in the scientific bureaucracy of the federal government as well as his intellectual accomplishments and contributions made him a central figure in American anthropology from the 1880s onward (Mark 1980:131–71; Meltzer and Dunnell 1992).

Holmes was an innovator in American archaeology. After surveying the remains of cliff dwellers near Mesa Verde in 1875–6, he concluded that the cliff dwellers were the ancestors of the modern Pueblos rather than of the nomadic Navaho and Apache who then inhabited the area (Holmes 1878:408). His study of textile impressions on pottery from earthen mounds in the Mississippi Valley led him to conclude that the Moundbuilders were no more advanced technologically than aboriginal peoples who inhabited the area at the time of White settlement (Holmes 1884). In 1884, Holmes (1885) was one of the first to recognize the chronological and historical significance of superimposed cultural assemblages containing stylistically distinct pottery types. From 1887 onwards, he and his colleagues at the National Museum scrutinized all assertions of the existence of human beings in the Americas during the ice age and subjected the evidence supporting such claims to rigorous scientific examination (e.g., Hrdlička, Holmes, Willis, Wright, and Fenner 1912). He believed that archaeology was a science and examined archaeological evidence through a theoretical lens that was shaped by positivism and by Morgan's theory of progressive human development from savagery through barbarism to civilization (Holmes 1892).

7. For example, in 1903, W. H. Holmes wrote that "It is customary with anthropologists to regard the physical and cultural phenomena as constituting a single unit, *the correlation between race and culture being intimate and vital*, and it is a cherished idea to present this unit with the completeness and effectiveness that its importance warrants" (quoted by Hinsley 1981:113).

8. While students at Harvard, Kidder and Morley attended Hewett's field school in 1907; however, Kidder learned archaeological research techniques from George A. Reisner (1867–1942), a German-trained Egyptologist whose investigations were supported by Phoebe Apperson Hearst. Nelson, who studied with Kroeber and Putnam at the University of California, excavated shellmounds around San Francisco Bay using techniques he had learned from Max Uhle (1856–1944), another archaeologist trained in Germany whose investigations in Peru at the turn of the century were supported financially by Hearst and William Pepper.

9. Hrdlička, trained as a physician in New York, was also sponsored by F. W. Putnam, who sponsored his anthropometric studies in the American Southwest in the 1890s. Holmes hired him in 1903 to direct the Division of Physical Anthropology at the National Museum. Hrdlička long felt that anthropologists teaching in universities did not pay sufficient attention to physical anthropology in general and especially to how it was practiced in France where he studied somatology and anthropometry. He wanted to establish an institute of physical anthropology in Washington and a journal devoted to the subject to correct this oversight (Spencer 1979:628).

Hrdlička measured 140 men and 135 women of old American families – i.e. all of their grandparents had been born in the United States – in order to test the conclusions of Boas's (1911) study of "Changes in the Bodily Form of the Descendants of Immigrants." Boas had claimed that, within the space of a single generation, far-reaching changes occurred in the configuration of the headform of the immigrant groups he studied. Hrdlička argued that Boas's study had defects – e.g. he had not measured the parents and grandparents of his subjects nor were the subjects studied at different times in their development. Hrdlička believed that the form of the human skeleton changed at a much slower rate than Boas suggested (Spencer 1979:628–32). Hrdlička (1917:600–1) argued that his "Old American Families" study showed a great deal of variation among the subjects, which was not surprising given their ethnic diversity, and "that no definite, already formed, strictly American type or sub-type of the whites as yet exists."

10. Davenport was the Director of the Carnegie-sponsored Eugenics Record Office and Station for the Experimental Study of Evolution at Cold Spring Harbor and a leading exponent of eugenics in the United States (Allen 1986).

11. By 1935, twenty-six states had sterilization laws, and California had already sterilized more than 12,000 individuals (Allen 1983:122).

–3–

Anthropology and the Search for Social Order, 1929–1945

The Depression and then the Second World War dominated everyday life during the 1930s and 1940s. In the four years following the crash of the stock market in 1929, nearly a million farmers went bankrupt; seventeen million workers, nearly a third of the total workforce, were fully unemployed, and one in three of those with jobs worked reduced hours; industrial output declined by fifty percent; and the volume of foreign trade fell by seventy percent. The international position of the United States was weakened, and its capitalists struggled with their British counterparts for markets and investment opportunities in Latin America and Canada.

In 1933, newly elected President Franklin D. Roosevelt (1882–1945) and a Congress controlled by the Democrats launched a series of programs, called the New Deal, that attempted to resolve the crisis. The federal government expanded its role as a consumer of goods and services, created relief programs for workers and reorganized business and labor relations in ways that would promote industrial growth and favorable investment opportunities at home and abroad (Ekirch 1969; Pels 1973). It also established public corporations, most notably the Tennessee Valley Authority which built a network of dams and canals to protect the area from floods and a series of hydroelectric projects in the Western states; in the process, the federal government became a major producer of hydroelectric power and the employer of large numbers of specialists and technicians (Higgs 1987:159–95). Big business and the investment banks sought and received the government's support for every phase of their internationalization and overseas expansion into new markets, especially in Latin America and the Pacific (Williams 1961:451–78; 1972:162–201).

The regulatory policies initiated by the federal government during the 1930s promoted continuous economic growth after the Second World War broke out. However, after 1940, the government intervened in the economy in unprecedented ways. The Selective Service Act of 1940 underwrote the conscription of ten million men for military service during the war. The War Powers Acts of 1941 and 1942 permitted the President to reassign personnel; to negotiate cost-plus, no-bid contracts with private suppliers of war-related products; to use the Treasury as a printing press to finance deficits; and to censor communications between the United States and foreign countries. The Office of Price Administration, established in 1941, fixed rents and prices and used indirect sanctions to enforce its regulations. The Labor Disputes Act of 1944 permitted the federal government to seize production facilities and to intrude in labor markets (Higgs 1987:199–225).

These and others policies provided the foundations for the military-industrial complex that emerged during the Second World War and that still continues to dominate everyday life in the United States. In the process, Congress surrendered constitutional powers to the executive branch of the government. Civil rights were trampled as the Supreme Court upheld the incarceration of 110,000 Japanese-Americans in concentration camps in the West. Companies that supplied products for the government, especially large ones such as General Electric, made enormous profits – billions of dollars – from the war.

Anthropology on the Eve of the Deperession

Three initiatives shaped the direction of anthropological research in the United States after the First World War. Their importance derived from the research funds and resources that were associated with them. One was the effort of the Rockefeller philanthropies – notably the Social Science Research Council (SSRC) established in Chicago in 1923, the Laura Spelman Rockefeller Memorial (LSRM) and the Rockefeller Foundation – to promote problem-oriented, interdisciplinary research in the social sciences (Fisher 1983, 1986, 1993). The second was the National Research Council's (NRC) effort to promote the study of racial groups and race mixture in the United States. The third was the American Council of Learned Societies' (ACLS) Committee on Research in American Native Languages, funded mainly by an $80,000 grant from the Carnegie Corporation in 1927, to "collect data on those languages which were near extinction and also to try to develop the comparative study of diversified linguistics stocks" (quoted by Leeds-Hurwitz 1985:129; Darnell 1990:277–87).

The three initiatives concentrated money and resources at universities that already had established graduate training programs. They sped up the process of professionalization of anthropology as an increasingly academic discipline. They also selected a small number of social scientists who would set research agendas and allocate the funds necessary to support them through conferences, grants, and fellowships. A few anthropologists – notably Edward Sapir and, to a lesser extent, Franz Boas – were involved with more than one of the initiatives in the 1920s and 1930s. During this period, Sapir, for example, was a member of the Social Science Research Council (1928–34) and the ACLS's Committee on Research in American Native Languages (1927–37) and chaired the NRC's Division of Psychology and Anthropology (1934–36) when the SSRC projects that he proposed on the study of acculturation and the relationship of the individual and culture came to fruition (Darnell 1990:277–87, 303–8; Fisher 1993:78, 80, 283).

The initiative of the Rockefeller philanthropies had the most profound effect on the development of anthropology and the other social sciences, especially at the University of Chicago which John D. Rockefeller founded in 1892 (Richardson and Fisher 1999:6; Stocking 1982, 1985). First, the philanthropies injected more than fifty million dollars into the advancement of the social sciences in the United States during the 1920s and early 1930s. They were concerned with making the social sciences more scientific in order to promote social and economic stability, to eliminate subjective studies of social phenomena, and to develop more effective methods of social control (Fisher 1983:215). To achieve these goals, they supported studies concerned with curbing crime and delinquency (Fisher 1993:57–9).[1] Second, they designated a select number of universities – Chicago, Columbia, Yale, Harvard, North Carolina at Chapel Hill, Stanford, Berkeley, and Pennsylvania – as "centers of excellence" and provided the funds and resources required to develop them as "prototypical research institutions"; they also funded the development of anthropology programs overseas – most notably at the London School of Economics and at the University of Sydney (Fisher 1993:199ff). Third, since John D. Rockefeller had financed the emergence of the University of Chicago as a major center of learning and research in the 1890s, there was a close relationship between the Rockefeller philanthropies and the University. As a result, Chicago-based anthropologists – such as Fay-Cooper Cole (1881–1961), Melville J. Herskovits, Ralph Linton, Robert Redfield (1897–1958), and Edward Sapir – figured prominently in the development of the field during the late 1920s and 1930s.

The interest of the Rockefeller philanthropies in anthropology, especially in colonial policies and the social management of natives, was apparent by 1926, when they invited Bronislaw Malinowski (1884–1942) and A. R. Radcliffe-Brown (1881–1952) to discuss their views with colleagues at selected universities in the United States. At the end of the summer, Radcliffe-Brown sailed to Australia to assume the newly created, Rockefeller-funded chair in social anthropology at the University of Sydney. He saw to it that W. Lloyd Warner (1898–1970) – who had studied anthropology with Kroeber and Lowie at the University of California – received a fellowship provided by the LSRM through the Australian National Research Council to continue his studies in Sydney. After studying an aboriginal society in northern Australia for three years, Warner accepted a position at Harvard University, where he would begin to apply the ideas of Radcliffe-Brown and Malinowski to the study of contemporary American society.

In Cambridge, Warner met Elton Mayo (1880–1949), the Australian psychiatrist who was employed by the Harvard Business School and who was a close friend of Malinowski and Radcliffe-Brown. Mayo had co-founded Harvard's Committee on Industrial Physiology whose research in the 1920s and 1930s was completely underwritten by the LSRM. Mayo was studying the effects of fatigue among workers at Western Electric's Hawthorne plant, where he discovered that productivity was tied in important ways to the participation of individuals in groups, to interpersonal relations, and to cultural factors (Spicer 1977:120–4). He brought Warner into the Committee in 1930 to consult on the Hawthorne project and to investigate the relationship of the industry to the community in which the workers lived (Richardson 1979). Warner turned his attention to the town of Newburyport, Massachusetts (Yankee City) whose largest employer was a shoe factory. With the financial support of the Committee (and hence of the Rockefeller philanthropies), Warner and students[2] from Harvard conducted a series of community studies in Newburyport from 1931 to 1936. The project came to a close in 1936 when Warner accepted a position at the University of Chicago. A study of industrial relations in the shoe factory was merely one aspect of the investigations (Chapple 1953; Whyte 1987). While much of Warner's subsequent work focused on social stratification in American society, he nevertheless remained interested in industrial relations and subsequently co-founded the University of Chicago's interdisciplinary Committee on Industrial Relations (Warner 1937, 1940; Warner and Davis 1939; Szwed 1979).

While the Yankee City investigations were landmark studies of an American community, they were neither the first community studies conducted by American social scientists nor the first studies of American communities. They were preceded by W. E. B. Du Bois's (1899/1967) *The Philadelphia Negro: A Social Study*; Robert S. and Helen M. Lynd's (1929) *Middletown: A Study of Contemporary American Culture*; Robert Redfield's (1930) *Tepoztlan: A Mexican Village*; and Louis E. King's (1951) study of an African American community in rural West Virginia between 1927 and 1931 (Harrison 1999). The importance of the Yankee City studies derives partly from their thoroughness and partly from subsequent community studies that were undertaken by participants in the project. For example, as Warner was moving to the University of Chicago in 1936, his student collaborators in Newburyport – Allison Davis, Burleigh Gardner, and Mary Gardner (1941) – were engaged in a multi-year study of race and class relations from both sides of the color line in Natchez, Mississippi (Old City). Their inquiry into race relations in a Southern town followed recommendations made by both the Rockefeller philanthropies and the National Research Council in the 1920s.[3]

In December 1920, a committee of the NRC's Division of Psychology and Anthropology chaired by Clark Wissler issued a confidential report recommending six areas for future anthropological research. The committee gave top priority to the study of racial groups in the United States. This was partly in response to race riots in the late 1910s, the integrationist arguments of the National Association for the Advancement of Colored People, the black nationalist arguments of Marcus Garvey's United Negro Improvement Association, and the rapidly growing number of African Americans who had migrated from the South to the northern industrial cities in search of work during and after the First World War. They took the unskilled jobs that, only a few years earlier, had been filled by the steady stream of immigrants from Eastern and Southern Europe – a stream that the war reduced to a mere trickle after 1914 (Williams 1989:92). It was the first time that African Americans had entered the industrial work force in the northern cities in significant numbers.

The NRC initiative coincided in the 1920s with the gradual triumph, at least in the social sciences, of the views of Boas and others regarding race, culture, and their interconnections. In their perspective, races existed, races were variable, and races were equal. Furthermore, while there was no direct relation between race and culture, hereditary physical features, such as skin color, were socially and culturally significant in American society because of racial discrimination and racism. Such views helped to underpin the emergence and gradual ascendancy of an assimilationist perspective in the social sciences during the 1930s and 1940s. At the same time, a number of African Americans, some of whom had received advanced degrees in anthropology, used this perspective to develop an increasingly trenchant critique of American society (Williams 1989).

The NRC initiative stimulated both biological and cultural determinists. Aleš Hrdlička published a number of articles on race mixture and the physical anthropology of the American Negro in his *American Journal of Physical Anthropology* during the 1920s. Although Earnest Hooton at Harvard was also interested in race mixture between Negroes and Whites, he did not initially undertake research on this topic.[4] He believed that it was necessary to employ black researchers in order to gain access to black communities (Ross, Adams, and Williams 1999:43), and there were no African-American students interested in physical anthropology at Harvard until Carolyn Bond Day (1898–1948) arrived in the late 1920s. While Day worked within the vindicationist perspective[5] she had refined during her undergraduate years at Atlanta University where W. E. B. Du Bois was a dominant intellectual force, she was also constrained by Hooton's beliefs – i.e. race is a biological reality, the white race is superior, and the future of humankind depends on biology rather than cultural practices (Hooton 1931: Barkan 1992:101–8; Montagu 1942/1997:105). In *A Study of Some Negro-White Families in the United States*, Day (1932) described similarities between the black and white middle classes and attributed the differences between them to racial segregation rather than biology. She also dealt with the issue of African Americans' passing for white and the implications this had for racial typology (Day 1930).

In 1923, Melville J. Herskovits, one of Boas's students at Columbia, received a three-year fellowship from the National Research Council to study the effect of race crossing on the American Negro.[6] Herskovits, who was concerned primarily at this point in his career with the anthropometry of hybridization, taught at Howard University during this period. There he was exposed to the views of black intellectuals – Alain L. Locke (1886–1954), the spiritual guide of the Harlem Renaissance, and biologist Ernest E. Just (1883–1941) – and to the results of the ongoing dialogue between intellectuals such as W. E. B. Du Bois and Franz Boas.

Herskovits relied on the efforts of African-American research assistants – Zora Neale Hurston (1903–60) and Louis E. King (1898–1981) – to collect the measurements of the school children and adults (Herskovits 1928:x; 1930:xiv). He discussed the quantitative differences observed among individuals in his sample in terms of the interplay of biological, social, and cultural factors. In his view, race was a fuzzy biological category but an important cultural one in a country where there was growing segregation by skin color which reinforced a certain homogeneity of beliefs in black communities – e.g. lighter skin tones were valued more highly than darker ones. While his biological explanations were not sophisticated by today's standards, Herskovits in fact challenged the idea of pure races; he attempted to explain the patterns he observed in terms of political-economic, social, and cultural processes that were manifest in the preceding half century (Herskovits 1928:51–68; Barkan 1992:111–9). This was already evident in his critique of racial-intelligence testing mentioned in the last chapter.

Hurston and King had been encouraged by Alain Locke (1886–1954) and Ernest Just (1883–1941) – their mentors at Howard University – to pursue their anthropological interests with Boas at Columbia. Boas sent them to Harlem to collect anthropometric measurements for Herskovits. At the same time, Boas and Elsie Clews Parsons were collaborating on the collection of black folklore for the American Folk-Lore Society; during the 1920s and 1930s, the independently wealthy Parsons subsidized the work and publications of a number of Boas's students including those of Hurston (Willis 1975:319–23).[7] After her work in Harlem, Hurston continued to collect black folklore and music in the Deep South. In the mid-1930s, she received a Guggenheim fellowship to investigate folk rituals, gender roles, women's activities, and exploitation in Haiti and Jamaica. While her books were widely acclaimed by lay audiences, they were not well-received by scholars. Hurston did not complete her dissertation, and, by the late 1930s, she was beginning to support herself as a dramatic coach, playwright, and part-time lecturer and was gradually lost to and by the profession during the 1940s (Mikell 1989).

Louis E. King undertook one of the first community studies by an American anthropologist. In a rural community in West Virginia, he documented the importance of social relationships and activities that were involved in the satisfaction of basic needs. He also questioned the validity of intelligence tests, writing that

> Emerging from a cultural background almost wholly influenced by slavery, Negro life in this area presents at this time a pattern similar to the life in the white community . . . The investigation reveals that there exists in the development of Negro life limited educational, economic, and social opportunities. These cultural limitations, in turn, created drastic psychological effects and inhibit the full development of the Negro's potentialities. Under these circumstances it becomes a pertinent question whether any instrument can be devised that can determine accurately the relative superiority or inferiority of intelligence, without first securing an intimate and thorough knowledge of the background of those for whom the instrument is intended as a measure (King 1951:1–2, quoted by Harrison 1999:76–7).

When he completed his dissertation in 1932, King did not have enough money to publish the thesis and provide Columbia with the twenty-seven copies it required; as a result, he did not receive his doctorate until 1952 after Columbia had eliminated the rule requiring that dissertations be published. King, who was unable to secure a teaching or research position during and after the Depression, worked at a variety of jobs to support his family; consequently, he too was effectively lost to and by the profession (Harrison 1999).

The third initiative was the formation of the ACLS's Committee on Research in American Native Languages in 1927. The ground had already been prepared by the appearance of the *International Journal of American Linguistics* a decade earlier in 1917 and by the formation of the Linguistics Society of America in December 1924. Boas, Edward Sapir, and Leonard Bloomfield (1887–1949), who were on the editorial board of the journal, recognized that the existing professional organizations and traditional divisions within universities made it difficult for individuals who conducted linguistic research to meet and discuss common problems (Bloomfield 1925). During the next three months, 264 scholars – teachers of English, German, and Romance and Slavic languages, philologists, psychologists, and anthropologists – joined the new organization. The goals of the American Linguistics Society were to promote the science of linguistics, to develop its methods, and to relate the results of its inquiries to other disciplines (Hymes 1971:230–1).

In 1927, Boas, Sapir, Kroeber, and Bloomfield played instrumental roles in the creation of the ACLS's Committee on Research in American Native Languages. At the time, Boas complained that there were not enough individuals with sufficient training to carry out the mandate of the committee. However, the mere existence of the committee with its promise of funding for research stimulated student interest in linguistics; as a result, Boas and Sapir trained more students in linguistics, and this in turn led to the expansion of the number of linguistics programs in the country. By 1930, Columbia, Chicago, Berkeley, Pennsylvania, Washington, and Yale provided training in linguistics. Between 1927 and 1937, the committee subsidized the research of thirty-eight scholars who collected native-language texts and various kinds of information on the phonology, morphology, grammar, and vocabulary of seventy-five American Indian languages (Hoijer 1973; Leeds-Hurwitz 1985). Researchers supported by the committee – such as Morris Swadesh (1909–67), for instance – would develop modern linguistic analysis in the United States during the 1930s and 1940s, building on theoretical foundations established earlier by Sapir (e.g. 1921/1984, 1925/1949), Bloomfield (1926), and others (Golla 1986; Hymes and Fought 1975; Murray 1993). The Committee also provided significant levels of financial support (more than $10,000 of the $80,000 it allocated) to two Native American scholars – Ella Deloria (1888–1971), the Yankon Dakota anthropologist and linguist, and Jaime de Angulo (1888–1950), the Modoc linguist and shaman (Medicine 1989; Leeds-Hurwitz 1983).

The University of Chicago emerged as a major center in the development of American anthropology in the 1920s, partly because of the financial support provided directly and indirectly by the Rockefeller philanthropies and partly because of the organizational and intellectual prowess of Fay-Cooper Cole and Edward Sapir. In the formative years of the University before the First World War, anthropology and sociology co-existed in the same department (Miller 1975; Stocking 1979:9–19). While Chicago sociologists – notably Albion Small (1854–1926), William I. Thomas (1863–1947) and Robert E. Park (1864–1944) – were pre-eminent in their field and trained the vast majority of the sociologists with academic credentials, anthropology led by anti-imperialist critic Frederick W. Starr (1858–1933) languished after the turn of the century. Fay-Cooper Cole, who had arrived at the Field Museum in the late 1910s and came to the university after Starr's retirement in 1923, was largely responsible for building the anthropology program in the combined department and for overseeing the formation of a separate department six years later. One of Cole's first moves in 1925 was to hire Edward Sapir who was widely regarded at the time as the most thought-provoking of Boas's students and whose salary was paid for three years by the LSRM. With the financial support of the Rockefeller Foundation from 1929 to 1934, Cole, Sapir, and Redfield – Robert Park's son-in-law who joined the anthropology faculty in 1929 – attracted graduate students and were able to fund their ethnological, archaeological, and linguistic research during the early years of the Depression (Darnell 1990:223–37).

Sapir's two interrelated research interests during his years at Chicago were the psychology of culture, which soon came to be called culture and personality, and American Indian languages (Aberle 1960). The former built on the reformulation of the culture concept that occurred during the 1920s; it was fueled after 1926 by his close friendship with psychiatrist Harry Stack Sullivan (1892–1949), an advocate of interdisciplinary collaboration between psychiatrists and social scientists (Perry 1982:242–60); and it was supported directly and indirectly by the Rockefeller philanthropies which promoted interdisciplinary, problem-oriented inquiries.[8] Sapir's linguistic studies and those of his students were financed by the ACLS's Committee on Research in American Native Languages.

Sapir had an important role in the reformulation of the culture concept during the 1920s; however, he was not the only one in that milieu in which a number of anthropologists – Boas, Alexander Goldenweiser (1880–1940), Ruth Benedict (1887–1948), and Margaret Mead (1901–78) to name only a few – perceived a close relationship between their discipline and psychology. As you will recall, English anthropologist Edward B. Tylor's (1832–1917) definition of culture in *Primitive Society* as all of the learned behavior "acquired by man as a member of society . . . [including] knowledge, belief, art, morals, custom, and any other capabilities and habits" implied that culture was an organic whole composed of interconnected parts. Tylor also believed that culture evolved in a linear fashion from lower to higher states and that it had reached its highest level in Western Europe and the

United States (Tylor 1871/1958 vol. 1:1). Boas and his students, who mostly rejected the racialist implications of Tylor's evolutionary scheme, often viewed the culture of a people in terms of accretions of outside elements, what Robert Lowie (1917/1966:441) described as "that hodge-podge, that thing of shreds and patches." They began to realize the limitations of a perspective that saw culture mainly as a collection of traits brought together by chance, and to move slowly toward one that saw it in terms of shared mental patterns or collective conscience (Caffrey 1989:152–3). Such a view would allow them to examine how the activities and psychic states of a people were connected and to look at the "inner forces" and "dynamic conditions" involved in change (Goldenweiser 1913:267–70; Boas 1919, 1920/1940). In a word, they were beginning to look at culture as a totality whose elements were interconnected, integrated, and patterned.

By the mid-1920s, Benedict, Mead, Sapir, and others were seizing upon the insights of psychoanalysts and Gestalt psychologists in order to portray the forms of integration between various behaviors in a society and the deeply held attitudes and beliefs of their members (Caffrey 1989:154–7). They called these connections configurations or patterns.

Benedict (1930) described cultural configurations in a pathbreaking paper presented at the International Congress of Americanists in 1928. She pointed out that the Pueblo cultures of the Southwest were strikingly different from those of neighboring groups and from most other Indian cultures in North America. She argued that they possessed "an *ethos* distinguished by its sobriety, by its distrust of excess, that minimizes to the last possible vanishing point any challenging or dangerous experiences" (Benedict 1930:573). While acts of ritual or personal experience leading to disruptive psychological states such as frenzy and ecstasy were absent in the Pueblo cultures, they were present in myriad forms in most other American Indian cultures. Benedict (1930:572) extended the idea of individual psychological types to whole cultures and, in the case of the Southwest, pointed out that the Pueblos and the neighboring Pima had selected "two diametrically different ways of arriving at the values of existence." While the Apollonian Pueblos sought to minimize disruption, their Dionysian neighbors used various disruptive means to achieve excess. She subsequently wrote that the development of these configurations

> was [no] more difficult to understand than, for example, the development of an art style. In both, if we have the available material we can see the gradual integration of elements, and growing dominance of some few stylistic drives. In both, also if we had the material, we could without doubt trace the influence of gifted individuals who have bent the culture in the direction of their own capacities. But the configuration of a culture always transcends the individual elements that have gone to its making. The cultural configuration builds itself up over generations discarding, as no individual may, the traits that are uncongenial to it. It takes to itself ritual and artistic and activational modes of expression that solidify its attitude and make it explicit. Many cultures have never achieved this thoroughgoing harmony (Benedict 1932:26).

Benedict's essays focused attention on the emotional and value orientations that underpinned everyday life and showed that not all cultures were integrated in the same manner or even to the same degree. While she was aware of the issues, Benedict did not answer questions concerned with how cultural configurations develop or how they influence individual behavior, or with the effects of individual differences in behavior and beliefs in particular contexts, nor did she particularly share Sapir's emphasis on the importance of the individual. Nevertheless, her views and those of Sapir would gain adherents in the SSRC's interdisciplinary seminars on culture and personality (Stocking 1976:16). Thus, by late 1920s, the ideas shaped by Benedict, Sapir, and others – that culture was the product of both psychic and historical factors, that it was functionally integrated to some extent, that it was patterned, and that cultural configurations were historically emergent – were commonplace in the field.

It is clear that ideas about language played an important role in the reconcept-ualization of culture that occurred in the 1920s (Aberle 1960). The new theory of culture followed a linguistic model: both select a small number of elements out of a larger range of possibilities; both are patterned; both change through time; and both are shared or participated in by the members of a community. This should not be particularly surprising, because many anthropologists from the first generation of academically certified professionals routinely carried out both ethnographic and linguistic research, and some, such as Kroeber or J. Alden Mason (1885–1967), did archaeology as well.

As the Great Depression of 1929 wore on, fewer and fewer young men and women attended college. This slowed and almost brought to a halt the development of anthro-pology as an increasingly academic discipline in the 1930s. In spite of this, 149 men and 30 women obtained Ph.D. degrees in anthropology between 1929 and 1941 (Thomas 1955). More than half of them found their first jobs not in the university but rather in the government or in one of the private or public relief agencies that were attempting to alleviate the miserable conditions being experienced by a majority of the American population in the 1930s. That social science research should be relevant and practical was a basic tenet of both the Rockefeller and Carnegie philanthropies. The dire conditions of the American people also brought a number of anthropologists into contact with community-based organizations, labor unions, and leftist political parties. In the process, some of them became outspoken critics of the racism and classism of American society, while others spoke out against fascism in Germany, Italy, Spain and the United States.

Anthropology and the New Deal, 1933–1941

The hundred or so anthropologists hired by the government after 1933 were typically employed by a work relief agency, the Bureau of Indian Affairs (BIA), or the Depart-ment of Agriculture (Partridge and Eddy 1987; Spicer 1977; van Willigen 1993).

They were asked to apply their knowledge to problems confronting the country – unemployment, the conditions on Indian reservations, or the circumstances of small farmers. That social science knowledge should have an immediate practical utility was, of course, the dominant viewpoint of the Rockefeller philanthropies, and most of the anthropologists employed by the government had already participated in Rockefeller-funded projects. In practical terms, this meant that a significant number of them came from the University of Chicago or had participated in Warner's Yankee City project at Harvard, both of which received financial support from the Rockefeller philanthropies. They would bring their knowledge to bear on problems facing government agencies. By the end of the decade, the term "applied anthropology" was commonplace, and the individuals who shared this perspective formed the Society for Applied Anthropology in 1941.

However, archaeologists were the first anthropologists to benefit from New Deal legislation. In the summer of 1933, the local office of the Federal Emergency Relief Administration (FERA) in Marksville, Louisiana requested that the Smithsonian Institution send two archaeologists – Frank M. Setzler (1902–1975) and James A. Ford (1911–1968) – to supervise a crew of more than one hundred employed to excavate and restore prehistoric mounds in the area. In November 1933, the Civil Works Administration (CWA) called on the Smithsonian Institution to provide additional archaeologists to direct field projects in states with warm winters and high unemployment; during the next two months, eleven projects employing 1500 men and women were initiated in California, Georgia, Florida, North Carolina, and Tennessee, and another 1,000 workers were engaged in archaeological survey and excavation projects sponsored by the Tennessee Valley Authority. These pilot projects showed that "large numbers of laborers supported by federal relief funds could be used fruitfully in the excavation of large archaeological sites" (Quimby 1979:111). As a result, archaeological research became an integral part of the programs of the Work Projects Administration (WPA) from 1934 to 1943. Archaeology appealed to the relief agencies, because it was labor-intensive and did not produce a commodity that competed with the private sector (Faguette 1985; Lyon 1996).

The relief archaeology programs were actually multi-tiered bureaucracies that operated simultaneously at both federal and state levels. Congressional audits from 1938 onwards meant that the WPA and the archaeologists it employed had to develop criteria for evaluating performance. While the federal archaeologists employed by the Smithsonian or the National Park Service and most of those working through state-level WPA offices supported standardization, archaeologists in New Mexico and Tennessee opposed uniform criteria, arguing that control of the archaeological research should be vested at the level of individual states and that such efforts represented federal interference and insufficient appreciation of local circumstances. The need to organize data and to establish procedures for comparing information from different sites sparked a theoretical debate over typology, classification, and the meaning of various concepts that would last more than two decades (e.g. Ford 1938; Willey and Phillips 1958:11–56). The data collected by WPA archaeology programs also underwrote the first historical synthesis of Native American cultural development in the eastern United States (Ford and Willey 1941).

The sudden demand in the mid-1930s for competently trained archaeologists to supervise workers outstripped the supply and stretched the ability of the universities to produce them on short notice. At the time, only two universities – Chicago and Kentucky – had summer field schools that provided students with hands-on training at nearby archaeological sites. Many of the men and women employed as archaeological supervisors participated in the University of Chicago field school, and virtually all of the men and women trained in Americanist archaeology during the 1930s worked at one time or another on a WPA-funded project. The demand for archaeologists also led Fay-Cooper Cole and others to form the Society for American Archaeology in December 1934 in order to gain a voice in policy-making and to curb the activities of looters (Patterson 1995:73–8).

In 1933, John Collier (1884–1968) was appointed Commissioner of Indian Affairs. He found himself in charge of a sprawling bureaucracy with more than 5,000 employees across the country whose activities were organized into a series of administrative departments. His aim was to reverse the assimilationist policies of his predecessors in the office, to grant tribes a greater degree of self-reliance, and to make the bureau more responsive to the people it was supposed to serve. To accomplish this he lobbied for the passage of the Indian Reorganization Act of 1934 (IRA) and employed a handful of anthropologists in varying capacities. One of his first initiatives was an experimental school in which Gladys Reichard (1893–1955) and Ruth Underhill (1883–1984) were involved with the Indian Service in teaching Navajos to write in the Navajo language. The success of this program led Edward Kennard to develop orthographies for other Indian languages and Underhill and others to prepare historical ethnologies for several tribes. Anthropologists employed by the Indian Service also studied the adjustment of men and women who had graduated from the Indian boarding schools (Griffen 1989; Kennard and Macgregor 1953).

In December 1934, Collier outlined the provisions of the Indian Reorganization Act of 1934 (IRA) at the annual meeting of the American Anthropological Association.[9] Eight months earlier, he had met with the officers of the association and a small group of anthropologists interested in practical or applied anthropology in order to enlist their aid in his effort to revitalize Indian life; the group included Fay-Cooper Cole and A. R. Radcliffe-Brown from Chicago; W. Lloyd Warner from Harvard; John M. Cooper (1881–1949), the association's secretary; and William Duncan Strong (1899–1962) from the BAE (Kelly 1980:8).

As soon as Collier received a congressional appropriation to implement provisions of the IRA, he began to employ anthropologists sympathetic to his aims. His first hire in 1935 was H. Scudder Mekeel (1902–47), one of Wissler's students at Yale, whose dissertation had dealt with the psychological effects of acculturation among the Sioux. Mekeel and five additional anthropologists hired the following year formed the Applied Anthropology Unit of the BIA.[10] The primary task of the unit, which was located in Washington, was to provide information about the social organization of those Indian groups that had elected to adopt charters; they sent this information to lawyers in the BIA's Tribal Reorganization Division who were charged with drafting their tribal constitutions. Various problems were present from the inception of the unit, and tensions quickly developed between the anthropologists and the lawyers. For example, on one hand, anthropologist Morris Opler (1907–96) pointed out that tribes, such as the Creek, traditionally did not have the kind of centralized political organization called for in the IRA (Opler 1952); on the other, the agents and lawyers paid no attention to the findings and recommendations of the anthropologists.

The anthropologists of the Applied Anthropology Unit increasingly found themselves in an untenable position. Their intentions were seen as suspect both by the BIA officials with whom they had to deal and by the Indians from whom they were collecting information. Neither Collier nor the anthropologists fully appreciated the resistance to change or inertia of the BIA bureaucracy itself which was thoroughly imbued, except possibly at the upper levels, with an assimilationist worldview that stood in stark opposition to the kind of controlled cultural diversity mandated by IRA provisions. The unit was disbanded in 1938 as a result of congressional budget cuts and opposition within the BIA itself to the anthropologists and their activities.

The anthropologists employed in the Technical Cooperation unit (TC-BIA) – a program funded jointly by the BIA and the Soil Conservation Service of the Department of Agriculture – fared little better (Kelly 1985b).[11] The roots of this unit dated back to 1933, when the federal government began to express concern that soil erosion resulting from overgrazing in the western part of the Navajo Reservation threatened to silt up the Hoover Dam reservoir. Collier had appeared before the Navajo Tribal Council in 1933 to announce that the federal government had mandated $1 million for soil-conservation studies and that these funds were tied to reductions in the size of their sheep and goat herds. The Navajo opposed stock reduction and soon resisted all programs emanating from the BIA offices. In 1936, Collier employed anthropologists – Burleigh Gardner (1902–88) and Solon T. Kimball (1909–82), who were Warner's students, and John Provinse from Chicago – to conduct human dependency studies focusing on land use, land ownership, and population distribution in one district of the Navajo reservation. In 1936, Kimball and Provinse (1942) discovered that the basic land-use units in Navajo society were small groups of matrilineally related families that came to be called "outfits." They recommended that the economic and political programs among the Navajo be organized along the same lines. From Collier's perspective, this was the highpoint of anthropology's involvement in the BIA. Nevertheless, the advice of Kimball and Provinse went unheeded by the BIA lawyers and government officials committed to the existing administrative structure and policies. The budget cuts of 1938 ultimately doomed the TC-BIA, and at least twenty other human dependency studies were not completed after the unit was disbanded in 1939.

In 1939, M. L. Wilson (1885–1969), Undersecretary of Agriculture, and Carl Taylor (1884–1975), chief of the Bureau of Agricultural Economics, invited Conrad Arensberg (1910–97), John Provinse from the BIA and W. Lloyd Warner, Robert Redfield, and Horace Miner (1912–93) from the University of Chicago to meet with them to discuss how cultural anthropologists could contribute to problems of concern to the Department of Agriculture (USDA). In the wake of the meeting, the Department sponsored Rural Life Studies in 70 counties across the country (Spicer 1977:127–9). However, because of the war looming on the horizon and the consequent diversion of resources and personnel, only six of the Rural Life Studies were actually completed. The most important and controversial was Walter Goldschmidt's (b. 1913) *As You Sow* (1947). Goldschmidt examined the development of agribusiness and the profound shaping effects it had on class and race relations in the Central Valley of California. His study drew the ire of both corporations and politicians who saw it as a threat to established practices and relations in the region.

The cultural anthropologists employed by the federal government in the 1930s had to confront two major problems: (1) the social organization of various American Indian tribes, and (2) the changes that were taking place or had occurred in the recent past among native peoples as a result of assimilation and acculturation (Eggan 1937). A significant number of the government anthropologists were attracted to the functionalist views of Malinowski and Radcliffe-Brown, both of whom believed that the discipline should be scientific, practical, and responsive to the needs of colonial administration (Radcliffe-Brown 1924/1986).[12] It should also be, in their view, comparative and non-historical – a perspective that contrasted with the historical thrust of much of American anthropology at the time. Malinowski and Radcliffe-Brown had already made their views known during Rockefeller-sponsored lecture tours of the United States in 1926.

The University of Chicago became the beachhead for British functionalism in the 1930s. The government anthropologists who were trained there were further exposed to structural functionalism by Radcliffe-Brown who taught at the university from 1931 to 1937 and by W. Lloyd Warner who moved to Chicago from Harvard in 1936; however, Radcliffe-Brown and Warner were not the only functionalists at Chicago. Robert Redfield, who had joined the department in 1928, was also making use of functionalist arguments in his analyses of peasant communities in Mexico. Unlike his English colleague, Redfield did not subordinate culture to social structure.

Redfield was hired as a part-time research associate by the Carnegie Institute of Washington in 1929 to direct a comparative study of Yucatecan Maya communities that would complement and extend its multidisciplinary investigations centered on the archaeological excavations and restoration at Chichén Itzá (Castañeda 1996:35–65; Sullivan 1989). Redfield and his collaborators studied four "folk" or peasant communities with distinctive cultures and whose residents were isolated to varying degrees from the city of Mérida (Hansen 1934, 1976; Redfield 1941; Redfield and Villa Rojas 1934; Villa Rojas 1945). In 1934, Redfield employed Sol Tax (1907–95) – who had studied with Linton and Radcliffe-Brown – to extend the CIW's ethnological fieldwork into Guatemala where highland communities exhibited different cultural practices from those found in Yucatán (Rubenstein 1991). Their publications echoed the cultural pluralism of the anti-incorporationist *indigenista* movement in Mexico during the 1930s as well as the anti-assimilationist views of John Collier in the United States (Hewitt de Alcántara 1984:19–39).

Redfield (1934, 1941) believed that the most powerful force underlying the changes taking place in the rural communities of Yucatán was that they were simultaneously less isolated and in greater contact with urban centers such as Mérida. However, the changes were not occurring uniformly across the peninsula. The residents of Tusik in Quintana Roo were still quite isolated relative to the other villages, and barely affected by the demands of the state; they spoke Maya and followed traditional Maya lifeways. Other communities, such as Chan Kom or Dzitas, were more influenced by the cultural practices of modern Mexican society; some residents spoke Spanish, read newspapers, went to school, and worked for individual gain rather than for the benefit of the community as a whole.

Redfield viewed the cultural diversity of Yucatán in terms of a "folk-urban continuum," one end of which was anchored in remote, tribal villages such as Tusik. The other end of the continuum was firmly tied to modern urban centers such as Mérida, whose cultural practices differentially influenced the residents of "folk" or peasant communities, some of whom had already adopted or were in the process of adopting features of the modern national culture. Thus, rural communities – such as Chan Kom or Dzitas – with their amalgams of Spanish and Indian cultural elements occupied points midway along the folk-urban continuum. Cities, in Redfield's view, were the source of change, and the folk communities, depending on the intensity and frequency of their contact with the urban culture, differentially exhibited the disorganization, secularization, and alienation resulting from their increased communication with modern cities. The values of their residents were transformed as the folk communities were increasingly enmeshed in the lifeways of the city.

As a contrast to the remote, relatively self-sufficient villages of Yucatán, Tax (1937, 1939) described the *municipios* in highland Guatemala in terms of economic specialization and mutual interdependence. Each community grew a particular crop, part of which was consumed by the farmers and part of which was sold in a nearby market for cash that was used to purchase other necessities. He also distinguished Indians and Ladinos, partly in cultural terms and partly in terms of the technical division of labor that existed in communities where both resided. He further noted that the Indians from some communities also worked seasonally elsewhere as wage workers, and that the members of other *municipios*, such as Atitlán or Chichicast-enango, bought "the produce of other communities in wholesale quantities to take to other markets to sell" (Tax 1952:48). While the local cultures of the Guatemala communities were relatively homogeneous and isolated, families were less integrated into them and exhibited more impersonal relations and individualistic behavior than their Yucatecan counterparts. In other words, the Guatemalan communities did not fit neatly into Redfield's folk-urban continuum.

The functionalist theoretical perspectives of Redfield and Tax led them to empha-size the relative cultural homogeneity of the communities, the harmony of social and interpersonal relations and the value orientations shared by the majority of their members. Stressing the functional interrelations of the local cultural elements, they did not consider fully the implications of rural class structures, exploitation, or the disputes and conflicts that disrupted everyday life in these communities. Some critics – such as Oscar Lewis (1914–70) – would point out that these folk societies were in fact peasant villages that were never isolated from urban centers but always existed in a symbiotic and dependent relation with them (Lewis 1951); others, notably Sidney Mintz (b. 1922), would show that Redfield's folk-urban continuum failed to account for the rural proletarian communities associated with the modern henequen plantations in Yucatán (Mintz 1953).

Redfield's attention to processes of culture change and their effects on the indi-viduals experiencing it resonated with a wider concern of American anthropologists in the 1930s – acculturation, or what happened when groups of individuals with different cultures came into continuous contact resulting in changes in the original cultural patterns of one or both groups. Before the First World War, some assumed that the American Indians would either assimilate or disappear, that European immi-grant groups with the passage of enough time would disappear in the American melting pot, and that the "Negro problem" would somehow resolve itself. However, none of these came to pass, and many Indians, Blacks, and ethnic minorities actively resisted acculturation and assimilation. As a result, in 1935, the SSRC's Committee on Personality and Culture established a subcommittee on acculturation composed of anthropologists from the greater Chicago area – Redfield, Linton, and Herskovits (1936) – to access the current status of acculturation studies in the United States and to identify fruitful lines of inquiry. The committee found that, while the literature dealing with acculturation was extensive, it was difficult to compare cases, because the published accounts often emphasized different aspects of the process or features of larger totalities. The subcommittee "felt that a series of studies prepared in accord-ance with a single plan or outline would be extremely useful for the testing of certain hypotheses" (Linton 1940:viii).

The subcommittee raised a series of questions for consideration: (1) what was the nature of the contact – for instance, was it friendly and between entire groups or certain kinds of individuals; (2) what circumstances surrounded the contact and subsequent acculturative processes – were there, for example, inequalities between the groups or was force involved; (3) what processes of acculturation were involved – that is, how were traits selected by the donor and recipient culture, and how were they integrated into the cultural configuration of the recipient groups; (4) what psychological mechanisms underpinned the acceptance, rejection, and integration of the new elements; and (5) what were the results of acculturation – in other words, were large numbers of new traits accepted, were original traits from both cultures combined to produce a newly smoothly functioning whole, or was the acceptance of new traits resisted? Their recommendations built on anthropological studies concerned with the interplay of personality and culture and with the idealist conceptions of culture that stressed the patterning of its elements and the unconscious, core value-orientations that shaped and brought consistency and a distinctive integration of those cultural configurations.

The subcommittee was particularly concerned with the psychology of acculturation – that is, with determining the covert value orientations of the recipient cultures as well as the psychological characteristics of individuals from those cultures who might accept or reject elements from the donor culture under the particular circumstances of contact. They wanted to determine why some societies adopted new elements and others did not, or why some individuals in a particular society adopted foreign traits while others rejected them. A few years later, Clyde Kluckhohn (1905–60) would point out how important it was for administrators in the BIA to understand the covert culture – i.e. the unconscious value-orientations – of a society in situations where acculturation was taking place or where the adoption of new traits was being resisted (Kluckhohn 1943).

The subcommittee's emphasis on reciprocity and the shifts in value patterns that occurred during moments of acculturation deflected attention away from an important fact. Alexander Lesser (1902–82), a Columbia-trained anthropologist sympathetic to the left at the time, had already described it in the following way:

> The problem of acculturation, when we are considering the American Indians in relation to their adjustment to European culture, is a problem of assimilation . . .
>
> In acculturation, the cultural groups involved are in an essentially reciprocal relationship. Both give and take . . . In assimilation the tendency is for the ruling cultural group to enforce the adoption of certain externals, in terms of which [its] superior adjustment seems to be attained. The adopting culture is not in a position to choose (Lesser 1933:ix).

Lesser, the leftist, was clearer than his liberal colleagues on the importance of power relations during episodes of cultural change. So was Malinowski (1938:xxii–xxiii) who wrote

The whole concept of European culture as a cornucopia from which things are freely given is misleading. It does not take a specialist in anthropology to see that the European "give" is always highly selective. We never give any native people under our control – and we never shall, for it would be sheer folly as long as we stand on the basis of our present Realpolitik – the following elements of our culture:

1. The instruments of physical power: fire-arms, bombing planes, poison gas, and all that makes an effective defence or aggression possible.
2. We do not give out instruments of political mastery [i.e. sovereignty or voting rights] . . .
3. We do not share with them the substance of economic wealth and advantages . . . Even when under indirect economic exploitation . . . we allow the native a share of the profits, the full control of the economic organization remains in the hands of Western enterprise.
4. We do not admit them as equals to Church, Assembly, school, or drawing room . . . Full political, social and even religious equality is nowhere granted.

The dominant orientation of acculturation studies resonated with a major third focus of American anthropologists during the 1930s – the interpenetration of culture and personality. New Haven and New York were centers for these inquiries, particularly after Sapir left Chicago in 1931 to accept a position at Yale (Darnell 1986, 1990:327–97). From 1932 to 1936, Sapir taught seminars dealing with the impact of culture on personality and the psychology of culture; however, his focus on the formative power of culture on personality was ultimately overwhelmed by the evolutionary sociology and behavioralist approaches of the social scientists in Yale's Institute of Human Relations which was well-funded by the Rockefeller philanthropies (Capshew 1999). As a result, Sapir pursued his agenda in 1935 through an interdisciplinary conference he organized in New York for the NRC's Committee on Personality in Relation to Culture; however, a year later, the NRC declined to fund further activities planned by Sapir and the committee. Following a heart attack in 1936, Sapir recuperated in New York and spent increasing amounts of time there until his death a year later.

The arrival of émigré pyschoanalysts from Central Europe in the early 1930s coincided with Ruth Benedict's (1934/1989) interest in cultural configurations manifest in her *Patterns of Culture* to stimulate the interest of a number of New York-based anthropologists in the interplay of culture and personality by the mid-1930s. Benedict and psychoanalyst Abram Kardiner (1891–1981) taught seminars on the cultural determinants of personality adaptation at the New York Psychoanalytic Institute and Columbia; these were continued after 1937 by Kardiner and Ralph Linton as Benedict dropped out of the seminar and worked with other psychoanalysts, notably Harry Stack Sullivan and Karen Horney (Caffrey 1989:243–4; Manson 1986). The seminars yielded a small but influential number of publications including Kardiner's (1939/1974) *The Individual and His Society*, Cora DuBois's (1903–91)

(1944/1960) *The People of Alor* and Linton's (1945) *The Cultural Background of Personality*. The explorations of Benedict and Sapir regarding the interconnections between culture and personality development were also the medium in which Margaret Mead (1928, 1930, 1935) produced studies of the cultural conditioning of the behavior of teenage girls in Samoa, the cultural processes by which children become adults in Manus, and the cultural determination of sex roles.

The ongoing concern with race relations and racism discussed earlier constituted the fourth major focus of American anthropologists during the 1930s. From 1932 to 1934, Hortense Powdermaker (1896–1970), a former union organizer trained by Malinowski, carried out an SSRC-supported ethnographic study of race relations in Indianola, Mississippi – John Dollard's (1937) Southerntown. In 1935, Allison Davis (1902–83), supported by Rockefeller funds channeled to Warner through Harvard's Committee on Industrial Physiology, worked with white colleagues, Burleigh and Mary Gardner, in Natchez, Mississippi to study the linkages between social classes and racial castes from both sides of the color line (Davis, Gardner, and Gardner 1941). Davis and his wife, who had worked among the more affluent members of the black community, found it difficult to establish rapport with the black lower classes so in 1935 they invited St. Clair Drake (1911–90) to work with members of the lower classes. During the two years he was in Natchez, Drake spent part of his time organizing sharecroppers (Harrison and Harrison 1999:17). After returning to Chicago in 1937, Drake met Horace Cayton (1903–70), a black sociologist and socialist; together they would launch a theoretically sophisticated two-year study of the black community in Chicago financed by the WPA (Drake and Cayton 1945).

Anthropologists from New York City were involved also in a series of projects, including the Carnegie Corporation's "Negro in America" project which culminated with the publication of Swedish economist Gunnar Myrdal's (1944/1962) *An American Dilemma: The Negro Problem and Modern Democracy* (1944/1962). In 1937, the Carnegie Corporation appointed Myrdal (1898–1987) – a former fellow of the Rockefeller Foundation recommended by its director, Beardsley Ruml – to carry out a study of the "Negro problem;" the project which would cost nearly $300,000 over the next seven years (Lagemann 1989:123–46; Jackson 1990; Southern 1987). Myrdal discussed the project with a number of African-American scholars – Ralph Bunche, E. Franklin Frazier, Allison Davis, Horace Cayton, St. Clair Drake, Abram Harris, Alain Locke, and W. E. B. Du Bois among others. He also solicited criticisms and suggestions from anthropologists including Boas, Benedict, Herskovits, Linton, and Powdermaker. In addition, he employed Columbia-trained anthropologists Ashley Montagu (1905–99) and Bernhard J. Stern (1894–1956) among others to prepare research memoranda on particular subjects (Myrdal 1944/1962:lx–lxiii). Simply put, many of the scholars that Myrdal consulted were socialists inspired by the writings of Karl Marx; in fact, Du Bois, the Howard University Circle (Bunche,

Frazier, Harris, and Locke) and the anthropologists at Columbia and Chicago held more radical views than Myrdal who was a Social Democrat (Baker 1998:176–87; Jackson 1990:88–134, 186–230, 257–61). Many of them – including Benedict (1940) and Montagu (1942/1997) – would subsequently publish books depicting the fallacy of race and the politics of racial prejudice in the United States. Benedict and Mildred Ellis (1942) wrote a pamphlet for the National Education Association addressing the myth of the master race; and Benedict and Gene Weltfish (1943) wrote a pamphlet for the Public Affairs Committee on the races of mankind that was distributed to inductees in the armed services and USO centers until Southern Congressmen on the Military Affairs Committee of the House of Representatives denounced the pamphlet, claiming it showed "all the techniques . . . of Communist propaganda"; they banned it from all military installations (Dower 1986:120; Caffrey 1989:297–301).

The rising tides of anti-Semitism and fascism in Europe increasingly became matters of concern for American anthropologists in the 1930s. Boas was already involved by the spring of 1933; his were among the first books burned by the Nazis. By the fall of that year, Boas and Benedict were already engaged in discussions with colleagues about how best to attack the ideologies of fascism, racism, and anti-semitism. Their concern was to prevent fascism from taking hold in the United States. They found allies, such as Albert Einstein, in organizations that were concerned with fascism and the Spanish Civil War; they founded organizations, such as the American Committee for Democracy and Intellectual Freedom, which was labelled a Communist-front organization by the Dies Committee in 1942 (Caffrey 1989:282–301). Because of their anti-fascism, the FBI kept files on the activities of both Boas and Benedict from 1936 onward (Krook 1993). While neither Boas nor Benedict belonged to the Communist Party of the United States (CPUSA), several of their students did, and they were certainly sympathetic to many aims of the party. In a letter to Earl Browder, the incarcerated National Secretary of the party, Boas wrote:

> A long life has taught me that the hope of the future lies in our willingness to rise above prejudices that separate man, one social group from the other. We must learn to see a common goal for humanity as a whole, a goal diversified in form, but a unit because it is based on the love of mankind and the loyalty to ideals, not on the loyalties to group interests, whatever these may be. This ideal is not easily attained, for it seems to be an ancient, biological characteristic of animal life that group consciousness implies group conflict. However, the history of mankind shows that the group limits can expand so as to include millions, and the purest minds have always envisaged a group consciousness that must embrace humankind as a whole and forbid group conflict. However much I may disagree with the methods of your party and the demand of obedience of party members, I recognize that the final ideal of your party agrees with this lofty aim. If you set this above party disciplines and allow your party members free set discussion of

party procedure you fulfill a useful function in society. I have met many young people who profess to be Communists, and my judgment is that they are attracted to the ideals of equality of all members of mankind. Among them are the best of our youth (Boas letter to Earl Browder May 17, 1941 quoted by Krook 1993:95).

A number of anthropology students in American universities during the late 1930s also belonged to various anti-fascist organizations. Several – John Murra (b. 1916), Elman Service (1915–96), and Clifton Amsbury among them – enlisted in the Lincoln Brigade in 1936 and saw action in the Spanish Civil War; others, such as Stanley Diamond (1922–91), were turned away by recruiters, because they were too young – barely into their teens – when the war broke out (Gailey 1992:4). Eleanor Leacock (1922–87) described being denied a security clearance in 1944 by the FBI because of her anti-fascist political activities as an undergraduate at Radcliffe and Barnard (Leacock 1993:11). Others who belonged to leftist and anti-fascist organ-izations in the late 1930s – Gene Weltfish (1902–80) and Morris Swadesh to name only two – would later lose their jobs to the anti-Communist fervor of zealots who carried out the wishes of Senator Joseph McCarthy's Senate Internal Security Com-mittee in the early 1950s (Hymes 1971; Pathé 1979).

War clouds loomed on the horizon with steadily increasing intensity from the time of Japan's invasion of Manchuria in 1931 and the Nazis' rise to power in Ger-many in 1933. As the threat of the Second World War grew more imminent, American anthropologists continued to work for various government agencies, but their activities also began to merge subtly with new undertakings toward the end of the decade that involved mobilizing the American people for war. The war economy set in motion in the late 1930s ended the Depression and boosted the productivity of American firms beyond the levels of the boom years of the 1920s. By 1940, the demands of the economy and the approaching war were already affecting almost every aspect of daily life in the United States. In the process, the worldviews of anthropologists shifted almost overnight from matters of national interest to inter-national concerns, and the focus of the profession would be changed forever.

During the early 1940s, some anthropologists investigated education, personality development, and administration on Indian reservations, while others examined food habits or conducted studies of national morale. Others organized the development of foreign area and language studies. When war was finally declared, many went to work in diverse capacities for the government – such as data analysts, researchers for the War Relocation Authority, advisers to aircraft manufacturers who designed seats for the Army Air Force that reduced fatigue and discomfort, or forensic spec-ialists who identified individuals from their remains after the war. A number served with the Office of Strategic Services (OSS) in Europe and Africa while others were employed by the FBI or military intelligence in Latin America. Many more, however, served in the military as average citizens who either enlisted or were drafted.

Anthropology and the War Years, 1941–1945

Let us review some of the institutional settings in which anthropologists were employed during the war years. What made anthropologists particularly attractive to various federal agencies was their holistic, cross-cultural perspective, and the anthropologists made use of the opportunities that were created by the war.

The second phase of the BIA's involvement with anthropology began in the fall of 1941. John Collier contracted with W. Lloyd Warner of the University of Chicago's Committee on Human Development to study education, personality development, and administration on six Indian reservations (Kelly 1980:19–23). Laura Thompson (1905–2000), who had studied with Kroeber and Lowie at Berkeley before working in the Pacific during the 1930s, coordinated the project, while Warner directed and supervised the research. In 1944, supervision of the project shifted to the officers of the Society for Applied Anthropology. Building on the culture and personality studies of Sapir and others in the 1930s, the six projects involved cooperative investigations by anthropologists, psychiatrists, and physicians that focused on child-rearing, education, and the growth of interpersonal relations.[13] Their studies of the Hopi, Sioux, Navajo, Zuñi, and Papago were completed and published in the mid-1940s.

Thompson (1951) then reviewed the effectiveness of various Indian Service policies and programs and made a number of recommendations that were designed to improve the welfare of the communities: integrate the services at the community level recognizing that there are differences between tribes and that what might be ideal on one reservation might be disastrous on another; integrate tribal members, especially traditional health practitioners, into the Indian Service; pay attention to existing child-rearing practices; develop the resources of the reservations; and decentralize the BIA. At the time, her recommendations went largely unheeded.

Concern over the welfare of poor rural populations led to a second area of employment. In late 1940, Vice-President Henry Wallace and M. L. Wilson of the USDA expressed concern over the well-being of rural populations in the country. With SSRC funding, a pilot study was designed and directed by Wilson, W. Lloyd Warner, Margaret Mead, and others. John Bennett (b. 1915) who studied the food habits of rural peoples in southern Illinois emphasized the determinant roles played by social and economic factors. After war was declared on December 7, 1941, attention shifted from the welfare of rural populations to that of the American population as a whole, and control over research on nutrition was taken over by the NRC's Committee on Food Habits of which Margaret Mead was Executive Secretary and John Cooper, Ruth Benedict, and Warner were members. Investigators shifted their attention to low-income groups in the Eastern industrial states, low-income rural and Black communities in the Southeast, and various racial, national, and cultural groups in isolated areas. Fred Eggan of the University of Chicago, for example, investigated the food habits of Indians and Hispanics in the Southwest. Given the wartime food shortages, the NRC Committee was concerned with assessing dietary changes, the resistance or readiness of the American population to adopt new consumption patterns, and attitudes toward food relief. The committee focused its advertising on housewives. While few if any changes resulted from the food-habits research conducted during the war, the studies did have an effect on the federal government's nutrition and food policies (Montgomery and Bennett 1979).

A number of wartime agencies established by executive orders during the winter and spring months of 1942 employed the services of anthropologists. These agencies were major sources of employment during the war.

About twenty anthropologists were employed by the most infamous of the new agencies, the War Relocation Authority (WRA), which was established in March to administer the ten concentration camps where about 140,000 Japanese-Americans from the West Coast, who had been dispossessed of their property and deprived of their civil rights, were interned during the early years of the war (Drinnon 1987; Feeley 1999; Hirabayashi and Hirabayashi 1989; Ichioka 1989; Nishimoto 1995). Nine of the camps were under the authority of the WRA from its inception; since the tenth – at Poston, Arizona – was located on the Papago Indian Reservation, it was under the jurisdiction of John Collier, the Commissioner of Indian Affairs until February 1943 when management passed to the WRA. Anthropologists were involved from the inception of the camps in three separate research projects that would provide administrators with information they needed to run the camps efficiently (Ichioka 1989:3)

In March 1942, John Provinse from the Bureau of Agricultural Economics was named Chief of the Community Management Division, and John F. Embree (1908–50), a Chicago-trained anthropologist with research experience in Japan, headed the Documentation Section. Believing in the necessity for social science research at the relocation camps, they lobbied for the creation of the Community Analysis Section (CAS) which was established in February 1943. Social unrest at the camps under-scored the need for social analysis at the centers (Embree 1944; Suzuki 1981:23–5). The CAS employed twenty anthropologists to investigate and analyze the causes of social unrest. In August 1942, six months after assuming control of the center at Postan, Collier named psychiatrist-anthropologist Alexander Leighton (b. 1908) – already a consultant on the Indian Personality and Education Project – to investigate everyday life in the camp; Leighton employed two anthropologists and fifteen Japanese-Americans to carry out the research.

The third – the Japanese American Evacuation and Resettlement Study (JERS) – was independent of the other two. It was directed by sociologist Dorothy Swaine Thomas (1899–1977) who had earlier worked on Myrdal's Carnegie-funded study of the "Negro problem" in America. With the support of Milton Eisenhower – who was Director of the WRA – and the University of California, Thomas received about $90,000 from various foundations to study the effects that the enforced "mass migration" of Japanese-Americans in California might have in the postwar years. She was particularly concerned with cultural conflict, assimilation, how the Japanese communities adjusted to their incarceration, and the impact that these might have on California agriculture. Robert Lowie and other UC faculty members served initially as consultants, and five graduate students, including two anthropologists, were employed to collect information, some as participant observers in the camps (Ichioka 1989). Thomas required that the analysts refrain from publishing any data they collected until after the war. At that time, she refused to recommend the publication of Morton Grozdins's doctoral dissertation in political science, "Political Aspects of the Japanese Evacuation," because he argued that "in California, state and local politicians [including Earl Warren] and economic interest groups had applied pressure on the military to remove all Japanese from the state" (Ichioka 1989:17). Grozdins's work was ultimately published by the University of Chicago Press in 1949 as *American Betrayed: Politics and the Japanese Evacuation* (Suzuki 1989).

The other two government agencies that employed significant numbers of anthropologists were the Office of War Information (OWI) and the Office of Strategic Services (OSS) – the precursor of the Central Intelligence Agency (CIA) – both of which were established in the early months of 1942 (Winkler 1978). Ruth Benedict, Margaret Mead, Alexander Leighton, Gregory Bateson (1904–80), and Clyde Kluckhohn were prominent analysts in the Foreign Morale Analysis Division of the OWI (Caffrey 1989:318–26; Dower 1986:118–47; Leighton 1949:223–5). They produced a series of national character studies that attempted to predict the behavior of the citizens of nation-states – Thailand, Burma, Japan, Germany and Rumania. The impetus for the national character studies came from earlier investigations of the linkages between culture and personality development. They had a number of distinctive features. In Mead's (1979:148) words, they covered "those aspects of personality that could be referred to national institutions that transcended regional, class, or ethnic subdivisions within a nation-state." The analysts frequently had no first-hand knowledge of the citizens of those countries; they relied instead on information that could be gleaned from published accounts, diaries, movies, and interviews with individuals residing in the United States. They focused on those aspects of the cultures that were relevant to the war – such as the attitudes of their citizens regarding victory or defeat or, in the case of Japan, the importance of the emperor as a universally respected symbol that "had to be retained as both a rallying point for surrender and the vehicle for postwar change" (Dower 1986:138).

The most enduring of the OWI's national character studies was probably Benedict's (1946) *The Chrysanthemum and the Sword: Patterns of Japanese Culture.* While she appreciated the significance of cultural differences and the subtle dynamics of change, Benedict was also aware of the difficulties of applying the psychiatric analysis of an individual to the entire undifferentiated citizenry of a nation-state.

The same cannot be said for Geoffrey Gorer's (1905–85) analysis of the Japanese, which received more publicity at the time. Gorer (1942) depicted the Japanese as primitive, infantile, abnormal, and tormented by an inferiority complex; he was convinced that their values and patterns of behavior were shaped by child-rearing and early-childhood experiences. In an internal OWI memo, Kluckhohn expressed his disapproval, referring to this approach as the "Scott Tissue interpretation of history" (Dower 1986:138, 122–3).

Earlier, by the 1930s, the SSRC and ACLS were already acutely aware that the United States was ill-prepared to wage war on a global basis. Its citizens knew woefully little about the cultures and languages of peoples living outside the United States and Europe. Throughout the 1930s, the two foundations advocated the need to develop inter-disciplinary area studies in American universities. Earlier in the decade, they had created a series of committees to coordinate research and resources on China, Japan, the Pacific, and Latin America. The activities of these committees expanded as the threat of war grew (Patterson and Lauria-Perricelli 1999).

For example, in 1935, the ACLS established its Committee on Latin America Studies with 29 members, seven of whom were anthropologists: Robert Redfield, A. V. Kidder, A. L. Kroeber, Clark Wissler, Alfred M. Tozzer, Carl Guthe, and John M. Cooper. At the same time, the Advisory Committee for the *Handbook of Latin American Studies* was established by the ACLS, SSRC, American Geographical Society, and the Universities of Chicago and Michigan. The handbook was a periodic survey of knowledge in all fields on a major world area. By the end of the 1930s, the Rockefeller Foundation and other philanthropies increased their support for work on Latin America. In 1940, the ACLS-SSRC Joint Committee on Latin American Studies was established as the NRC's more specialized Committee on Latin American Anthropology whose charge was to coordinate research and resources with government needs. Projects such as these articulated with those of government agencies such as the Office of the Coordinator of Interamerican Affairs (OCIAA) which was established by the federal government in 1940 to promote its good-neighbor policies with Latin American countries.

Nelson Rockefeller (1908–79), who had gained extensive knowledge of Latin America and its people during the 1930s, was named to head the OCIAA (Erb 1982). He implemented a series of policies that involved anthropologists. He provided $114,000 in federal funding for ten archaeological projects in Latin America in 1940–1941, which were coordinated by Wendell Bennett (1905–53) and George Vaillant (1901–45) of the American Museum of Natural History.[14] He lobbied Congress for funds to publish the *Handbook of South American Indians* as a symbol of hemispheric unity during the war; Julian Steward edited the *Handbook* for the BAE and the Smithsonian Institution. Rockefeller and John Collier supported the formation of the Inter-American Indian Institute in 1941 to carry out research on "Indian problems" of countries in the Western Hemisphere. In 1943, Steward established and directed the Smithsonian's Institute of Social Anthropology to carry out research on the Indian question in the countries south of the Río Grande; at the same time, Steward helped Ralph Beals (1901–85) organize the Inter-American Society of Anthropology and History and its journal *Acta Americana*. During this period, Steward also maintained close ties with the Institute of Andean Research investigations and with William D. Strong's Ethnogeographic Board which was established by the NRC, ACLS, SSRC, and Smithsonian Institution in 1942

> to make readily accessible to Washington military and war agencies such specific regional information and evaluated personnel data as may be available to the sponsoring institutions and the numerous other governmental and outside scientific organizations with which they are affiliated on in contact (Bennett 1947:v).

Before the war, the ACLS received $100,000 from the Rockefeller Foundation to study Chinese, Japanese, Russian, and other languages such as Thai that were not taught in American universities. In 1942, the ACLS established its Intensive Language Program to apply linguistics techniques developed by Bloomfield, Sapir, and others to the problems of language-learning and -teaching (Haas 1953). A year later, the army incorporated the procedures and training manuals developed by the ACLS linguists as well as the linguists themselves into its Specialized Language Training Program; in the next year, they trained nearly 15,000 enlisted personnel in foreign area and language studies at 55 universities across the country. In 1944, roughly 80 of the 96 linguists attending the annual meeting of the Linguistics Society of America "were being paid by the Government or by the ACLS for militarily crucial work" (Martin Joos quoted by Murray 1994:151). In addition, anthropologists – e.g. George P. Murdock (1897–1985) and John M. Whiting (1908–99) of Yale's Institute of Human Relations – taught in Army or Navy programs established at a dozen universities to train administrative officers for occupied territories after the war (Fenton 1947:v-vi).

At the fortieth annual meeting of the American Anthropological Association (1942:289) held three weeks after the declaration of war, the association resolved to "place itself and its resources and the specialized skills and knowledge of its members at the disposal of the country for the successful prosecution of the war." Indeed, for the next four years, the federal government made extensive use of anthropologists and their specialized knowledge. By the end of the war, many social scientists apparently felt the same way about their experiences with the administrators of government agencies as Alexander Leighton (1949:127–8) did. One of Leighton's colleagues remarked that

> You always get one of two requests: to show that some policy the executive has already decided upon is badly needed; or, to show that some policy the executive is already employing is working well.

Another suggested that

> The administrator uses social science the way a drunk uses a lamppost, for support rather than illumination.

Discussion

Two lines of inquiry that emerged from the late 1920s onward endured after the war ended. One was concerned with social class and race relations in the United States. The other focused on the future of colonial rule in Africa, Asia, and Oceania.

Anthropologists began to examine social stratification and the class structure of American society in ways that did not treat Indians and Blacks as isolated communities within the larger society but rather as integral parts of the larger society itself. Such analyses which began with the Lynds' discussion of Muncie were honed by W. Lloyd Warner and his associates in their accounts of Newburyport and Natchez. Warner and his associates focused their attention on how individuals and families viewed their social status and those of other members of the local community. They did not pay sufficient attention to the fact that whole categories of individuals – such as international bankers or corporate presidents – did not reside in the relatively small communities they studied. In a word, the class structures they discerned were defined in terms of families or cliques. They did not pay sufficient attention to the economic conditions and circumstances of these groups and their ownership or possession of the means of production.

Walter Goldschmidt's (1947) study of the agricultural communities in the Central Valley of California was almost unique at the time because of the emphasis he placed on economic relations and ownership of the instruments of production as a means of discerning class position and relations with the class structure of the wider society. He further pointed out that social mobility, when it did take place, occurred mainly between different layers of the same social class. While Goldschmidt effectively related the class structure manifested in the local communities with those of the wider society, he was not the only anthropologist who conceptualized class in terms of distinctive economic activities or relationships with the means of production. Allison Davis and the Gardners' (1941) did this in their investigation of Natchez, and St. Clair Drake and Horace Cayton (1945) also made use of economic criteria in their study of the Black Community in Chicago's South Side. Simply put, a number of anthropologists made Marxist class analyses in the late 1930s and early 1940s.

Warner's (1937) functionalist conceptualization viewed race relations in American society in terms of cross-cutting systems of class and caste. In his view, the class system which regulated marriage relations between the higher and lower orders of the society allowed some mobility between the various social strata; the caste system which prohibited intercaste marriages prevented upward or downward social mobility. In other words, while an individual's class position might change, his or her caste status would remain constant. Warner's view stood in opposition to the Marxist perspective found in *Deep South* or *Black Metropolis*; it also contrasted with the views of Myrdal (1944/1962) for that matter, regarding the utility of caste as a means of describing race relations in American society (Harrison 1992). Drake and Cayton perceived American society as relatively caste-free; they and Davis saw race relations in terms of an historically organized, technical division of labor structured by race and gender.

Davis, more than the anthropologists who worked on the BIA's education and personality development studies in the early 1940s, had a clear understanding of the interconnections of class, race and education (Browne 1999). He and John Dollard observed:

> In their efforts to teach, lower-class Negro parents punish children with great energy and frequency and reward them seldom. They cannot offer the more effective status rewards to their children because both economic and educational privileges are class-bound and there are very few to which the child in the lower class has access. The chief reason for the relative lack of socialization of lower-class children seems to be that their incitement to learn, which means in part to renounce direct impulse gratification and to build up more complex habits and skills, is crippled by the scarcity of available rewards (Davis and Dollard 1940:267).

A few years later, Davis (1948:10–11) described the linkages in the following way:

> If a child associates intimately with no one but slum adults and children, he will learn only slum culture . . .
>
> Because the slum individual usually is responding to a different physical, economic, and cultural reality from that in which the middle-class individual is trained, the slum individual's habits and values also must be different if they are to be realistic. The behavior which we regard as "delinquent" or "shiftless" or "unmotivated" in slum groups is usually a perfectly realistic, adaptive and – in slum life – respectable response to reality.
>
> His social instigations and goals, his symbolic world and its evaluation are largely selected from the narrow culture of that class with which alone he can associate freely.

The other anthropological insight from the war years was concerned with the crisis of colonial regimes and their future after the war. At a conference sponsored by the Viking Fund (now the Wenner-Gren Foundation for Anthropological Research) in 1944 on the science of man [*sic*] in the world crisis, sociologist Raymond Kennedy (1906–50) observed that three developments were preparing the way for the dissolution of colonial states. The first involved the growing political discontent and awareness of colonial subjects themselves and their insistence upon better wages and economic opportunities. The second was that colonial peoples were taking seriously Western statements about democratic ideals and were beginning to demand these privileges for themselves. The third was that

> the institution of colonialism is being weakened by the rising tide of democratic enthusiasm in the Western world, where the ideal of democracy is itself undergoing a change. The new concept of democracy is international. . . . The people of the Western countries are coming to feel that a world half-slave and half-free is a constant danger to the survival of liberty everywhere (Kennedy 1945:345–6).

Looking back to the decolonization and national liberation movements of the postwar years, these were prophetic words.

Notes

1. Psychologists supported by corporations and by the Rockefeller philanthropies in the 1920s were at the center of the industrial relations movement that sought to control shop-floor inefficiency and worker discontent. The single most important study was undertaken at the Hawthorne Works, a Western Electric plant in Chicago (Baritz 1960:76–116). The management of American Telephone and Telegraph provided more than one million dollars to researchers from MIT, the Harvard Business School, and the NRC to learn about the employees at Hawthorne. The LSRM financed the entire career of Australian psychiatrist Elton Mayo (1880–1949) in the United States, including his studies at Hawthorne in the late 1920s and 1930s, and the Yankee City studies of W. Lloyd Warner and his students in Newburyport, Massachusetts. Mayo was concerned with eliminating the the deleterious aspects of industrial organization that affected productivity (Kelly 1985a:124–5; Trahair 1984).
2. The Yankee City staff included Conrad Arensberg, J. O. Brew, Eliot Chapple, Allison Davis, Burleigh Gardner, Solon Kimball, Paul Lunt, and Leo Srole.
3. King's work was an important link in a chain of black community studies that stretched back to Du Bois's (1899/1967) *The Philadelphia Negro: A Social Study*, and that would soon include the investigations of other black communities by African-American anthropologists – notably Allison Davis and St. Clair Drake (Baber 1999; Browne 1999).
4. Five of Earnest Hooton's physical anthropology students completed dissertations on race and racial mixture: Biraja Guha (India); Harry Shapiro (Pitcairn Island),

Carleton Coon (North Africa), Arthur Kelly (Mexican communities in Texas), and George Williams (Yucatan Peninsula) during the late 1920s (Thomas 1955:710–11).

5. The vindicationist perspective according to St. Clair Drake was set in motion in the mid-nineteenth by African-American intellectuals to rebut "the criticism, slurs, ridicule and racial derogation that was hurled upon black people as the contest between abolitionists and defenders of slavery sharpened. 'Vindicationists' were concerned with sins of omission, too, e.g., the failure to recognize the contributions that black people had made in the Nile Valley civilizations" (Drake quoted by Harrison and Harrison 1999:13). Du Bois, Boas and others used it to challenge the ideology of the superiority of Anglo-Saxon culture (Drake 1980).

6. Herskovits, who moved to Northwestern University in 1928, focused his attention increasingly on race relations, African-American culture, African and Caribbean ethnology, and African cultural survivals in the New World. During the 1930s he continued to work with a group of young black scholars that included Abram L. Harris (1899–1963) who had assisted him earlier in his anthropometric studies and Ralph Bunche (1904–71) who would subsequently become the American representative to the United Nations after the war. At various times in the 1930s, he publicly argued for desegregation, supported civil rights and "praised the interracial unionism of the C.I.O. and the Southern Tenant Farmers' Union" (Jackson 1986:117; Simpson 1973:1–41). Herskovits (1941/1958) wrote *The Myth of the Negro Past* at the request of Gunnar Myrdal (1898–1987) who directed the Carnegie Corporation's "The Negro in America" project.

7. Hurston was not the only African-American scholar who received financial assistance from Parsons. She also supported Arthur H. Fauset's (1899–1983) investigations of black folklore in Nova Scotia, the Deep South, and the Caribbean between 1923 and 1927. Fauset, who eventually completed his dissertation at the University of Pennsylvania in 1942, was a trade-unionist activist involved in the reorganization of the teachers' union in Philadelphia in the early 1930s; he subsequently became vice-president of the American Federation of Teachers Local 192 (Carpenter 1999:233).

8. By the mid-1930s, culture and personality studies were supported by the SSRC's Committee on Personality and Culture and by the NRC's Committee on Culture and Personality that Sapir chaired. The Rockefeller Foundation funded the Institute of Human Relations at Yale and underwrote Sapir's seminar on culture and personality when he moved there in 1931 (Caffrey 1989:214–15).

9. From the early 1920s onward, John Collier had been an outspoken critic of the Bureau of Indian Affairs, charging that its assimilationist policy was flawed because it was based on a false premise – i.e. that all groups "should conform to a single, uniform cultural standard" (Kelly 1975:292). Because of his persuasiveness, Roosevelt appointed him Commissioner of Indian Affairs, a position he

held from 1933 to 1945. The changes he proposed in the federal Indian policy were advanced in the Indian Reorganization Act of 1934; they included the end of individual land allotments, the formation of tribal governments, guaranteed federal loans to groups that formed tribal governments, and the purchase of additional land for incorporated groups. Kroeber and Lowie were enthusiastic about Collier's appointment; Boas, among others, opposed it, arguing that the changes he proposed would do more harm than good. Boas believed that allotments among Northwest Coast and Great Plains groups "had created vested interests in individual land ownership and that the communal ties binding these Indians had been largely destroyed" (Kelly 1980:7).

10. The Applied Anthropology Unit was headed by Scudder Mekeel (Ph.D. Yale 1932) whose doctoral dissertation dealt with Sioux acculturation. The other employees of the unit were Morris Opler (Ph.D. Chicago, 1936) who had studied Apache social organization; David Rodnick (Ph.D. Penn, 1936) whose dissert-ation examined Assiniboine acculturation; Charles Wisdom, a doctoral candidate at Chicago who had worked previously with the Chorti in Guatemala; Gordon Macgregor (Ph.D. Harvard, 1935) a physical anthropologist from Harvard; and Julian Steward (Ph.D. California, 1929) who was a specialist in Great Basin ethnography and who was on loan from the BAE.

11. The Anthropologists employed by the TC-BIA unit included Solon Kimball (Ph.D. Harvard, 1936) who had worked with W. Lloyd Warner in Newburyport and whose dissertation dealt with the economic structure of an Irish town; Bur-leigh Gardner (Ph.D. Harvard, 1936), another Warner student who had already worked in the Hawthorne Plant, Newburyport, and Natchez; and John Provinse (Ph.D. Chicago, 1934) who examined the mechanisms of social control in Sioux culture. Gardner left the unit in 1936 to accept a position with Warner at the University of Chicago. Ruth Underhill (Ph.D. Columbia, 1939) and Frederica de Laguna (Ph.D. Columbia, 1932) also worked for the Soil Conservation Service before the summer of 1937.

12. Malinowski's functionalism was concerned with culture, the interrelations of institutions, and the needs of the individual. Radcliffe-Brown's structural-functionalism focused on the concepts of society, social structure, and social relations and sought to discern general laws that were framed in sociological rather than psychological terms; he advocated a natural science of society. In this non-historical, comparative science of society, Radcliffe-Brown (1937/1956) argued that culture (a set of rules for behavior and associated symbols, senti-ments, and beliefs) could only be studied in relation to social structure (Stocking 1995:361–426).

13. The six anthropologists besides Thompson were Gordon Macgregor (1902–83), Clyde Kluckhohn (1905–60), Rosamond Spicer (1913–98), Jane Chesky, John Adair, and Florence Hawley Ellis (1906–91).

14. These funds were allocated to the Institute of Andean Research which was estab-
    lished in the wake of Rockefeller's visit to Peru in 1936, where he intervened
    to secure the support of Peru's president for Julio C. Tello's plan to build a new
    archaeology museum in Lima. Tello and Kroeber organized the Institute with
    the financial backing of Mrs. Truxton Beale and Robert Woods Bliss. The invest-
    igators whose OCIAA-funded archaeological research was coordinated by
    Bennett and Vaillant included Gordon Willey (b. 1913), James Ford (1911–
    68), William Duncan Strong (1899–1962), Junius Bird (1907–82), John Rowe
    (b. 1917), Theodore D. McCown (1908–69), Alfred Kidder II (1911–84),
    Marion Tschopik (1910–91), Isabel Kelly (1906–83), Donald Collier (1911–
    95), John Murra, Cornelius Osgood (1905–85), George Howard, Irving Rouse
    (b. 1913), John Longyear (b. 1914), and Gordon Ekholm (1909–87).

$-4-$

Anthropology in the Postwar Era, 1945–1973

Optimism greeted the war's end in 1945. The GI Bill of Rights of 1944 guaranteed veterans college educations and low-interest loans to purchase homes, and the Full Employment Act of 1946 promised jobs for everyone. American corporations, whose factories had reaped enormous profits from the war effort, would soon collaborate with the federal government to rebuild the destroyed economies of capitalist Europe and Japan, and this postwar reconstruction, once under way, promised even greater profits for such companies. However, there were threats to these optimistic visions of the future. The military was slow to discharge soldiers and sailors for fear of flooding the labor market, and more than 600 strikes in 1946 alone threatened corporate profits.

By the spring of 1947, a number of Americans took these as omens of the fact that civilization itself was in peril. In their view, the threat was both internal and external. A communist "Fifth-Column" threatened America at home, and the Communists' seizure of power in Czechoslovakia and China as well as the Soviet Union's efforts to thwart the creation of an independent state in West Germany imperiled civilization abroad. After the Soviet Union exploded an atomic bomb in 1949, they spoke even more passionately of the need to contain the threats they perceived. The government assented to their demands, narrowed free political discussion, and trampled the rights of thousands of citizens and foreigners alike as it implemented policies of containment. In the process, the government spent trillions of dollars fueling corporate profits, and the military stockpiled weapons of every imaginable kind. For the next fifty years, every American was caught up in an eerie movie simultaneously directed by optimism and by the fear of nuclear annihilation.

The Cold War, precipitated by the United States and England and adopted by the other capitalist countries to halt the advance of socialism, was one of the two shaping features of the postwar era (Montgomery 1997). The other was decolonization. The colonial subjects of the United States, Britain, France, and the Netherlands used the opportunities provided by the overall weakness of the imperial states in the wake of the Second World War to proclaim political independence or to launch popular movements, armed and otherwise, to gain autonomy. By 1960, more than 1.3 billion people – more than a third of the world's population at the time – had gained independence as a result of successful national liberation movements. If the socialist

Second World was forged in the crucible of the Cold War, then the Third World – composed of the newly independent countries – was created as struggles for political independence spread across Africa, Asia, Latin America, and the Pacific Islands.

American anthropology was transformed in the years following the war. American Indians and rural communities in the United States were no longer the primary objects of inquiry for American anthropologists. The internationalism forged during the war was now fueled by postwar reconstruction, the Cold War, and national liberation struggles. The GI Bill sent nearly 2.2 million veterans – 2.1 million men, mostly white, and 67,000 women – back to school after 1946. The veterans doubled the number of college students in the United States and significantly altered campus sex ratios through the late 1950s (Solomon 1985:188–9). More than 2000 new college and university campuses opened their doors during the 1950s and 1960s. The new schools constituted the primary labor market for anthropologists with advanced degrees and underwrote the shift in the profession's center of gravity from government work back to the academy, effectively reversing the trend of the preceding fifteen years.

The growth and transformation of academic activity from the late 1940s onward was fueled mostly by the Cold War expenditures that provided fellowships as well as research funds and incentives (Lewontin 1997). It had a number of dimensions. First, it underwrote the organization of knowledge and the development of new fields of learning – such as computer science, primate studies, or paleoanthropology. Second, the discourses of established areas of learning were shaped and transformed in tandem with the changing needs of the state; for instance, the Rockefeller, Ford, and Carnegie Foundations which linked their overseas programs to the policy objectives of the United States shifted their support for area studies shifted from Latin America to the Soviet Union and China after 1947, then to the newly emergent nations of Africa, the Middle East, and South Asia, in the words of a Ford Foundation official "situated along the periphery of the Soviet-Communist orbit" in 1952, and finally to international studies (Berman 1983:56; McCaughey 1984:111–67; Wallerstein 1997).[1] Third, the foundations supported lines of inquiry – such as behavioralism or functionalism – that countered more radical social theories which had gained prominence during the Depression (Berman 1983:108). Fourth, graduate students and faculty members received steadily increasing levels of support for study and research from both the federal government and private philanthropies; for example, the National Science Foundation budget grew from $100,000 in 1951 to $100 million a decade later, and by 1953 the Ford Foundation was already spending $2 million a year on foreign area studies (Gerstein 1986; Klausner 1986; Price 1998). Fifth, certain subjects, such as Marxist contributions to anthropology or social thought, could not be discussed openly in the academy for fear of political reprisal; as a result, academic discourse and research were narrowed as they were channeled in certain directions and not others (e.g. Hymes 1999:vi; Leacock 1982a). The repercussions of this channeling are still felt today. Sixth, in the late 1940s and early 1950s, a number of anthropologists lost their jobs in the academy because of their political beliefs and activities. Two decades later, a number of anti-war graduate students in anthropology were blocked from academic positions for the same reasons. In both periods, some anthropologists acted as gatekeepers; some were informants who provided the FBI and other investigative agencies with (mis)information about their colleagues and students; and some, fearing for their livelihood, used pseudonyms, avoided conflict, or wrote in ways that obscured their political and theoretical beliefs (Diamond 1992; Leacock 1982a; Peace 1993; Price 1998; Schrecker 1986).

The Reorganization of American Anthropology, 1945–1953

At war's end, more than 100 anthropologists – roughly a sixth of the profession – worked in Washington. About 25 of them met during the summer of 1945 to found a new society that would be composed exclusively of professional anthropologists who could define

> the "essential core" of anthropology ("the comparative study of human biology, culture, and language")[,] . . . counteract the centrifugal tendencies in the discipline and mobilize the resources of the whole profession for a broad range of internally and externally oriented activities. Its provisional constitution required all members to have either the doctorate, or (having a degree in an allied field) to be employed as anthropologists; their membership would have to be approved both by a membership committee and two-thirds of a proposed Executive Board, which could subsequently disqualify them for "violation of scientific ethics" (Stocking 1976:38).

Many of the Washington anthropologists believed that the profession could have been more involved in the war effort and policy-related activities. They also believed that the discipline would have received higher levels of financial support from various research councils if anthropologists had been more engaged. An organizing committee composed of Julian Steward, Clyde Kluckhohn, John Provinse, Frank Roberts (1897–1966), and Homer Barnett (b. 1906) sent the proposal to their professional colleagues in anthropology, many of whom responded angrily. They saw it as a threat to the integrity of the American Anthropological Association (AAA).

Nevertheless, the proposal touched on important concerns. By the time of the 1945 annual meeting of the AAA, the proposal had been replaced by one concerned with reorganizing the association itself. A Committee on Reorganization chaired by Steward was named to examine the issues involved. Its aim was to reintegrate the linguists, archaeologists, physical anthropologists, and applied anthropologists into the association. At the 1946 annual meeting in Chicago, which was the first of the large meetings and whose organizers had to deal with the de facto Jim Crow segregation of the hotels, the constitution and by-laws recommended by Steward's committee were adopted. The new constitution created a two-tier society. It distinguished "Fellows" (those with doctorates) from members (students and those who were not employed as anthropologists), and it placed control of AAA in the hands of the Fellows who elected officers selected from slates that were provided by an Executive Board composed exclusively of Fellows (Stocking 1976:39–42).

Steward's committee also made a series of recommendations to the Executive Committee. These included developing area studies programs for foreign service-personnel, creating a plan that would benefit anthropology if a National Science Foundation were established, surveying anthropological curricula in universities and opportunities for introducing it into schools below the college level, broadening the scope of the *American Anthropologist*, and forging closer relations with other anthropological organizations – such as the Society for American Archaeology, the American Folklore Society, the Linguistics Society of America, and the American Association of Physical Anthropologists – to explore matters of mutual interest (American Anthropological Association 1947:352–7).

What the AAA did not do in the late 1940s and early 1950s was come to the aid of those fellows and members – such as Gene Weltfish or Richard Morgan – who lost their jobs because they had been called to testify before state and federal legislative committees investigating "un-American activities." While the Executive Board of the AAA claimed neutrality in Morgan's case, one of its members, George P. Murdock, actually wrote a four-page letter to J. Edgar Hoover that contained a list of anthropologists who [he believed] were communists or communist sympathizers (William Peace, David Price, personal communications).

Anthropology was redefined, Much of the progressive or overtly radical thrust it had in the 1930s was muted, partially suppressed but not completely eradicated. The new version of anthropology borrowed Boas's vision and came to view itself as a discipline that was divided into four fields: ethnology or cultural anthropology, linguistics, archaeology, and physical anthropology. Alfred L. Kroeber, the doyen of American anthropology in 1940s and 1950s, wrote the mythic charter for this newly reconstituted endeavor. It was his *Anthropology*, a thick, green-covered volume published in 1948, that juxtaposed, if not integrated, chapters on ethnology, linguistics, archaeology, and physical anthropology. This was followed five years later by the proceedings of a Wenner-Gren conference, called *Anthropology Today: An Encyclopedic Inventory*, which Kroeber (1953) edited. It contained several dozen papers by leading practitioners in each subdiscipline. It was followed immediately by the publication of a commentary volume, appropriately called *An Appraisal of Anthropology Today*, in which the participants described and explored the implications of four-field anthropology (Tax 1953). A few years later, Sol Tax (1955, 1964), Sherwood Washburn (1911–2000) and others began to examine in more detail how four-field anthropology was integrated (Haraway 1989).

The postwar years witnessed a veritable explosion in the number of anthropologists. The individual membership of the American Anthropological Association more than doubled between 1945 and 1948, increasing from 678 to 1,723. By 1960, it had grown to 3,174 men and women. By 1967, it had risen to 4,678 – 3,510 men and 1,168 women. The growth of the profession was underwritten from 1945 through the late 1950s by the GI Bill students, 97 percent of whom were men. From the mid 1960s onward, it was sustained by young men and women born during the postwar "baby boom" – the children of veterans – who attended college in roughly equal percentages.

The postwar years also witnessed a rapid increase in the number of undergraduate and graduate anthropology programs. In the 1950s and less so in the 1960s, many of the new programs were housed in joint departments where anthropologists and sociologists shared resources under circumstances that they themselves did not create. These conditions were the bureaucratic and budgetary constructs of deans and provosts. In 1958, Alfred Kroeber and Talcott Parsons (1902–79), the leading figures in American anthropology and sociology at the time, provided their colleagues with a rationale for distinguishing the two disciplines. Many academic bureaucrats were convinced by the weight of Kroeber's and Parsons's reputations if not by the strength of their arguments. As a result, many of the joint anthropology-sociology departments – Temple and UCLA, for instance – were dissolved and replaced by separate degree-granting departments. These newly created, free-standing budgetary units were distorting mirrors that reflected in complex ways the autonomy proclaimed for the two disciplines.

A common pattern in the postwar expansion of anthropology programs was that cultural anthropologists who received their degrees in the 1940s or early 1950s founded the new programs. They hired another ethnologist or two, then an archaeologist, a physical anthropologist, and a linguist to round out the curriculum. The rapid growth of the other fields began about five years later than that of the AAA. For example, the demand for archaeologists, judging by the membership levels of the Society for American Archaeology, intensified after 1957 and persisted at high levels into the early 1970s. Given this history, it seems likely that fewer archeologists, physical anthropologists, and linguists had experience in joint departments where the divisions followed disciplinary lines separating anthropologists and sociologists. Instead, they were hired into academic settings where the separation was either already a fait accompli or imminent. Thus, the ever-finer distinctions anthropologists began to draw were within the discipline itself. As a result, anthropology departments increasingly became the loci of subdisciplinary turf wars once their budgetary linkages with sociology were dissolved (Wolf 1980).

The growing importance of area studies from the late 1930s onward transformed the organization of anthropological research. By the early 1940s, large research projects involving the collaboration of a number of anthropologists became commonplace. Myrdal's study of race relations and Office of War Information's (OWI) studies of national character were two examples. The large projects of the postwar years built on the experiences gained earlier in the decade. Let us look at the object of inquiry and institutional support for a few of the "big science" area studies projects undertaken by anthropologists in the postwar years. These enterprises had a shaping effect on anthropological research. By selecting certain problems and modes of inquiry as important, they had channeled their own inquiries and those of some contemporaries in particular directions.

Ruth Benedict (1946) whose *The Chrysanthemum and the Sword* was widely acclaimed after the war was contacted in 1946 by the Office of Naval Research (ONR) which urged her to expand the national character research she had done for the OWI during the war (Janssens 1999). The ONR provided nearly $100,000 for the Columbia University Research in Contemporary Cultures project that Benedict developed in collaboration with Margaret Mead, Ruth Bunzel (1898–1990), and Ruth Valentine (Caffrey 1989:329–30). It employed more than sixty individuals – graduate students, professional anthropologists and social scientists as well as émigrés, displaced persons, and refugees from Russia, Eastern Europe, and China – who were organized into a series of work groups that met regularly for the next year and a half. Like their predecessors in the OWI, the teams were concerned with societies that were inaccessible to researchers, not because of war but rather because of revolutions (Indonesia), destruction (East European Jewish communities), and travel restrictions imposed by the American government. In Mead's (1953:3) words,

> We then faced a situation in which we have access on the one hand to many living and articulate individuals whose character was formed in the inaccessible society and on the other to large amounts of other sorts of materials – books, newspapers, periodicals, films, works of popular and fine art, diaries, letters – the sort of materials with which the social historian has learned to deal without the benefit of interviews with living persons. By combining the methods of the historian with those of the anthropologist, who is accustomed to work without any documented time perspective, we have developed a new approach.

After Benedict's untimely death in 1948, Mead continued the study of cultures at a distance in two successor projects that were carried out under the auspices of the American Museum of Natural History: Studies in Soviet Culture funded by the RAND Corporation (a Cold War think tank that carried out classified research for the government), and Studies in Contemporary Cultures funded jointly by the ONR and the Center for International Studies at Massachusetts Institute of Technology (MIT). Mead and Rhoda Métraux (1953) summarized the results of these investigations in their *Study of Culture at a Distance*.

In 1946, Clyde Kluckhohn, Talcott Parsons, and others at Harvard established the Department of Social Relations in order to promote interdisciplinary collaboration between social anthropologists, sociologists, and social and clinical psychologists (Parsons 1973). A year later, Kluckhohn was named director of Harvard's Russian Research Center which was established with $740,000 ostensibly provided by the Carnegie Corporation (Berman 1983:101). Kluckhohn was involved in a web of relations that linked the Social Relations Department and the Russian Research Center with various government agencies, philanthropies, and academic programs including the FBI, the CIA, the Air Force's Air University, Harvard's Department of Anthropology, and MIT's Center for International Studies (Diamond 1992:68–93; Price 1998:402–7). In 1950, he directed the Center's project on the Soviet social system which was based on interviews with refugees and defectors from the Soviet Union as well as Eastern and Central Europe; he and his associates at the center were also concerned with understanding Russian national character and "the distinctive character of the Bolshevik elite" (Inkeles 1973:65; Bauer, Inkeles, and Kluckhohn 1956). At the same time, Kluckhohn organized and gained funding from the Rockefeller Foundation for Harvard's Comparative Study of Values in Five Cultures Project that was carried out between 1949 and 1955 by graduate students and junior faculty affiliated with the university's departments of social relations and anthropology (Vogt 1994:49–57; Vogt and Albert 1966).

One goal of the national character studies of Soviet society undertaken by the New York and Harvard groups was to be able to predict how its leaders and rank and file were likely to act when confronted with particular situations. Benedict, Mead, Kluckhohn, and their associates assumed that

> the members of a given culture share certain common, sufficiently distinct ways of handling emotional drives and regulating social conduct which form a unique life style that differs, often markedly, from the life style of other cultural groups. The "norms" of the group specify how an individual must manage the key tensions generated in social living (i.e., attitudes to authority, frustration of impulses, aggression, etc.) and how the social control of violations of those norms (i.e., mechanisms of guilt and shame, disposal of repressed hate, etc.) operate (Bell 1960/1988:316).

Both the New York and Harvard researchers pointed to differences in the character of the Soviet elite and the mass of the Russian population. However, they presented the results of their investigations in different ways (Kluckhohn 1955/1961). The New York researchers focused on the cultural character of Russian society; they sought to discern the relation between Russian culture and the dominant personality types that were produced in individuals by primary institutions such as child-rearing practices or family organization and that were expressed in secondary institutions such as folklore, art, or religion (Gorer and Rickman 1949/1962). In contrast, the

Harvard group framed their analyses of Soviet society in terms of how unspecified changes in the social system affected the modal personality patterns and adaptive patterns of behavior among the rank and file that allowed its members to participate in and adjust to the Communist socio-political order (Bauer, Inkeles, and Kluckhohn 1956:135; Inkeles, Hanfmann, and Beier 1961).

Benedict, Mead, Kluckhohn, and their associates were relativists who believed that the culture of one society often differed markedly from the lifestyles of other groups because of the different ways in which their members learned to deal with their emotions and to regulate their conduct. They viewed culture, forms of social consciousness, and their manifestations in language and material objects, as the principle force shaping human interpersonal and social relations. Thus, theirs was a limited relativism that did not subvert objectivity. The idealism of their perspective resonated with the views of Émile Durkheim (1858–1917) who believed that morality and religion dictated the sentiments and ideas of a group and regulated the actions of its members (Durkheim 1886:61–9; 1887:138).

The culturalist perspective of the area studies conducted in New York and Harvard contrasted with those of social or cultural evolutionists – notably Julian Steward, Leslie White, and a number of archaeologists – who stressed cross-cultural regularities and adopted a base-superstructure or layer-cake image of society in which the base was seen as narrowly economic – i.e. subsistence technologies, organizational forms and strategies – and as determining the contours of the social and cultural layers of the group (Steward 1941/1977; 1949; White 1949:363–93). Thus, for the evolutionists, Benedict, Mead, and Kluckhohn were in error when they located the driving motor of change in the cultural superstructure rather than the economic base of society. Furthermore, their cultural relativism, regardless of how limited it was, obscured regularities in human social and cultural development and important correspondences between the social institutions and cultures of societies at the same level of economic development.

Several of the "big science" area studies projects carried out in the late 1940s eschewed cultural relativism and sought instead cross-cultural or societal regularities. These studies were framed in terms of economic determinist and evolutionist perspectives. The earliest of these was the Institute of Andean Research's Virú Valley Project that was carried out in 1946 by Wendell Bennett, William Strong, Gordon Willey, and other archaeologists in a small valley on the north coast of Peru. Their goal was to uncover a complete historical sequence from the remains left by earliest residents through those of the first farmers to the rise of civilization. They were largely successful in this effort, and by 1947 they had already adopted an evolutionist perspective to organize the presentation and discussion of their evidence (e.g. Bennett 1948; Willey 1974).

The archaeologists recognized that their discussions about the rise of civilization in the Virú Valley manifested an elaborate conception of history as a series of cultural stages that began with hunting and foraging bands and culminated with modern civilization. By 1950, Julian Steward had elaborated this scheme. In his view, following the hunters and foragers,

> there were small communities of incipient farmers. Later the communities cooperated in the construction of irrigation works and the population became larger and more settled. Villages amalgamated into states under theocratic rulers. . . . Finally culture ceased to develop, and the states in each area entered into competition with one another. . . . One or another state succeeded in dominating the others, that is, in building an empire, but such empires ran their course and collapsed after some . . . years only to be succeeded by another empire not very different from the first.
>
> For the historian this era of cyclical conquests is filled with great men, wars and battle strategy, shifting power centers, and other social events. For the culture historian the changes are much less significant than those of the previous era when the basic civilizations developed . . . or those of the subsequent Iron Age when the cultural patterns changed again and the centers of civilization shifted to new areas [i.e. Europe].
>
> . . . The industrial revolution brought profound cultural changes to Western Europe and caused competition for colonies and for areas of exploitation. Japan entered the competition as soon as she acquired the general pattern. The realignments of power caused by Germany's losses in the first world war and by Italy's and Japan's in the second are of a social order. What new cultural patterns will result from these remains to be seen.
>
> The general assumption today seems to be that we are in danger of basic cultural changes caused by the spread of communism. Russia acquired drastically new cultural patterns as a result of her revolution. Whether communism has the same meaning in other nations remains to be seen (Steward 1950:103–5).

Steward recognized limitations of this conception of world history. It was too general, and certain areas, such as colonial possessions, did not fit neatly into it. Thus in 1947 Steward, who had moved from the BAE to Columbia University, sought and soon received funding from the SSRC and the Rockefeller Foundation to investigate the effects of 50 years of American culture contact on Puerto Rican society; it was to be a joint venture with the Social Science Research Center of the University of Puerto Rico. The Rockefeller Foundation believed that the Puerto Rico Project would contribute information useful for guiding and assessing its programs of social and economic transformation/stabilization at home and abroad and would further the development of universal theories of social change (Lauria-Perricelli 1989). The goal of the project was to study the social anthropology of a country

> with modern civilizations of different kinds of with folk cultures that have come under some form of Euro-American or Russian dominance. . . . [It was concerned with finding out] how the influences emanating from a highly industrialized society [such as the United States] affected the local and regional varieties of culture found in one of its agrarian dependencies (Steward 1950:154).

Steward described Puerto Rico as an American colony that was

> agrarian, rural, and economically part of a capitalist world in that it depends upon an export crop and imports nearly all of its manufactured goods and about half of its food. . . . [The cultural heterogeneity of the society was due to the differential penetration of] the processes by which production, social patterns and related modes of life are selectively borrowed from the outside and adapted to local needs (Steward 1950:129, 133–4).

The result of the investigations carried out by Steward and his associates appeared in *The People of Puerto Rico* (Steward 1956/1972), which was one of the first attempts by anthropologists to portray a national society. In Steward's view the social structure of the island was composed of two interdependent features. One consisted of a series of distinctive, localized sociocultural subgroups that were crosscut by class, ethnic, and other social categories that were arranged hierarchically throughout the island. The other was a set of formal institutions – such as economic relations or the legal and government system – that constituted binding and regulating forces. "These institutions," he wrote, "have aspects which are national and sometimes international in scope and which must be understood apart from the behavior of the individuals connected with them" (Steward 1955:47). Furthermore, the engines of change penetrated Puerto Rican society through these institutions.

Research carried out by Sidney Mintz (b. 1922) and Eric Wolf (1923–99) on Steward's Puerto Rico Project laid the foundations for a critique, couched in unacknowledged Marxist analytical categories, of Redfield's and Tax's prewar discussions of folk societies in Yucatán and Guatemala. It also solidified the bases for studying peasant communities. Mintz (1953) challenged the utility of Redfield's folk-urban continuum which viewed culture change in terms of increasing complexity resulting from increased communication between folk (peasant) communities and city-dwellers. While agreeing that typological characterizations were useful, Mintz pointed out that Redfield did not take into account the rural proletarian communities found on the henequen plantations which constituted the backbone of Yucatecan economy. Wolf (1955) showed that the types of peasant communities in Latin America were more diverse than Redfield and Tax had supposed. Some peasant communities were concerned with subsistence; others consisted of farmers who sold some or all of their produce in the market; and still others were composed of rural wage workers. Mintz and Wolf provided an alternative understanding of the linkages that existed between various types of rural cultivators and national economic and political structures. They did not view these peasant communities as exploited producers left over from a precapitalist system of production, nor did they see them as a class rooted in tradition that was disappearing in the wake of capitalist social relations. They saw them instead as communities that were molded by the same social forces that were shaping urban societies in Latin America.

Micronesia – the Pacific island groups captured from the Japanese during the war – constituted a third kind of area study for anthropologists. The United States established military governments on these islands as they fell under its control. Early in the war, officials in the State Department and the Department of the Interior had favored establishing a series of trusteeships in Micronesia under which the island groups would be prepared for independence, whereas those in the Navy Department advocated their annexation. George P. Murdock who, along with his Yale colleagues John Whiting and Clellan S. Ford (1909–72), had taught at the Navy School of Military Government and Administration since its inception, was a leading advocate of the Navy's viewpoint. After providing the Navy with the Cross-Cultural Survey research on Micronesia, Murdock, Whiting, and Ford transferred to the Naval Office of Occupied Areas for Micronesia in the closing months of the war to set up military governments. In 1946, Murdock supported a plan drafted by Harvard anthropologist Douglas Oliver (b. 1913), which called for a central organization to administer scientific research and "close control over [the] activities of civilian visitors – in regard to mobility and access to native populations" (quoted by Bashkow 1991:182). Felix Keesing (1902–61), Edward C. Handy (1892–1980), and others who had already worked in the islands opposed the plan. At the same time, Laura Thompson, John Embree (1908–50), and John Useem (b. 1911) expressed their dismay at the arrogance and insensitivity of the military governments already established by the Navy (Bashkow 1991:178–90; Petersen 1999:147–54).

President Truman's announcement in 1946 that the United States would retain control over the islands of Micronesia after the war signaled the victory of the Navy's agenda over the internationalist and anticolonialist views found in the State Department and the Department of the Interior. The Navy also found the proposals of Murdock and Oliver more to its liking than those of the anthropologists who had already worked in the Pacific; consequently, they supported the agenda of the academic veterans of the war agencies. In November 1946, Murdock received $100,000 from the Navy to collect data that were relevant for island government. He established the Coordinated Investigation of Micronesian Anthropology (CIMA) which employed 25 cultural anthropologists, 3 linguists, and 4 physical anthropologists to collect these data in the late 1940s (Kiste and Marshall 1999:467–73). A number of CIMA employees subsequently became administrators or staff anthropologists employed by the governments of the Trust Territories.

"The anthropologist in the Trust Territories was," as Robert Redfield (1957/1960:418) commented a decade later, "an arm of administrative action . . . [who] provided the administrator with special knowledge to guide his action." Redfield made this remark in the context of a discussion of "action anthropology." The term "action anthropology" was coined and used by Sol Tax and his students in relation to their work among the Fox Indians of Iowa which had two overarching goals – to understand the processes of acculturation that were taking place in the late 1940s and to intervene in those processes to help the Fox community improve the quality of everyday life (Blanchard 1979; Gearing, Netting, and Peattie 1960:166–7; Tax 1951/1960). Action anthropology in their view involved helping communities create the possibility of choice; it also involved solving problems and learning something in the process.

Two action anthropology projects were initiated in the late 1940s and the early 1950s. One was the Fox Project which achieved certain educational benefits for the community and helped to establish a community-owned craft company. The other was the Cornell-Peru Project (1951–66) launched by Allan R. Holmberg (1909– 66). In collaboration with the Peruvian Indian Institute, Cornell University rented the Vicos hacienda and its serf-bound labor force for a period of five years. The goals of the project were twofold:

> on the theoretical side, it was hoped to conduct some form of experimental research on the process of modernization now on the march in so many parts of the world; on the practical side, it was hoped to assist the community from a position of relative dependence and submission in a highly restricted and provincial world to a position of relative independence and freedom within the larger framework of Peruvian national life (Holmberg 1955/1964:22).

Over the next decade, the anthropologists directing the project would intervene in the everyday life of the community in various ways: training leaders, developing decision-making skills, introducing new crops, supporting the community's efforts to purchase the hacienda, and inadvertently fomenting gender inequality among its members (Holmberg 1964; Babb 1976).

Anti-racist arguments gained ground in the United States after the war, partly because of anti-Nazi sentiments and racism's unsavory connections with Nazism and partly because of the improved standards of living experienced by many Americans. In October 1949, the Director-General of UNESCO convened the Committee of Experts on Race Problems – a panel of anthropologists and sociologists – to collect materials concerning problems of race, disseminate this information, and prepare an educational campaign based on the data. Ashley Montagu, the reporter elected by the group, circulated the statement prepared by the committee to a number of scientists for criticisms and suggestions. The revised Statement on Race drafted by Montagu was finally released on July 18, 1950 by UNESCO's Mass Communications Department (Montagu 1951:3–10). On the same day, a *New York Times* headline announced that "No Scientific Basis for Race Bias Found by World Panel of Experts." The UNESCO Statement asserted

> that the mental capacities of all races are similar; that no evidence for biological deterioration as a result of hybridization existed; that there was no correlation between national

or religious groups and any race; . . . [and] that "race was less a biological fact that a social myth" (Barkan 1996:97).

The UNESCO Statement on Race attracted immediate attention. It indicated a significant shift in the United States with regards to the concept of race. Nevertheless, its claims that "biological studies lend support to the ethic of universal brotherhood" and that "man is born with drives toward co-operation, and unless those drives are satisfied, men and nations alike fall ill" provoked criticism from the Right (Montagu 1951:17–18). A second UNESCO committee composed of physical anthropologists and geneticists, including Montagu, was convened to deal with these criticisms and issued its "Statement on the Nature of Race and Race Differences" in July 1951. The second statement retreated from the claims of the first. It accepted the ideas of race mixture and racial classification but reserved judgment on the question of whether there had ever been pure races and ignored altogether the statements about universal brotherhood and co-operation (Barkan 1992:341–6; 1996:102–4). The second UNESCO statement signaled that the issues of race and racism would continue to attract the attention of anthropologists in the years to come.

American Anthropology and the Cold War, 1954–1964

The rising tensions of the Cold War led the Ford, Carnegie, and Rockefeller foundations to consider carefully the relation between their overseas programs and the foreign-policy objectives of the United States government. From 1953 through the mid-1960s, the Ford Foundation provided $138 million to fifteen American universities, all of which had doctoral programs in anthropology, to develop non-Western language and area studies programs. The goal of these programs was to train American scholars in particular areas – notably Africa, Latin America, South Asia, the Near East, the Soviet Union, and Eastern Europe. The Ford Foundation also funded the development of international studies programs at MIT, Harvard, Georgetown, Berkeley, Princeton, and Stanford. Ford and the other foundations saw themselves as intermediaries between the overseas specialists they supported and the federal government; they believed that the specialists should provide the government with information about the nations they studied (Berman 1983:55, 101–3; Cumings 1998).

As a result, many scholars in the newly established area and international studies programs had close ties with government agencies. For example, Max Millikan (1913–69), the first director of MIT's Center for International Studies which was established in 1952 with Ford Foundation and CIA funds, co-authored a report with Walt Rostow (b. 1916) for the Director of the CIA regarding the economic policies the government should promote in Southeast Asia and the Far East (Millikan and Rostow 1954/1998; Needell 1998:22–4; Ransom 1974; Simpson 1994:81–4). Other scholars had offices down the hall from Millikan and Rostow, and received their salaries from the same sources (Simpson 1998:xix).

Millikan and Rostow provided a blueprint for the interdisciplinary development and modernization studies that were carried out by social scientists, including anthropologists, in Asia, Africa, and Latin America during the 1950s and 1960s. American foreign aid programs should, in their view, combine economic and political agendas to develop the infrastructures of underdeveloped countries and to support the export-oriented sectors of the local elites in order to promote capitalist modernity and to create "an environment in which societies which directly or indirectly menace ours will not evolve" (Millikan and Rostow 1954:1998:41; Gendzier 1998). The important questions for modernization theorists were how to identify and how to support those classes or groups in the underdeveloped countries that would promote capitalist economic development. Many modernization studies carried out in the 1950s and 1960s presumed the superiority of the political culture of the United States and implied the cultural and racial inferiority of peoples in the underdeveloped countries.

Such perspectives were not shared by the leaders of the newly independent nations in Asia and Africa who met in Bandung, Indonesia in April 1955 to discuss common problems such as maintaining their independence and resisting Western domination. They advocated instead non-intervention or interference in the internal affairs of other countries, the peaceful settlement of international disputes, respect for the human rights outlined in the UN Charter and recognition of the equality of all races. Their belief that the newly independent states had the right "to choose their own political, economic and social system" would become the cornerstone of the movement of non-aligned countries in the 1960s (Singham and Hune 1986:66). In other words, there was a fundamental difference of opinion between the American advocates of modernization and the leaders of the non-aligned nations of Asia, Africa, Europe, and Latin America who wanted to pursue independent lines of economic and social development.

Indonesia was an early focus of American modernization studies. From 1952 to 1954, Harvard anthropologist Douglas Oliver directed the Ford Foundation-funded Modjukuto Project sponsored by MIT's Center for International Studies. Clifford Geertz (b. 1927), then a student in Harvard's Social Relations Department, participated in the project. In his early publications, Geertz focused on the historical development of the Javanese economy and how it shaped the postwar situation in Indonesia. The economy, in his estimation, was "part of a broader process of social, political, and cultural change" (Geertz 1956:4); consequently, "a search for the true diagnosis of the Indonesian malaise takes one, thus, far beyond the analysis of ecological and economic processes to an investigation into the nation's political, social, and cultural dynamics" (Geertz 1963a:154). His analysis of the Javanese rural economy was couched in terms of marginal utility theory: What happens to productivity or output when a worker is added to or subtracted from the work force? What effect does this have when the land has already reached its maximum output?

Geertz ultimately saw modernization as part of broad process of change that was shaped at some fundamental level by the values of the cultural system. Thus, he rejected materialist conceptions of history that were concerned with economic growth and gave primary importance to the economic base. These included not only Marxist analyses but also the economic determinist arguments of Julian Steward, Leslie White, and other cultural evolutionists in the 1950s and 1960s. By relocating the motor of development from the economic base to the cultural realm, he incorporated most immediately the views of Clyde Kluckhohn and Talcott Parsons, his teachers at Harvard, and more distantly of Émile Durkheim – who believed that morality, religion and law dictated the ideas of a group and regulated the action of its members. The important transition for modernization theorists such as Geertz was the shift from traditional society – a catch-all category composed of diverse groups with primitive technologies oriented toward agricultural production – to a dynamic, modern social type whose cultural values promoted economic growth and high mass consumption (Rostow 1960).

During the early 1960s, modernization theorists such as Geertz, who was by then affiliated with the New Nations Project at the University of Chicago, became increasingly concerned with what happened after nationalist movements succeeded and they had to confront the effects of primordial attachments on the constitution of the new civic or national identity (Geertz 1963b, 1971). These primordial attachments were the culturally assumed "givens" of social existence – ethnicity, tribe, race, language, region, culture, or religion – that shaped the search for identity and the demands that those identities be acknowledged publicly in the new states. They were unleashed by the same forces that buttressed movements for political independence. While they could be a motor for progress, rising standards of living, and a more effective political order, they could also impede or block the creation of new civic identities and values. Some new states attempted to domesticate culturally prescribed identities in their social statistics, dress, official histories, and symbols of public authority in order to aggregate them into larger, more diffuse units so the state bureaucracy could continue to function without serious impediments. Other modernization theorists such as the political scientists on the SSRC's Comparative Politics Committee were less concerned with the developing democratic institutions in the new states than with creating political regimes, even authoritarian ones, that could maintain political order and promote conditions that were favorable to American interests (O'Brien 1972; Bernstein 1972).

From the perspective of the modernization theorists, Steward, White, and the other cultural evolutionists had missed the proverbial boat. The cultural evolutionists did not address the problem that rose increasingly during the 1950s as a result of decolonization, Soviet foreign aid, and political opposition to capitalist development in the non-aligned nations: how to identify and support those groups that would promote capitalist development in the Third World. At the same time, however, cultural evolutionism and the idea of progress were becoming the dominant theoretical framework of archaeologists as exemplified by Gordon Willey (b. 1913) and Philip Phillips's (1900–82) widely read *Method and Theory in American Archaeology* (Willey and Phillips 1958). The different theoretical underpinnings of those anthropologists concerned with modernization, on one hand, and the archaeologists, on the other, exacerbated centrifugal tendencies that already existed within the discipline and fueled the almost complete separation of the two subfields that prevailed at Harvard after the formation of the Social Relations Department and at the University of Chicago after Geertz and other anthropological theorists of modernization arrived en masse in 1958 and Sherwood Washburn departed for Berkeley.

Because of the anti-Communist hysteria and repression provoked by the FBI and the Cold War, few American archaeologists writing in the 1950s actually used the terms "cultural evolution" or "social evolution" because of linkages widely perceived at the time between evolutionist and Marxist social thought. Such sentiments are conveyed in Morris Opler's (1909–96) red-baiting of a discussion of Leslie White's cultural evolutionism: "Apparently the 'practical tool kit' Dr. Meggers [1960:302–3] urges upon the field is not quite as new as she represents, and its main contents seem to be a somewhat shopworn hammer and sickle" (Opler 1961:13).[2] With some caution, the archaeologists elaborated two strands of evolutionist thought in the 1950s, even though they rarely made use of the term in the repressive political climate of the decade. One was rooted in the economic determinism of Steward and White; the other built on Spencer's and Durkheim's notions of increasing social differentiation. Willey at Harvard was a leading proponent of the former, and Robert Braidwood (b. 1907) of the University of Chicago championed the latter. Both took to heart Walter Taylor's (1948) assertions that archaeologists needed to move beyond the construction of cultural sequences and that they should begin to explore the cultural and social dimensions of the societies whose artifactual remains they had excavated. Both adopted a kind of developmental functionalism that focused attention on the functional interconnections between the different parts of culture. Both examined the rise of civilization in terms of a succession of social types that were characterized by particular subsistence techniques and functionally related forms of social organization and culture. Both assumed that civilization – i.e. class-stratified, state-based society – was a natural outcome of human social evolution that was achieved in some areas and blocked in others because of natural environments that limited or prevented agricultural production.

Willey used the concept of "settlement patterns" to develop a series of snapshots of everyday life, first on the Peruvian coast and then in the lowlands of eastern Guatemala. Settlement patterns referred to the way in which man disposed himself over the landscape on which he lived. It [the concept] refers to dwellings, to their arrangement, and to the nature and disposition of other buildings pertaining to community life. These settlements reflect the natural environment, the level of technology on which the builders operated, and various institutions of social interaction and control which the culture maintained. Because settlement patterns are, to a large extent, directly shaped by widely held cultural needs, they offer a strategic starting point for the functional interpretation of archaeological cultures (Willey 1953:1).

In Willey's view, the existence of permanent villages, fortified towns, temple mounds, irrigation works, or cities refracts the economic and sociopolitical organization of particular ancient communities. Stable villages, which were based on the capacity of agricultural economies to produce surpluses, were prerequisites for increases in population size and density and for social differentiation. The internal organization of these stable farming villages ultimately underpinned the rise of class structures and states (Willey 1960a). In the mid 1950s, archaeologists began to consider the functional and evolutionary implications of community settlement patterns (e.g. Beardsley, Meggers, Holder, Krieger, Rinaldo, and Kutsche 1956).

While Willey focused largely on the synchronic relations that constituted particular communities, Braidwood's functionalism was mainly diachronic. He was concerned with the processes of change that led to the development of food-producing economies in the Near East. In his view, civilization appeared not because of the increased efficiency of the early food-producing villages but rather because of the elaboration "and further development of social, political, moral, and religious forces that made possible the integration of the growing population into a functioning civilization" (Braidwood 1952:6). The appearance of new social institutions and more diverse understandings about the nature and purpose of life within the community underwrote the rise of civilization after permanent agricultural villages, temples, and market towns appeared in both the hilly flank and riverine areas of the Near East.

The comparative evolutionary perspective deployed with increasing frequency by archaeologists from the late 1950s onward was concerned with explaining the underlying similarities of development in different cultural traditions rather than their divergent or unique features (Braidwood 1960; Willey 1960b). They sought cross-cultural regularities at the same time as paying attention to the historic specificity of each tradition. Their perspective was regional and comparative, and their methodology was avowedly scientific. Because of this, Braidwood and Willey were the first anthropologists to receive research grants from the National Science Foundation (Patterson 1986:16).

By the late 1950s, anthropologists were using cultural evolutionists' arguments to explore questions posed by Marx and Engels. For Robert McC. Adams (b. 1926), Braidwood's student, the early stages of civilization were characterized by regional networks of agricultural villages that were integrated

by individuals whose authority devolved from their positions as religious spokesmen.
. . . For a time, it seems probably that the religious elite played an increasingly important
role in the administration of group activities as communities grew larger and more
complex (Adams 1956:228).

The increased complexity and heterogeneity of the community – i.e. the products
of increased social differentiation – which was partly a product of the elaboration
of the temple establishments, slowly eroded the effectiveness of purely religious
sanctions as the glue that underpinned the moral order and mechanical solidarity
of the community. In the process, other forms of authority – militaristic or civil –
arose at the expense of the temple figures and in opposition to their activities. The
centrifugal effects of this struggle underwrote the formation of a social class structure and the state. Adams (1960:275–80), who engaged the writings of Marx as
well as those of Durkheim, observed that these class and state structures were sustained and reproduced by goods and services wrung from the farmers and artisans
who were engaged directly in production (Adams 1960:275–80; 1966).

In *Sons of the Shaking Earth*, Eric Wolf examined the dialectics of class and
state formation on the one hand and resistance on the other. He described circumstances in prehispanic Mesoamerica, where the elite class

hungry for surpluses, begin to look beyond the confines of its domain to other domains.
Power exercised within the society grows into political and military power exercised
against the outside. Through widening conquest and widening trade, the solar system
of the favored area becomes a galaxy, absorbing the constellations of villages and towns
beyond its limits, building a supra-regional ecology under the aegis of the growing
state (Wolf 1959:20).

Class and state formation in Wolf's view was a two-way street in ancient Mesoamerica. The humble way of life found in the communities of direct producers was
never completely suppressed by emergent states. It resurfaced repeatedly, often in
a fury of burning and destruction which left the temples and cities in ruin and relegated
their ruling classes to bad memories. Once Mesoamerican villages were enmeshed
in capitalist social relations, he wondered whether the processes of class and state
formation had become a one-way street, and whether the classes of direct producers
would find it increasingly more difficult to reduce or eliminate exploitation (Wolf
1959:67–8).

As the Darwin centenary approached, other anthropologists also considered the
implications of Marxist social thought for the elaboration, refinement, and further
development of cultural evolutionary theory. In 1959, Marshall Sahlins (b. 1930)
at Michigan drew a distinction between specific and general evolution. Specific
cultural evolution recognized the historic specificity of the developmental trajectories
that occurred in particular places. General cultural evolution focused on the processes

underlying "the successive transformations of culture through its several stages of overall progress" (Sahlins 1960:29). While Sahlins acknowledged the connections between contemporary cultural evolutionary thought and Marx's analysis of the rise of capitalism, his colleague Elman Service (1915–96) explored the linkage in more detail.

Service was concerned with two features of cultural evolution: the developmental potential that existed within a given form of society, and phylogenetic or local discontinuities in cultural development. To elucidate principles he turned to Leon Trotsky's (1879–1940) discussion of the "law of uneven and combined development" which he elaborated in his *History of the Revolution*. This law meant "that an 'underdeveloped' civilization has certain evolutionary potentials that an advanced one lacks." Service quotes Trotsky to the effect that

> Although compelled to follow after the advanced countries, a backward country does not take things in the same order. The privilege of historic backwardness – and such a privilege exists – permits, or rather compels, the adoption of whatever is ready in advance of any specified date, skipping a whole series of intermediate stages . . .
>
> The law of combined development reveals itself most indubitably . . . in the history of and character of Russian industry. Arising late, Russian industry did not repeat the development of the advanced [industrial capitalist] countries, but inserted itself into this development, adapting their latest achievements to its own backwardness. . . . Thanks to this, Russian industry developed at certain periods with extraordinary speed (Leon Trotsky quoted by Service 1960:99–100).

Later in the paper, Service (1960:109) quoted with approval Mao Zedong's rendering of Trotsky's law: "Nothing is written on a sheet of paper which is still blank, but it lends itself admirably to receive the latest and most beautiful words and the latest and most beautiful pictures." In a phrase, Service's discussion was both a critique of modernization theory and a radical alternative to their views about the potential for change possessed by the underdeveloped nations of the Third World. At the time, his message was largely unheard by the profession whose members were more interested in the evolution of social organization (Fried 1967; Service 1962).

Archaeologists and cultural anthropologists were not the only ones paying attention to cultural evolutionary thought at the time. From the late 1940s onward, Sherwood Washburn had urged his physical anthropology colleagues to replace their typological constructs with the core ideas of the new synthesis of evolutionary theory – the genetic diversity of populations and the modification of gene frequencies through selection, mutation, and drift (Washburn 1951a, 1953). He was successful in this effort partly because of the persuasiveness of his arguments and partly because of the summer seminars in physical anthropology he had organized with the financial support of the Wenner-Gren Foundation for Anthropological Research (Haraway 1989:206–11).

Washburn had started his career teaching comparative anatomy at the Columbia University Medical School. His early research was concerned with how behavioral patterns were manifested in anatomical structures such as the pelvis or the hand (Washburn 1951b). In the mid-1950s, Washburn and Virginia Avis (1958) pointed out that bipedalism, tool use, and speech distinguished human beings from apes. While these behaviors did not fossilize, they could be inferred from anatomical structures and from reconstructions based on close studies of fossil forms and modern primates. In their discussion of the evolution of human behavior, they reconceptualized the biological notion of a population as a functionally integrated social group and redefined "the key problem of evolutionary behavioral science . . . as the origin of adaptive behavior in a functioning social group, with adaptation seen more in terms of the integration of groups than in terms of differential reproductive success" (Haraway 1989:213). Culture was the human adaptation. It was manifested in repetitive behavior that could be inferred from pelvis, brain, and anatomical structures. These linkages allowed Washburn and his students in the 1960s to focus their attention on the origins of human sociality – i.e. on those features that were characteristic of all human groups (Lee and DeVore 1968). The foundational features involved cooperation, sharing and a gendered division of labor. Washburn's "man the hunter" hypothesis reaffirmed the biological basis of human sociality as well as the biological unity of humankind. The hypothesis sparked diverse kinds of research in the 1960s. The Ford Foundation provided financial support for field studies of primate social behavior; the National Science Foundation and private donors contributed more than $4 million to the search for new fossil hominids and their artifacts; and the National Science Foundation, the National Institute of Mental Health, and the Wenner-Gren Foundation, among others, underwrote field studies of hunter-forager societies such as the San of the Kalahari. Interpretations of such diverse studies provided impressions of what proto-human and early human societies were like. These societies resembled the idea of "universal man" embodied in the United Nations' Declaration of Human Rights that was adopted in 1948 (Haraway 1989:197–8).

In 1962, Washburn (1963:521) was asked by the Executive Board of the American Anthropological Association to address the subject of race in his presidential address to that body. The issues of race and racism were once again making front-page headlines in the United States because of the school integration mandated by the American Supreme Court's 1954 decision in *Brown v. Board of Education*. Race and racism were also debated in virtually every number of *Current Anthropology* published between October 1961 and October 1963. These issues were provoked initially by Juan Comas's (1961) discussion of articles in the first issue of *The Mankind Quarterly* which recycled old eugenics arguments that purported to support claims regarding the mental inferiority of non-Whites. The publication of Carleton Coon's (1904–81) *The Origin of Races* in 1962 added fuel to the fire. Coon classified the world's population into five races which, he argued, were already identifiable during the Middle Pleistocene; furthermore, each race had its own nature and characteristics implying that they had evolved more or less independently of one another for the last 500,000 years.

Washburn (1963), among others, argued that the goal of physical anthropology should not be the classification of human diversity but rather explanation of the processes and mechanisms that gave rise to it. While Coon sorted people into a few types, Washburn advocated looking at how human variation was produced – selection, mutation, migration, and drift. For Washburn,

> Since races are open systems which are intergrading, the number of races will depend on the purpose of the classification. This is, I think, a tremendously important point. It is significant that as I was reviewing classifications in preparing for this lecture, I found that almost none of them mentioned any purpose for which people were being classified. Race isn't very important biologically (Washburn 1963:524).

Washburn reiterated his view that the members of the human species continue to survive through culture. He proceeded to argue that "racism is based on a profound misunderstanding of culture, of learning, and of the biology of the human species," and that racist arguments, such as the ones using differences in test scores, are not supported by modern sciences. He concluded his lecture with a statement couched in the language of classical liberalism: "Human biology finds its realization in a culturally determined way of life, and the infinite variety of genetic combinations can only express themselves efficiently in a free and open society" (Washburn 1963:528, 531).

The significant contribution of anthropologists during the years when one colony after another claimed political independence was that it was no longer possible to pretend that the world could be understood exclusively from the perspective of the West. They showed that other peoples had cultures and histories that were different from, but necessarily related to, their own. To understand the world properly, it was critical to know these cultures and histories in order to understand what was taking place and what had happened. Anthropologists provided a window of opportunity, a holistic perspective, through which to view the cultures and histories of others.

American Anthropology in Crisis, 1965–1973

The crises of American society were refracted in the dilemmas confronted by anthropologists from the mid-1960s through the early 1970s. These included the increasing polarization of the American people resulting from the U.S. war in Vietnam and its meddling in the internal affairs of other countries, the emergent and changing character of black and urban politics in the wake of *Brown v. Board of Education*, and the breakdown of the sustained economic growth of the postwar years (Harvey 1982:373–445; Reed 1999:55–116). This situation prompted Stanley Diamond (1922–91) to write that

> Anthropology, reified as the study of man, is the study of men in crisis by men in crisis. Anthropologists and their objects, the studied, despite opposing positions in the "scientific" equation, have this much in common: they are both, if not equally, objects of contemporary, imperial civilization. The anthropologist who treats the indigene as an object may define himself as relatively free and integrated, a person, but that is an illusion. In order to objectify the other, one is, at the same time, compelled to objectify the self (Diamond 1969:401).

By virtue of the problems they raised and the availability of funds for investigation, the crises that crystallized during the mid-1960s underwrote the appearance of new fields of anthropological inquiry. For example, anthropologists working in Latin America and Africa began to pay attention to the problems encountered by rural immigrants to cities, and those working in the United States began to investigate the poor and working-class immigrant and racialized communities and subcultures of urban neighborhoods. This led them to examine how these groups fit into larger structures through the social networks, class structures, and economic and political institutions and processes in which they participated (Eames and Goode 1977).

The crises also led anthropologists to recognize the inadequacies or limitations of prevailing theoretical perspectives and to explore other frameworks that potentially afforded more insightful understandings of the problems emerging in everyday life. They questioned the efforts of modernization theorists, structural-functionalists, cultural evolutionists, and structuralists to explain the world around them. They replaced their views with ideas borrowed from the dependency theorists of Latin America, with feminist perspectives derived from the women's movement, and with Marxist viewpoints that incorporated both domestic and foreign strands of the Marxist tradition.

Public disclosure of and reaction to Project Camelot was an early warning of the crisis looming in the anthropological profession. Project Camelot was a Department of Defense-funded study carried out by the Special Operations Research Office (SORO) at American University. SORO was a contract organization established in 1957 to serve the needs of the psychological warfare directorate of the American Army. Initially, it concentrated its attention on foreign areas, on social revolutions, on how communist party organizations worked, and on tribal groups in various countries. In 1962, SORO's mission was expanded to include social research on counterinsurgency. By 1964, projects involving anthropologists or individuals representing themselves as anthropologists had been launched in Chile, Colombia, and

Peru. The existence of Project Camelot – the research in Chile – became public in June 1965. The project was immediately canceled because of outcries from the Chilean legislature, the State Department, social scientists in the United States and Latin America, and the press (Deitchman 1976:64–188; Horowitz 1967).

At the fall 1965 meeting of the American Anthropological Association (AAA), the Executive Board appointed a committee to examine

> issues involving the relationship between anthropologists and agencies, both govern-
> mental and private that sponsor their research. Among these issues are those of access to
> foreign areas, governmental clearance, professional ethics and our responsibilities toward
> colleagues at home and abroad, the peoples with whom we work, and the sponsoring
> agencies . . .
>
> The integrity of the field worker himself [*sic*]. Is he attempting to serve the cause of
> basic science, or the mission-directed role of a government agency, or both? Are these
> reconcilable? (*AAA Newsletter*, December 1965, pp. 1, 3 quoted by Wakin 1992:29–30).

Ralph Beals who headed the committee subsequently testified before the Congressional Subcommittee on Government Research in June 1966. He noted that marginalized peoples studied by anthropologists often feared reprisals from their governments, that anthropologists did not want the information they collected in confidence used against their informants, and that Camelot-like projects were creating difficulties for anthropologists. He recommended that the activities of intelligence and mission-oriented agencies be divorced from those of the scientist. At the same time, he suggested that anthropologists might be employed in staff positions to identify problems and to interpret research findings (Wakin 1992:30–1).

In January 1967, the Beals Committee on Research Problems and Ethics reported to the AAA. The voting members overwhelmingly adopted it as a non-binding statement on professional ethics, and the Executive Board established an Ad-Hoc Ethics Committee that would meet for the first time in January 1969. However, in the report, Beals warned that

> The Fellows should recognize that although Camelot is dead under that name, in a sense
> it has only gone underground. Similar types of projects have been conducted and are
> being planned under different names and through other kinds of agencies (*AAA
> Newsletter*, Jan. 1967, pp. 5–6 quoted by Wakin 1992:32).

Significant divisions appeared in the AAA at the 1966 annual meeting. AAA members who either supported the war in Vietnam or believed that the organization should not make political statements were incensed when their colleagues passed a resolution at the business meeting condemning the practices of the American military in its war against the people of Vietnam. The resolution stated that we condemn the use of napalm, chemical defoliants, harmful gases, bombing, the torture and killing of prisoners of war and political prisoners and the intentional or deliberate policies of genocide of forced transportation of population for the purpose of terminating their cultural and/or genetic heritages by anyone anywhere.

These methods of warfare deeply offend human nature. We ask that all governments put an end to their use at once and proceed as rapidly as possible to a peaceful settlement of the war in Vietnam (*AAA Newsletter*, December 1966, p. 2 quoted by Wakin 1992: 32–3).

While the supporters of the resolution condemned in the name of the Association the actions of the U.S. military in Vietnam, their opponents argued that it was improper to involve the organization in what was clearly a political controversy. David Aberle (b. 1918) and others who supported the resolution argued that anthropology had never been a value-free science and that genocide was or ought to be a concern of anthropologists.

Project Camelot would seem like a dress rehearsal in the wake of events that began to unfold in March 1970. At that time, the Student Mobilization Committee to End the War in Vietnam (SMC) obtained documents from the files of a UCLA anthropologist which indicated that the professional expertise of several anthropologists working in Southeast Asia was being harnessed to counterinsurgency efforts in Thailand. The SMC showed the documents to Marshall Sahlins, Gerald Berreman (b. 1930), Eric Wolf, and Joseph Jorgensen (b. 1934), all of whom were active in the anti-war movement and all of whom felt that the anthropologists named in the documents were violating the intent of the Beals Report adopted three years earlier. Their public statements about the documents spread like wildfire across the country and through the profession.

AAA President George Foster (b. 1913) and some members of the Executive Board were critical of the actions and remarks of Berreman, Wolf, and Jorgensen who, at the time, were members of the Ethics Committee. The Ethics Committee responded, saying that Wolf, Jorgensen, and Berreman had acted as individuals, and that the documents supported their claims regarding unethical behavior. In November 1970, the Executive Board established an ad hoc committee of inquiry, chaired by Margaret Mead, to deal with the controversy. The Mead Report was released in November 1971 in time for discussion at the annual meeting. It suggested that counterinsurgency research

is well within the traditional canons of acceptable behavior for the applied anthropologist, and is counterinsurgent only for present funding purposes; a decade ago it might have been called "mental health" (Report of the Ad Hoc Committee to Evaluate the Controversy Concerning Anthropological Activities in Thailand, September 1971, quoted by Wakin 1992:205).

After whitewashing the activities of the anthropologists involved in the counter-insurgency research, the Mead Report condemned Wolf and Jorgensen for the statements they made when the documents were released by SMC in March 1970. At the long, acrimonious business meeting, the voting members of the Association rejected the report section by section. Two days later, the Executive Board passed a motion stating that the issues raised by the Thailand Controversy remained unresolved (Wakin 1992:153–213). They are still unresolved thirty years later (Berreman 1991; Davenport 1985).

The Thailand Controversy which was a symptom of the wider crisis in American society was not the only expression of the crisis in the anthropological profession in the late 1960s. Kathleen Gough (1925–90) had already captured another facet of the problem in 1968 in her now-famous article "Anthropology: Child of Imperialism" which appeared in *Monthly Review*, the most influential of the American Marxist journals. Gough (1968a) pointed out that many Third World peoples involved in decolonization or national liberation movements saw anthropologists as part of the larger problem of American interference in the internal affairs of their countries. She argued persuasively that the "discipline was neither objective nor neutral, that its establishment in universities was in part to serve and justify politics of domination" (Lee and Sacks 1993:185). This was not the first time that Gough had been at the center of a political controversy and felt the wrath of the opposition. A few years earlier, at the time of the Cuban Missile Crisis, Gough had given an electrifying speech at Brandeis University in which she supported the Cuban revolution and expressed her fervent hope "that Cuba would defend itself against the United States' flagrant violation of international law" (Lee and Sacks 1993:187). The Brandeis administration retaliated by forcing Gough and David Aberle, her husband and colleague, out of the university in 1963 (Jorgensen 1993).

In a follow-up paper to "Anthropology: Child of Imperialism," Gough (1968b) argued that it was time for anthropologists to reassess critically the roots of their discipline and to examine the social and political interests which its practitioners have traditionally served. The concerns of this paper, controversial at the time, resonated with sentiments expressed in the pages of *Current Anthropology* and in three edited collections that were published between 1969 and 1973: Dell Hymes's (1969) *Reinventing Anthropology*; Robin Blackburn's (1972) *Ideology in Social Science: Readings in Critical Social Theory*; and Talal Asad's (1973) *Anthropology and the Colonial Encounter*. The authors whose work appeared in the Hymes volume, for example, called anthropology and its theories into question and advocated developing a reflexive, critical anthropology; they pointed to the relationship between anthropology and racism, on the one hand, and the politics of African-American culture, on the other. They deployed concepts – imperialism, exploitation, resistance, neo-colonialism, economic dependency, and hegemony among others – that were more at home in Marxist traditions of social thought than they were in the various strands of social theory taught in American universities at the time.

As the war continued, both left and right wings of the AAA tugged at the hearts and souls of liberals in the center. This temporarily weakened the influence of the centrists in the profession. One manifestation of this struggle was the appearance in 1968 of Marvin Harris's (b. 1927) history of the field, *The Rise of Anthropological Theory: A History of Theories of Culture* (Harris 1968). Harris used the historical development of anthropology in an effort to reestablish the political center of the deeply divided profession. There were two major dimensions to Harris's argument – one that was designed to appeal to the Right; the other to Liberals and elements of the New Left.

On the one hand, Harris (1968:250–318) claimed that Boas and his students were inductivists and eclectics who eschewed generalization in favor of particularism. They based their arguments on the collection of an ever-increasing number of facts and on the belief that conclusions about the significance of these facts would emerge from the data themselves. Their neo-Kantian philosophical stance prevented the Boasians from constructing and elaborating any systematic body of social thought.[3] The real appeal of Harris's arguments for the Right was that it afforded an opportunity to minimize Boas's influence in the field. They shifted attention away from the public outrage Boas had expressed when he discovered that American anthropologists engaged in espionage activities during the First World War; they downplayed his lifelong struggles against racism and anti-semitism and his fervid belief that anthropology should be a critical harnessing of the mind for promoting the general welfare of the most oppressed elements in the society. The Right used Harris's arguments to portray Boas as a muddle-headed collector of facts unconcerned with generalization or theory. This perspective is reproduced in the often-heard phrase "Boas was only an historical particularist." This phrase found a receptive audience among students who were receiving in their courses steady doses of social theory that was not linked to practice.

On the other hand, Harris appealed to the liberal and leftist students of the late 1960s by claiming that Marx was an important part of the intellectual heritage of modern anthropology. In his view, "cultural anthropology developed entirely in *reaction* to, instead of independently of, Marxism" (Harris 1968:249, emphasis in the original). While this was probably not a surprise to the members of Harris's generation and its predecessors, it was an important argument at the time, especially for students trained in the 1950s and 1960s whose understanding and appreciation of Western social thought were severely constrained by the repressive climate of the Cold War. However, Harris had a particular viewpoint regarding the significance of Marx's and Engels's work for anthropology. He portrayed Marx and Engels as historical functionalists, like Spencer and Morgan, who believed that the various parts of a culture were interrelated and that the cause-and-effect (i.e. determinant) relationship between the economic base and the superstructure provides the evolutionary consistency of social systems; in a phrase, "the decisive advantage of the Marxian model is that it is diachronic and functional, not that it is dialectic" (Harris 1968:236). Harris (1968:230) proposed to rid Marxism of the "Hegelian monkey on its back" – i.e. the idea that the social relations that exist in a class-based society at any given moment are the product of contradictory forces. In other words, class struggle was replaced with evolution.

Harris (1968:221) believed that Marxists, especially members of communist parties, "were fully prepared to corrupt scientific standards in order to prove by practice what their theories predicted . . . [and that they would not] hesitate to falsify data in order to make them more useful." His rejection of the dialectic of class struggle owed more to the anti-Communist sentiments of the Cold War than to any appreciation of the perspective that groups engaged in political activity need the most accurate assessments possible of the strengths and weaknesses of the forces they confront if they are to have any chance at all of making their own history (e.g. Leacock 1972:61–6).

Cultural materialism was Harris's (1968:643–87) proposal for overcoming the weaknesses he saw in historical particularism and dialectical Marxism. Cultural materialism was empirical and scientific. It formulated society in terms of a cultural superstructure and a largely economic, technological infrastructure that mediated the relations between the members of a society and their environment – relations that were understood partly in terms of a neo-Malthusian population pressure.

Cultural materialism, like modernization theory and cultural evolutionism, ultimately perceived human history in terms of a progression of stages. In the 1960s, the dependency theorists in Latin America questioned the validity of the idea that history could be portrayed as a regular succession of stages. Both the evolutionists and the modernization theorists had argued that, if certain levels of investment in the forces of production or in particular groups occurred, then a capitalist society resembling those of the industrialized West would emerge. By contrast, the dependency theorists pointed out that, in spite of high levels of investment, the countries of Latin America were not industrial capitalist societies. Their structures were, in fact, diverging from those of the industrial countries even as the amount of foreign investment increased. The reason for this, they argued, was that the developed, industrial capitalist states and the underdeveloped countries of Latin America occupied complementary positions in an international system of production and distribution that was bound together by unequal exchange relations. In their view, Third World countries would never become industrial capitalist states in the same sense that the United States or England were.

The Chicago-trained economist André Gunder Frank (b. 1929) did much to popularize dependency theory in the United States from the late 1960s onward through his critiques of mainstream development and modernization theory. Frank argued that economic underdevelopment of Latin American countries was a consequence of an exploitative relationship that extended from the capitalist metropoles in North America and Western Europe to the most remote reaches of their economically backward satellites in Latin America. He wrote that

> The now developed countries were never underdeveloped, though they may have been undeveloped. It is also widely believed that the contemporary underdevelopment of a country can be understood as the product or reflection solely of its own economic, political, social, and cultural characteristics or structure. Yet historical research demonstrates that contemporary underdevelopment is in large part the historical product of past and continuing economic and other relations between the satellite underdeveloped and the now developed metropolitan countries. Furthermore, these relations are an essential part of the structure and development of the capitalist system on a world scale (Frank 1966/1969:4).

The underdevelopment of the Latin American countries was, in Frank's view, reproduced by the contradictions inherent in capitalism. This challenged prevailing views that capitalist development and modernization were equally beneficial to all of the countries involved.

Peasantries perplexed liberal theorists of change who predicted that rural class structures would eventually disappear as industrialization proceeded and rural peoples moved to the cities in search of higher wages and better standards of living. What was perplexing was that peasant communities were not disappearing in countries experiencing economic development and modernization; in fact, they seemed to be resisting these processes. Thus, one consequence of the intensification of the Vietnam War was that a few social scientists, including Eric Wolf, began to explore the relationship between peasants and social revolution. What was most important about Wolf's (1969) widely acclaimed book, *Peasant Wars of the Twentieth Century*, was the close attention he paid to the historic specificity and particularities of peasant revolutions in Mexico, Russia, China, Cuba, Algeria, and Vietnam.

Wolf (1969:295) observed that the peasant rebellions just mentioned were "parochial reactions to major social dislocations, set in motion by major societal changes" associated with the spread of capitalism, markets, and capitalist economic rationality. They were launched by landholding peasants with the material and organizational advantages that their sharecropper and rural proletarian neighbors lacked. The battlefield of their rebellions was society itself:

> Where the peasantry has successfully rebelled against the established order – under its own banner and with its own leaders – it was sometimes able to reshape the social structure of the countryside closer to its heart's desire; but it did not lay hold of the state, of the cities which house the centers of control, of the strategic nonagricultural resources of the society. . . . Thus, a peasant rebellion which takes place in a complex society already

caught up in commercialization and industrialization tends to be self-limiting, and, hence, anachronistic (Wolf 1969:294).

The peasant's role in social revolution was, for Wolf (1969:304), both tragic and hopeful: tragic because their efforts ushered in even more uncertainty, and hopeful because "theirs is the party of humanity."

As Wolf turned his gaze toward peasant communities in distant lands, other anthropologists focused their attention on the intersection of class, culture, and inequality in urban America. In the early 1960s, Oscar Lewis (1914–70) had put forward a powerful thesis regarding the interrelations of class, culture, and inequality based on work in Mexico City and San Juan, Puerto Rico (Rigdon 1988:48–108). This was the "culture of poverty" thesis. In Lewis's view, the culture of poverty originated in class-stratified, rapidly developing capitalist societies and in colonial societies enmeshed in imperialist social relations:

> The most likely candidates for the culture of poverty are the people who come [to urban slums] from the lower strata of a rapidly changing society and are already partially alienated from it. The culture of poverty is not only an adaptation to a set of objective conditions in the larger society. Once it comes into existence it tends to perpetuate itself from generation to generation because of its effect on children. By the time slum children are age six or seven they have usually absorbed the basic values and attitudes of their subculture and are not psychologically geared to take full advantage of changing conditions or increased opportunities which may occur in their lifetime (Lewis 1966:xlv).

Senator Daniel P. Moynihan (b. 1927), who had held a number of subcabinet positions in the early 1960s and was director of the MIT-Harvard Joint Center for Urban Studies in the late 1960s, adopted the culture of poverty in his *Negro Family: The Case for National Action*. Moynihan (1965: 30) asserted that the African-American family was "at the center of a tangle of pathology . . . the principal source of most of the aberrant, inadequate or antisocial behavior that did not establish, but now serves to perpetuate the cycle of poverty and deprivation" (Moynihan 1965:30).

Eleanor B. Leacock (1922–87) was among the first anthropologists to critique the culture of poverty theses put forward by Lewis and Moynihan (Mullings 1993). She developed this critique in her introduction to an edited volume, *The Culture of Poverty: A Critique*, that appeared in 1971. Here, she sought to explain how and why the cultural differences between classes emerged and were reproduced. Leacock (1971:34) wrote that

> differences between the poor and nonpoor in a society stem from three sources. First, there are the different traditions of peoples with different histories; these are often reinforced by racial or religious segregation and discrimination. Second there are realistic attempts to deal with objective conditions that vary from one class to another. . . . There

is no hard fast line between this order of behavior and the third, which are those adaptive acts and attitudes that become institutionalized, and incorporated into internalized values and norms appropriate for living in a given position in the socio-economic system. It is, of course, the last – the subcultural variations along class lines – which come closest to what culture-of-poverty is supposedly documenting. However, . . . sociocentric methods of data collection and analysis, plus a nonhistorical theory of culture and its relation to personality, have contributed to stereotypical and distorted views of these class linked variations.

Thus, in her opinion, the culture of poverty theorists – i.e. Lewis and Moynihan – viewed the relation between culture and personality too narrowly; they imposed their own middle-class values on interactions with informants and, consequently, misrepresented working-class culture; and they did not adequately appreciate that middle-class solutions to the realities of everyday life were not necessarily available for members of the working class.

Leacock made other significant contributions to anthropology in the early 1970s besides her critique of the culture of poverty thesis. One of the more important was the introduction she wrote for a new edition of Frederick Engels's *Origin of the Family, Private Property and the State* that was published in 1972 by International Publishers, the publishing house of the Communist Party of the United States. In the introduction, she examined how anthropological research shed new light on arguments that Engels had made nearly a century earlier (Leacock 1972). These included the political implications of cultural or social evolutionary theory, primitive communism, and the emergence of the states. Most important, however, was her discussion of Engels's arguments about the subjugation of women and the emergence of monogamy, private property, and the state. This paved the way for subsequent discussions of women's issues and gender in American anthropology (Gailey 1998) and served as the basis for two important collections of essays that appeared in the mid 1970s – Michelle Rosaldo and Louise Lamphere's (1974) *Women, Culture and Society* and Rayna Rapp Reiter's (1975) *Toward an Anthropology of Women*.

Leacock (1972:30–46) suggested that Engels's arguments about the subordination of women were essentially correct and that they were supported by anthropological data. Engels had argued that "the position of women relative to men deteriorated with the advent of class society" and the state (Leacock 1972:30). Thus, the subordination of women was neither an integral feature of the human condition nor universal, as many cultural evolutionists implied. It was instead an integral feature of the historically contingent processes associated with class and state formation – i.e. the simultaneous dissolution of institutions and practices that benefit the community as a whole and the emergence of social relations that benefit the members of a particular group at the expense of their kin and neighbors. Leacock's exhortation to examine women's roles in kin-organized communities and class-stratified societies came at an opportune moment. It was during the political and social crises of the late 1960s that the traditional assumptions of anthropologists were being challenged from inside and outside the profession. What Leacock helped to establish at that instant was an explicitly Marxist-feminist perspective and practice.

Discussion

The optimism that greeted the end of the Second World War faded quickly in the United States and was replaced by the repressive atmosphere of the Cold War. Members of the Left were not the only ones who suffered. The anti-communist sentiments manifested in McCarthyism and fueled by the FBI narrowed both the political culture of the country and the traditions of social thought that were discussed in colleges and universities from the late 1940s onward. The Cold War also shaped the milieu in which the profession of anthropology was reorganized, and its center of gravity was shifted from the public political culture of the country to the academy. In this milieu, anthropology was increasingly seen as a practice divorced from the pressing issues of the day; it was a profession concerned with the ancient and the exotic. Studies of fossil hominids, the archaeology of ancient peoples, strange languages spoken by only a few dozen individuals, or the exotic customs of some remote tribe did little to dispel these perceptions as long as they remained only topics of conversation at cocktail parties and their significance was not clearly linked to broader issues that were of concern to the wider public.

Anthropology and anthropologists were radicalized in the context of the struggles that swept across the United States in the 1950s and 1960s. The Civil Rights struggles, resistance to the House Committee on Un-American Activities, campaigns to unionize farmworkers in California, opposition to the war in Vietnam, and the disillusionment of students with universities that were being transformed into commodity-producing factories all contributed to the growing disenchantment people felt toward what had become stock explanations for why people related to one another as they did. The process of radicalization was also fueled as students of anthropology spent time with peoples in distant lands who were often engaged in struggles to free themselves from colonial rule and who, by political necessity, needed more accurate accounts of the existing patterns of social relations and processes of social change than those provided by structural-functionalism, cultural evolution, or modernization theory.

A very different anthropology, enriched both by history and by a more sophisticated and textured appreciation of the social theory, loomed on the horizon by the early 1970s. It was enriched by Marxist thought, feminist critiques, and discussions of dependency, unequal exchange and other aspects of the human condition emanating from other parts of the world. For many of this generation, the anthropology they practiced was no longer divorced from the public sphere but was once more an integral part of the political culture of the country.

Notes

1. During the 1950s, top officials from the Rockefeller, Ford, and Carnegie Foundations often moved back and forth between the philanthropies and government service. For example, since 1952, three Rockefeller Foundation officials – John Foster Dulles, Dean Rusk, and Cyrus Vance – moved directly from the foundation to become Secretary of State. McGeorge Bundy moved from being President John F. Kennedy's National Security Advisor to the presidency of the Ford Foundation (Berman 1983:108; McCaughey 1984:182).
2. In a similar vein, I was told in all seriousness by a professor in graduate school that you could always identify communists, their sympathizers, and dupes because they were cultural evolutionists.
3. Leslie White, a long-time member of the Socialist Labor Party, had argued since the 1940s that Boas was an anti-evolutionist who attacked the evolutionary schemes of Spencer and Morgan. Right-wingers such as George P. Murdock argued that Boas's ethnographic research on the Kwakiutl not only lacked detail but also contained so many ambiguities that it was virtually impossible to cast Kwakiutl social organization in terms of the categories employed by the Human Relations Area Files.

–5–

Anthropology in the Neoliberal Era, 1974–2000

The crisis of American society during the last quarter of the twentieth century has been shaped by the intersection of several interrelated processes. These include the breakdown of the unwritten postwar compromise between capital and labor, the rise to prominence of finance capital, economic reorganization, and implementation of neoliberal austerity programs, immigration, the stalling out of the civil rights movement, and the appearance of new social movements rooted in identity politics, continued intervention in the internal affairs of Third World countries, and the on-going importance of Cold War policies even after the dissolution of the socialist states.

In the unwritten pact between capital and organized labor dating from the late 1940s, the capitalist class settled for aspects of a welfare state in return for labor peace. Labor agreed to participate in a capitalist growth economy shaped by Cold War rhetoric and xenophobia in return for regular cost-of-living increases, inexpensive education, and other social benefits. The compromise, which was unstable from its inception, became even more so through the 1960s and 1970s as serious restructuring of the American economy eroded the underlying logic and the political alliances that sustained it (Phillips 1993:3–31). Terms such as "deindustrialization," "rust belt," "offshoring," "the new international division of labor," "flexible production and accumulation," and "post-Fordism" were coined to describe the effects as industrial capital moved from the old industrial states in the Northeast to the southern states and Third World countries where inexpensive, non-union labor was plentiful.

The rise to prominence and hegemony of the finance sector by the early 1970s facilitated such transfers. The unilateral abrogation of the Bretton Woods Agreement by the United States in 1971 forced all of the capitalist states "to subordinate every aspect of [their] economic policy to the defence of currency" (van der Pilj 1984:262). This underwrote the emergence of the World Bank and the International Monetary Fund (IMF), both controlled by the United States, as major policy-making institutions whose experts promoted the development of export-oriented economies in Third World countries and advocated neoliberal policies – such as deregulation, free markets, privatization, and austerity – that facilitated the flow of capital (Kolko 1988).

Deregulation of the American banking industry in the 1970s coupled with tax concessions granted by federal, state, and local governments and the steadily higher interests rates banks charged for loans and debt servicing led to enormous profits by the middle of the decade. To increase profits even further, the banks made high-interest, high-risk loans to Second and Third World countries seeking to implement IMF and World Bank development strategies focused on export-oriented industries. By 1978, it appeared as if a number of the less-developed countries might default on loan repayments, which threatened the banks to their foundations. The banks responded to the threat by renegotiating some loans, writing off others, and forcing the governments involved to implement austerity programs that eliminated or severely curtailed the health, education, and welfare benefits enjoyed by their citizens. Austerity policies implemented in the United States also eliminated or weakened the "safety net" available to its citizens.

More than fifteen million immigrants entered the United States since 1969. The new arrivals, most from Latin America and Asia, were an internally diverse group: well-educated Koreans and Chinese, impoverished second-wave Cambodian and Hmong families, and working-class men and women from Mexico, Central America, and the Caribbean (Rumbaut 1991). The immigrants were slotted into a hierarchically organized working class historically structured by race, ethnicity, and gender. Class relations were reorganized by the appearance of the new groups composed of previously unconnected individuals who began to sense that they had something in common and by the identity politics unleashed as a result of this growing awareness. The immigrants constituting the new people classes were aware that Blacks, women, American Indians, Puerto Ricans, and gay men and lesbians were demanding recognition of rights and claims based on their identities. They participated in and were affected to varying degrees and in different ways by the new social movements.

The politics of the new social movements, like those of some civil rights activists in the 1950s and 1960s, celebrated differences and demanded recognition and rights because of them. Their goal was to ensure the survival of the community. Opponents of the collectivist goals of the new social movements appeared almost immediately and rooted their claims in another strand of liberal social thought that gave precedence to the rights of individuals; they demanded that differences be ignored. Such claims and counterclaims were the starting points from which new forms of social consciousness and identity were constructed in the 1970s and 1980s (Taylor 1992). They were buttressed by massive immigration and the changing complexion of the large cities, coupled with deindustrialization, growing unemployment, and capital flight. The politics of the new social movements also fueled the culture wars of the last thirty years of the twentieth century.

The Turn to Marx, 1974–1982

The development of anthropology training programs in the postwar era took place in a political-economic milieu underpinned by sustained economic growth. This reality changed abruptly with the restructuring of the American economy from the late 1960s onward. This reorganization had devastating implications for higher education and for anthropology training programs. By the early 1970s, the costs of higher education were rapidly being shifted from state and federal governments to the individual. At the same time, many university budgets, when adjusted for inflation, had already stopped growing or were actually beginning to decline – conditions that have persisted to the end of the twentieth century and beyond. By the mid-1970s, these no-growth budgets meant that college and university anthropology departments would no longer experience the sustained growth they had known since the early 1960s (d'Andrade, Hammel, Adkins, McDaniel 1975). New faculty were not added, and staff members who departed, retired, or died were not replaced. The increased reliance on marginally paid, part-time teachers quickly led to the formation of two-tier faculties composed of tenure-track slots and temporary positions with fewer benefits.

The erosion of academic jobs was accompanied by a decline in the levels of financial support available to graduate students. As a result, fewer students completed their doctorates; the number of Ph.D. degrees awarded fell from 468 in 1975–6 to 402 in the following year and remained at or below that level until 1992–3. Individuals with doctorates in anthropology were forced to seek employment outside the academy in positions where they could apply the skills they had acquired in graduate school. For example, many students of archaeology found employment in Cultural Resource Management (CRM) archaeology which was created by federal legislation between 1966 and 1974. These laws laid the foundations for a large bureaucracy that supervised the hundreds of private firms that were awarded money to record, recover, and preserve archaeological information in the United States. By 1980, an estimated 6000 men and women worked on CRM projects that cost about $300 million a year (Patterson 1999a:164–6).

The new labor market that emerged from the mid-1970s onward was internally stratified. At the top were tenure-track academics; temporary teachers and public and private-sector employees occupied lower rungs of the ladder. This internal stratification was sustained ideologically by all of the parties involved as they gave priority to pure over applied research and chose to ignore the conditions that underpinned the hierarchically ordered labor market in which they were participants.

The changes in the labor market were refracted in the membership lists of the American Anthropological Association (AAA) that were published yearly in the *Annual Report* during the 1970s and the *Anthropology Newsletter* from the 1980s onward. These numbers indicate that the AAA which had 4,678 individual members in 1967 grew rapidly to 7,750 members in 1973/4 and then more slowly to 8,404 members in 1976/7; the membership then fell steadily to 6486 individuals in 1983. The association has grown every year since then and now has more 11,000 members.

An increasing number and percentage of those entering the labor market from the late 1970s and early 1980s onward were women. For example, the number of Ph.D. degrees awarded in anthropology doubled from about 150 in the late 1960s to 301 in 1970/1. Women earned 28 percent of the degrees awarded that year; thirteen years later, they received 46 percent of the 403 Ph.D. degrees granted by American universities. This fact has several implications. One is that a steadily growing number of women entered the anthropological labor market during the period when it was being rapidly transformed. A second implication is that many of these women, regardless of their qualifications, were employed disproportionately as temporary or part-time teachers in the academy or as practicing anthropologists working outside the academy. In other words, many of them were forced by circumstances beyond their control to work in jobs viewed by the profession as less desirable than full-time, tenure-track positions in research universities. The privileging of academic over non-academic labor still plagues the field today.

Two of the three perspectives – symbolic anthropology and a broadly economistic, sometimes ecological, systems or process evolutionism – honed and refined by American anthropologists during the 1970s could not account adequately or at all for the conditions that were created by the new labor market (Sahlins 1976:55–125). Only the Marxist perspective had the theoretical tools required to do so. In fact, much of the work in the late 1970s can be understood as part of an ongoing dialogue between anthropologists inspired by Marx and those who were not.

The florescence of symbolic anthropology in the mid-1970s depended on the adoption of a perspective that distinguished culture from society, that viewed culture narrowly as a system of symbols and meanings, and that allowed culture to be studied as an autonomous domain. Such a perspective which was originally suggested by Alfred Kroeber and Talcott Parsons (1958) in the late 1950s was widely held by the 1970s. It was based on the belief that culture – the system of symbols and meanings which had a role in shaping the meaningful activity engaged in by people – could not be reduced to some other system. This implied, as David Schneider (1918–95) observed, that

> If one accepts the view that culture is an irreducible construct, one must also accept in principle some general social theory, for example, Parsons's theory of social action. Of course, the study of culture can articulate with theories other than the one developed by Parsons. But I would insist that to study culture without reference to some broader social theory is a pointless endeavor (Schneider 1976:198).

Schneider, Clifford Geertz, and Victor Turner (1920–83), all of whom were at the University of Chicago, used this viewpoint to develop distinctive versions of symbolic anthropology.

Geertz's interpretive anthropology was characterized by the adoption of Parsons's theory of social action and by the infusion of arguments developed by phenomenologists – notably Edmund Husserl (1859–1938), Paul Ricoeur (b. 1913), and Alfred Schutz (1899–1959). Culture, in Geertz's (1973) opinion, consisted of the systems of public symbols by which the members of a society communicated meaning to one another in the course of significant social activity. Cultural systems, for such exchanges to occur, must have at least a minimal degree of coherence – i.e. there was, in Durkheim's terms, a degree of consensus or solidarity. Meaning – i.e. culture – is thus constituted, in the course of symbolic or social action, as

> acting social beings [are] trying to make sense of the world in which they find themselves. . . . Culture is not some abstractly ordered system, deriving its logic from hidden structural principles, or from special symbols that provide the "keys" to its coherence. Its logic – the principles of relations that obtain among its elements – derives rather from the logic or organization of action, from people operating within certain institutional orders, interpreting their situations in order to act coherently within them (Ortner 1984/1994:375).

The version of symbolic anthropology developed by Schneider and his associates took a slightly different tack (Schneider 1969/1977; Dolgin, Kemnitzer, and Schneider 1977). They too combined the idea that culture was a system of symbols and meanings with Parsons's theory of social action. They argued that social action was orderly and understandable for both participants and observers and that social life – which is made up of people, actions, things, relationships, and institutions – had a degree of coherence "for those who live[d] it out in its particularity" (Dolgin, Kemnitzer, and Schneider 1977:5). Unlike Geertz, however, they tied social action and social life to an underlying, broadly Marxist perspective. They did not grant primacy

> in symbolic action to either the formal structures of collective representations or the individual processes of understanding, interpretation, adjustment, and expression. . . . [They focused] on the social processes in which these two sorts of force interact: the social relations of communication and interpretation, and those properties of the symbolic system itself, and of the social system of which the symbolic system is a part, which give coherence to communication: which either stabilize the symbolic order or which make change in it regular. The fact that such change is regular is proven by the fact that, even during periods of the most radical symbolic change, we have very little problem understanding each other (Dolgin, Kemnitzer, and Schneider 1977:16).

In their view, change

> is the natural state of existence of societies, which we now know not to be a succession of forms, but of arenas in which the *process of formation* of the social order itself is perpetually taking place. . . .
>
> For Marx, as for Hegel, the meaningfulness of social action for actors is part and parcel of their *creation* – in thought *and* action – of a social world, of what Ludwig Wittenstein called a "mode of life." In Marx's words, 'As people express their life, so they are . . ." (Dolgin, Kemnitzer, and Schneider 1977:17–8, emphasis in the original).

The foundations for Schneider's symbolic anthropology were his empirical studies of American kinship. He viewed the ideology of American kinship as a cultural system that was based

> on a distinction between the "pure" domain of kinship, defined in terms of the symbol of coitus and differentiated into two major aspects, relationships as a natural substance and a relationship as code for conduct, and a "conglomerate" domain of kinship, differentiated into "the family" on one hand and an articulated system of person-defined statuses (genealogical) on the other (Schneider 1969/1977:70).

The symbolic ties of substance/blood and shared codes of conduct between persons defined social groups and shaped action between their members and with outsiders. Schneider further argued that these concepts were in turn organized around the more encompassing core symbols of nature and rationality, and that collectively they undergirded relations of recruitment with regard not only to kinship but also to nationality and religion.

The issues that Schneider and his associates raised were why were certain symbols continually recreated in the course of meaningful social action, and how did they come to be seen as real or natural and imbued with a sense of inevitability? In Marxist terms, how were these abstractions reified and converted into sets of understandings that were repeatedly reproduced by social actors? They were not concerned, as Geertz was, with how symbolic forms were used by native and anthropologist to interpret particular episodes of social action but rather with how certain symbolic forms or sets of understandings about things, which are shaped by the desires of actors, became hegemonic and dominant in particular societies (Dolgin, Kemnitzer, and Schneider 1977:36–43).

The version of symbolic anthropology developed by Victor Turner (1975) was not rooted in Parsons's theory of social action; informed by Marxist social thought, it was a reaction against the structural-functionalist assumptions that cultural systems have a high degree of coherence, that consensus prevails in society, and that societies are harmoniously integrated as a result. In Turner's view, societies were shaped by conflict and contradiction. Like Schneider and his associates, Turner was interested in the dynamics and processes of symbolic action. He was concerned with how in particular events

> symbols can be detached from abstract systems of symbols . . . with which they have previously been connected and "hooked in" to new ad hoc combinations of symbols to constitute, legitimate, or undermine programs and protocols for collective action (Turner 1975:148).

He was also concerned with the social and historical processes by means of which symbols retained, added, or shed meaning in times of crisis (Turner 1974:98–155).

Another focus of Turner's symbolic anthropology was to determine the ways in which symbols put together in rituals performed in particular circumstances resolved social contradictions by bringing actors into line with the norms of the society. Here, he examined the spontaneous grouping or *communitas* that often appeared suddenly among marginal or liminal peoples, such as the millenarian movements that emerged among poor peoples or tribal peoples as they were enmeshed in the tributary relations of some state-based society (Turner 1969:94–130).

The second strand of anthropological thought that crystallized during the 1970s and the early 1980s was more concerned with the practical than with the symbolic coordinates of human activity (Friedman 1974; Sahlins 1976:vii–x; Vincent 1986). Its proponents, sometimes described as the Columbia-Michigan Axis, saw culture not as superorganic but rather as the "means by which human populations maintain themselves in ecological systems" (Rappaport 1971:245). Culture, in their view, was simultaneously the product of rational human beings interacting with one another, each attempting to maximize or optimize their own interests, and an instrument for reproducing or maintaining the human population within certain Malthusian limits (Nonini 1985). The ecological anthropologists built on the earlier work of Julian Steward and Leslie White. The various neofunctionalist, neoevolutionist perspectives constituting this viewpoint ranged from ecological anthropology and cultural materialism, on the one hand, to the concerns of the new archaeologists with the rise of civilization and the origins of states, on the other.[1] Its idiom included explanatory terms such as adaptation, system, feedback, homeostasis, carrying capacity, population pressure, evolution, and process.

Unlike Steward or White whose unit of analysis was culture, ecological anthropologists – such as Roy Rappaport (1926–97) or Andrew Vayda (b. 1931) – were concerned with populations, i.e. aggregates of autonomous human beings, whose culture and forms of social organization allowed them to adapt to the natural environments in which they lived and to make use of the resources offered by their real and perceived environments (Rappaport 1977; Vayda and McCay 1975). These human populations were constituent parts of an ecosystem along with other species and resources. Like the other populations, they captured energy from these relatively passive environments and reproduced in ways and numbers that tended to maintain the balance between themselves and the world in which they lived. This emphasis on how human populations survived and reproduced focused attention on nutrition, subsistence, and demography as their members went about acquiring the resources they needed for everyday life. The ecological anthropologists believed that cultural practices – such as the potlatch of the Northwest Coast – were adaptations that maintained the ecosystem in a homeostatic or dynamic equilibrium by redistributing food and other resources from peoples living in areas of relative abundance to those living in areas of relative scarcity (Orlove 1980:240–2, 253).

Explaining cultural change was a problem for the neofunctionalists. In their perspective, change occurred when some force impinged on the system from the outside and disrupted its equilibrium conditions. For example, Kent Flannery (b. 1934) – who introduced systems theory to the new archaeology – explained the shift from a food-collecting economy to one based on incipient cultivation in terms of

a series of genetic changes which took place in one or two species of Mesoamerican plants which were of use to man. The exploitation of these plants had been a relatively minor procurement system . . . , but positive feedback following these initial genetic changes causes one minor system to grow all out of proportion to the others, and eventually to change the whole ecosystem (Flannery 1968:79).

Flannery (1972:399) subsequently explored the cultural evolution of civilizations – i.e. states or those "human societies [that] have evolved to levels of great sociopolitical complexity." After describing antecedent forms of sociopolitical organization – bands, tribes and chiefdoms – he portrayed the state as a social type with a centralized government, a professional ruling class, social stratification, occupational specialization, monopoly of force, rule by law, and economic structures controlled by elites and characterized by reciprocal, redistributive, and market exchanges. States appeared because of the complex relationships and feedback among a series of variables or prime movers (Flannery 1972:408, 414). State formation was a long, slow process that involved increased internal differentiation and specialization of the cultural subsystems and denser linkages between the various subsystems and the highest-order controls of the society. He wrote that

the mechanisms and processes [by which states emerge] are universal, not merely of human society but in the evolution of complex systems in general. The *socioenvironmental stresses* [which select for those mechanisms] are not necessarily universal, but may be specific to particular regions and societies (Flannery 1972:409, emphasis in the original).

In other words, when socio-environmental stresses impinged on the adaptive milieu, evolutionary mechanisms changed the relationships among the higher- and lower-order controls that regulate the system. These mechanisms had the capacity to promote further stress and instability and to trigger social pathologies – two of which were usurpation and meddling – that underwrote even further transformations of the system. In Flannery's view, the evolution of civilizational systems was a slow, gradual, and continuous process of internal responses and adaptations, first to external socio-environmental stresses and then to the social pathologies that developed. The effect was that the components of the cultural system were the optimal or best-compromise solutions at any given moment to the problems produced by the natural and social environments.

While the neofunctionalists explained change in terms of exogenous factors, cultural materialists – such as Marvin Harris (1979) or Mark Cohen (b. 1943) – resorted to neo-Malthusian arguments. In their view, when a population surpassed the carrying capacity of its environment, some form of technological or organizational innovation was required to maintain it at its new level or density. Thus, Cohen explained the origin and development of agriculture in terms of population growth and reliance on more intensive forms of land or resource utilization. He wrote

> that human population has been growing throughout its history, and that such growth is the cause, rather than the result, of much of human "progress" or technological change. . . . While hunting and gathering is an extremely successful mode of adaptation for small hunting groups, it is not well adapted to the support of large or dense human populations. I suggest therefore that the development of agriculture was an adjustment which human populations were forced to make in response to their own increasing numbers. . . . [A]griculture is not easier than hunting and gathering and does not provide a higher quality, more palatable or more secure food base. . . . [It] has only one advantage . . . that of providing more calories. . . . [It] will thus be practiced only when necessitated by population pressure (Cohen 1977:14–15).

As the weaknesses of the ecosystems approach – its emphasis on functional integration and self-regulation and its difficulty in dealing with change – became increasingly apparent in the late 1970s, many of the ecological anthropologists and new archaeologists shifted their attention toward the analyses of individual decision-making and historical processes (Orlove 1980; Vincent 1986). This forced them to confront once again the specificity of the historical record and how people made their own history under conditions not of their own making. It also led many of them to examine critically how their own theoretical perspectives resonated with those of Marxist scholars whose work was developing along several different lines.

Dependency theory and subsequently world systems theory formed one bridge with Marxist social thought. Dependency theory, popularized in the United States during the late 1960s and early 1970s by Chicago-trained economist André Gunder Frank (b. 1929), was a critique of mainstream modernization and development theory. Frank (1966/1969:4) had argued that the forms of economic development in Third

World countries – such as Chile or Brazil – were the "historical product of past and continuing economic and other relations between the underdeveloped satellite and the now developed metropolitan countries." These relations were exploitative ones that drained economic surplus from the satellites and impregnated their domestic economies with the same capitalist structures and contradictions found in the Western industrialized countries (Frank 1967:10).

Historical sociologist Immanuel Wallerstein (b. 1930) continued the analysis of unequal exchange in his influential *The Modern World-System*, the first volume of which appeared in 1974 (Wallerstein 1974). Wallerstein argued that world economies linked by exchange relations were largely impossible before about 1500, because the bureaucracies of the constituent states absorbed surplus and precluded its accumulation for investment. The capitalist world economy which appeared around 1500 coincided with the expansion of commerce. By virtue of a series of accidents, the states of Northwestern Europe were able to impose a regional division of labor and specialization of production – e.g. sugar in the Caribbean, bullion in the Andes, and cereals in Eastern Europe – and, through increasingly powerful state bureaucracies, to consolidate the flow of surplus toward the core countries (Wallerstein 1974:38; 1979:18).

Joseph Jorgensen (1971, 1978) was the first American anthropologist to use dependency theory to examine the development of underdevelopment in the western United States. He focused not only on North American Indian economies but also on the consolidation and concentration of agricultural production in the hands of a steadily decreasing number of increasingly larger corporations. He showed that the same processes underpinned Indian battles for sovereignty, Chicano and Black protests about police brutality, and the steadily progressing immiseration of rural Anglos in many parts of the West. These were the rapacious development policies of corporations that were supported by federal, state, and local officials who enacted legislation that placed the burden of economic growth disproportionately on the members of the most marginalized communities and classes in the area. He wrote

> Whether at the hands of railroads, agribusiness, mining companies, or timber corporations, development has brought immense human suffering and environmental degradation to both Native American and Anglo communities. Today, many of those communities are skeptical of the promises of energy corporations and government officials and are seeking alternative models for revitalizing rural areas. Social scientists, if they so choose, can collaborate with Western tribes and communities in formulating and promoting these models (Jorgensen 1978:16).

The turn toward radical and Marxist analyses coincided with changes in the empirical base of the discipline – the fieldwork situation (Vincent 1986:100). These changes were underwritten by (1) the ongoing decolonization of Third World countries,

(2) the reorientation of funding opportunities toward social problems in the United States, (3) the politicization of native peoples at home and abroad, and (4) the emergence of various indigenous and advocacy groups including the International Work Group for Indigenous Affairs (IWGIA) in 1968 and Cultural Survival in 1972.

One advocacy group – the World Council of Indigenous Peoples, founded in 1975 – coined the term "Fourth World" to refer to "the disenfranchised Aboriginal peoples engulfed by nation-states" and called for the industrial states to reexamine their concepts of and claims to land, citizenship, and nation "in light of the cultural values and sentiments expressed in the arguments of the Fourth World" (Wright 1988:376). While the Council issued a moral challenge the Six Nations Iroquois went further and called for anthropologists for a critical analysis of "the West's historical processes, to seek out the actual nature of the roots of the exploitative and oppressive conditions which are forced on humanity" (quoted by Wright 1988:376).

Eric Wolf's (1982) *Europe and the People without History* and Stanley Diamond's (1974) *In Search of the Primitive: A Critique of Civilization* were early responses to such appeals. Wolf and Diamond developed different facets of Marxist social thought during the 1970s. Unlike Wallerstein's world-systems theory which stressed the importance of unequal exchange between the core and periphery, Wolf emphasized the importance of the social relations that structured the organization of production and the distribution of goods and labor within and between societies. He organized his discussion of

> the different social systems and varied cultural understandings that Europe would . . . encounter in the course of its expansion . . . [in terms of Marx's concept of the mode of production in order to delineate] the central processes at work in the interaction of Europeans with the majority of the world's peoples (Wolf 1982:73).

Wolf's analysis resonated with a wider debate that was taking place at the time among anthropologists inspired by Marxist social thought (Friedman 1974; Kohl 1981; O'Laughlin 1975). The debate was concerned with whether the conceptual framework that Marx had used to analyze the development of industrial capitalism was also applicable to the non-capitalist societies traditionally studied by anthropologists. Wolf and other American anthropologists – notably Janet Siskind (b. 1929) and Eleanor Leacock – concluded that it was applicable with modification and clarification in the light of anthropological inquiries to the study of band and tribal societies (Siskind 1978; Leacock 1982b).

Wolf's analysis of the political economy of the capitalist world bore similarities to the structural Marxism or Marxist structuralism being discussed in Europe in the emphasis he placed on the system as a complexly structured whole manifesting the articulation of societies with different modes of production and culture that define the deployment of social labor which set the terms of history. In his view, the motor for the rise of international capitalism was located in the West, and the system itself was built on exploitation, enslavement, genocide, and the formation of class structures and states. It also involved ethnogenesis – the creation of peoples without history both inside and outside Europe. Stanley Diamond's (1974:1) more dialectical analysis of capitalist civilization captured this dynamic in different words:

> Civilization originates in conquest abroad and repression at home. Each is an aspect of the other. Anthropologists who use, or misuse, words such as "acculturation" beg this basic question. For the major mode of acculturation, the direct shaping of one culture by another through which civilization develops, has been conquest.

Wolf and Diamond developed different facets of Marxist social thought. Wolf viewed anthropology as a science whose essential concepts were those of mode production and socioeconomic formations as structured totalities. It underwrote the formation of a comparative political economy. Diamond (1969:401) saw anthropology as the study of people in crisis by people who were themselves in crisis. Anthropology, in his view, was a humanist philosophy whose goals were to "penetrate the mystifications of genocide and bureaucratic repression, to understand the dimensions of an emancipatory politics" (Gailey 1992:7). This required taking seriously the notion that the social relations characteristic of kin-ordered communities constituted an archetype for struggles toward a more just and humane social order. *Dialectical Anthropology*, the journal he founded in 1975, contained articles that sought to hone and refine both facets of an anthropology informed by Marx's social and ethical theory.

Marxist social theory underpinned a number of developments in anthropology from the late 1970s onward, the most important, thought-provoking, and influential of which were a series of studies by Marxist-feminist anthropologists that examined the anthropology of work. They focused on the intersection of class, gender, and race in colonial settings as well as in contemporary capitalist, Third World and tribal societies (e.g. Etienne and Leacock 1980; Leacock and Safa 1986). By the early 1980s, they had clearly shown, for example, that labor markets were typically stratified by gender, race, and ethnicity; that gender relations were transformed as societies became increasingly enmeshed in tributary or capitalist social relations; and that appearance of gender inequities were integral aspects of class and state formation.

The Profession Reorganized, 1983–1993

In the fall of 1982, the AAA Executive Board presented a reorganization plan to the membership of the association. The impetus for the plan came from discussions between the AAA President and those of the cooperating organizations – e.g. the Society for American Archaeology (SAA) or the American Association of Physical

Anthropologists (AAPA) – about the increasingly impersonal nature of the annual meetings and about an IRS ruling which stated that the administrative services provided by the AAA to cooperating anthropological organizations were not tax-exempt. One aim of the plan was to allow the members to create a series of groups based on shared interests or region – such as humanistic anthropology, the anthropology of work, or the Central States Anthropological Association – which would elect officers and representatives to serve on a Council. The Council would share governance of the Association with an Executive Board whose members would be the presidents of cooperating organizations – e.g. the American Ethnological Society (AES) or the SAA – and the AAA officers elected by the members of the association; the implication of this was that cooperating organizations would relinquish their independent, corporate status in return for administrative services and representation on the Executive Board. A second aim was to enliven the annual meetings which would be organized by program chairs from each of the groups. A third aim was to give voice to the growing number of anthropologists who practiced their craft outside the academy (American Anthropological Association 1982).

The SAA withdrew in 1983 from further discussions about the proposed reorganization as the implications, financial and otherwise, of its loss of autonomy and corporate status became clear. Its Executive Board severed relations with the AAA and established an independent administrative office (Hymes 1983:2). The reorganization plan was subsequently approved in separate votes by members of the AAA and those of the AES in the fall of 1983. The adoption of the plan had a number of unintended consequences in the years that followed. For example, the number of interest groups proliferated rapidly and was ultimately capped in the early 1990s; the members of the Council felt subordinated by the Executive Board; the interest groups frequently felt themselves pitted against one another for resources – such as the number of panels they could organize for the annual meetings; and all of the groups objected to the costs of the administrative services provided by the AAA office. The adoption of the reorganization plan was ultimately divisive; it exacerbated divisions within the association and strained relations with the SAA and other organizations.

The reorganization plan also provided procedures that regulated the introduction of resolutions at the annual business meeting. Article XI, Section 4 of the proposed by-laws stipulated that

> New legislation or resolutions proposed by Members for consideration at the Annual Business Meeting must be received in writing by the Secretary of the Executive Board at least fifteen (15) days before the Annual Meeting to be placed on the agenda. . . . Resolutions passed at the Business Meeting shall be subject to a mail ballot of the Members (American Anthropological Association 1983:7).

The proposed by-law meant that it would take roughly a year to adopt any resolution introduced by a group of members. It was supported by individuals who wished to decant politics and ethics as legitimate concerns of the discipline's major professional organization. Its advocates were many of the same individuals who had supported the Mead Committee during the Thailand controversy a decade earlier (see Chapter 4). This group had long been angered by resolutions that were introduced by the Council of Marxist Anthropologists (CMA) and others at the business meetings and that were approved by those in attendance. These motions frequently dealt with politically sensitive topics – e.g. CIA recruitment, apartheid, and the massacres conducted by the Israeli army at Shatila and Sabra – that demanded timely responses. Open political discussion and resolutions from the floor that addressed important issues were effectively curbed when this proposal was adopted in the fall of 1983. Although the by-law was successfully challenged and amended in 1987, the AAA was effectively prevented from expressing opinions about what was happening in the world between 1984 and 1986 when it was in effect. By 1986, the business meeting had been reduced to a poorly attended, seemingly endless series of awards and reports.

The divide separating those anthropologists who believed the AAA should take principled stands on the issues of the day from those who preferred an apolitical, professional organization was mirrored by the subjects they wrote about and the theoretical frameworks they used. If the period from the mid-1970s through the early 1980s was characterized by a canter toward Marxist social thought, then the years from the mid-1980s onward were marked by simultaneous turns toward history and postmodernism. They also witnessed the emergence of a conscious self-awareness which viewed anthropology both as text and cultural critique.

In his 1988 Radcliffe-Brown Lecture to the British Academy, Marshall Sahlins (1989:2–3) was critical of

> the idea that the global expansion of Western capitalism, or the World System so-called, has made the colonized and "peripheral" peoples the passive objects of their own history and not its authors, and through tributary economic relations has turned their cultures into adulterated goods.

He proceeded to criticize the world systems theorists for not paying attention to the history of these peoples, for denying that they possessed their own laws of motion, and for claiming that they lacked any structure or system save those given to them by Western capitalist domination.

Sahlins reformulated the relation between people without history and the historical expansion of the capitalist world system as a cultural process. He wrote that

Western capitalism has loosed on the world enormous forces of production, coercion and destruction. Yet precisely because they cannot be resisted, the relations and goods of the larger system also take on meaningful places in local schemes of things. In the event, the historical changes in local society are also continuous with the superseded scheme, even as the new state of affairs acquires a cultural coherence of a distinct kind. So we shall have to examine how indigenous peoples struggle to integrate their experience of the world system in something that is logically and ontologically more inclusive: their own system of the world (Sahlins 1989:4).

The peoples without history who resided at different places on the periphery of the capitalist world system experienced its commodities and social relations differently and, initially at least, integrated them differently into their own practices and understandings of the world. From a slightly different perspective, the capitalist global economy was organized locally by the values of the indigenous communities. It was enmeshed differently in the various collectivities. In Sahlins's (1989:5) words, the "capitalist forces are realized in other forms and finalities, in exotic cultural logics far removed from the native-European commodity fetishism."

Sahlins, of course, was not the first to argue that attention must be paid to peoples living on the margins and in the interstices of the capitalist world. Eric Wolf (1982) had made the same point a few years earlier in his *Europe and the People without History*. However, Sahlins was gently critical of Wolf's work, remarking perceptively that it did not grant agency to collectivities on the periphery which "were drawn into the larger system to suffer its impact and become its agents" (Wolf 1982:23). The reason for this, he argued, was that Wolf – like many of the world systems theorists – had a reductive view of culture which saw it 'as a reflex of the 'mode of production,' a set of social appearances taken on by material forces that somehow possess their own instrumental rationality and necessity" (Sahlins 1989:3). Culture, in Sahlins's view, was more than a function of material circumstances; it was instead historically constituted as particular peoples went about satisfying their needs. It was a code "constructed in relation to pressures of the forces of nature – and typically also in relation to pressures of other societies" (Sahlins 1989:4).

Sahlins (1981) was concerned with the relation between structure and agency at those historical conjunctures in time when structural transformation occurred. In Marx's terms, he wanted to show how people made their own history under circumstances not of their own choice. In Sahlins's view, history was a cultural process. Change occurred when the relations among the oppositions in the cultural code were restructured. He buttressed this view with information derived from Hawaii in the late eighteenth century. Here, the behavior of the populace was shaped by a series of oppositions: man/woman, chief/commoner and *tabu* (ritually marked)/*noa* (ritually unmarked). When commoners, especially commoner women, consorted with Europeans, they transgressed the *tabus* established by the chiefs to protect their own relationships with the foreigners. This had a cascading effect that quickly led to modifications of other oppositions in the cultural code. While the meanings derived from the cultural code were transformed as the terms of the oppositions were altered, the code itself persisted in modified form.

Christine W. Gailey (b. 1950) was also interested in how peoples without history made their own histories. She too realized the importance of culture; however, she understood culture differently from Sahlins (Gailey 1983). In her view, Sahlins had adopted the "dominant ideology thesis" which asserted that the categories of the cultural code subsumed all meaning and ordered social relations. She argued instead for a more dialectical view of culture (Gailey 1987a, 1987b). In state-based societies, she maintained that

> the efforts . . . to legitimate rulership and class hierarchy through rituals and the idiom of kinship can be considered as an assertion. The politically dominant classes present their version of tradition as the culture, but among subject peoples, other meanings, other representations emerge or persist. . . . Thus, culture in state-based societies is not continuously created on a consensual basis; it is an arena of conflict. Where there is no open rebellion, there may be accommodation, an appearance of quietude. This does not mean that culture is thereby shared. If it were, there would be no need for the civil authorities or other nonproducing classes to sponsor a litany of ritual occasions, spectacles, or other forms of public indoctrination (Gailey 1987a:35–6).

In other words, culture was created spontaneously in contexts where states and ruling classes attempted to extend their control over production and reproduction and the subordinated classes and peoples resist their efforts. Culture – the meanings, values and practices that people continually renew and create to make the events and social relations of everyday life comprehensible – was one arena in which this dialectical process of class and state formation played itself out. While states attempted to organize dominant, universalizing, and homogenizing cultures, the members of subordinated groups renewed traditional cultural forms and created alternative, potentially oppositional cultures.[2]

Gailey's view of culture as a dialectic was well-received by historical archaeologists who were concerned with the social origins of inequality and its manifestation in the archaeological record (e.g. Paynter 1989; McGuire and Paynter 1991). It also resonated with the efforts of feminist anthropologists – notably Karen Brodkin Sacks (b. 1941) and Brackette F. Williams (b. 1951) – who were laying the foundations for exploring once again the linkages of class, gender, race, ethnicity, and nation (Brodkin Sacks 1989; Williams 1989).

Brodkin Sacks raised two questions: Were race and gender reducible in some way to class, or were "they separable and secondary dimensions of being in the context of theorizing social transformation" (Brodkin Sacks 1989:534)? The impetus for her questions came from the investigations of second-wave, socialist feminists who were concerned with women's unwaged labor; their efforts to theorize the domestic and community-based experiences of working-class women were responses to some Marxist and labor union studies that viewed class struggle almost exclusively in terms of struggles over control of the shop-floor. Brodkin Sacks focused her attention on social reproduction – i.e. how class structures were reproduced. She pointed out that the American working class had been organized hierarchically by gender, race and ethnicity since its inception. Wage differentials existed between men and women, between whites and non-whites, and between native English-speakers and immigrants.

From Brodkin Sack's perspective, the concept of social class was not a gender-neutral or race-neutral social category; it was instead a gendered, racially and ethnically specific concept. This meant that the class, racial, ethnic, and gender diversity in the United States was intimately related to the historical development of capitalism. It also implied that the categories themselves were cultural constructs that attempted to explain the existing social order rather than elements that were derived from some order imposed by the natural world. It indicated that social categories – such as bondsman, slave, Indian, Negro, or Italian-American – possessed historical specificity and attempted to address relations at particular moments (e.g. Epperson 1994; Gailey 1994; Patterson and Spencer 1994).

Williams (1989:401) noted that ethnicity – rather than class or race – had become in the 1970s a lightning rod for anthropologists who responded to decolonization by shifting their attention from the study of tribes, villages, and isolated communities to that of ethnic groups and nations. While many saw ethnicity as either a cultural or a situational phenomenon, a few viewed it as a relational phenomenon associated with the processes of class and state formation (e.g. Vincent 1974). Williams (1989: 428–9) suggested that

the ethnic aspect of any identity formation process, must be understood in relation to the societal production of enduring categorical distinctions and not simply in terms of individuals adopting and "shedding" particular manifestations of those categorical identities. . . . An adequate theory of ethnicity must account for the historical and contemporary ideological linkages among ethnicity and categorical aspects of identity formation processes in nation-states. Such a theory must help to reveal how the precepts of nationalism affect (a) how groups assess the amount of the "right blood" necessary to claim membership in the segmentary hierarchies of national society, (b) how the "bloods" of competing groups get into the mainstream of national society, and (c) how much cultural change is admissible before a group based on shared descent loses its distinctiveness.

Williams (1989:429–30) observed that the starting point for understanding the relationship between ethnicity and nationalism was to explore the "mythmaking and the material factors that motivate and rationalize its elements." In other words, how were the "impure" groups transformed or homogenized into a nation possessing particular characteristics such as a shared written or spoken language? She pointed out that the ideologies of nationalism and the subordinated subnational identities called ethnicity resulted from state-sponsored or promoted programs that called for the construction of myths that homogenized social and cultural diversity. Nation builders, in her view, were simultaneously mythmakers (see Chapter 1). These myths have taken myriad forms in different nation-states. For example, "real" Ecuadorians are committed to bringing Ecuador into the modern world of nation-states and are perceived as belonging to a mixed race that was created as a result of a history of miscegenation. In the United States, by contrast, race and ethnicity were differentiated as the Second World War loomed on the horizon and as the descendants of immigrants from Eastern Europe were subsumed into the dominant nationality and became white Americans in the process.

June Nash (b. 1927) among others launched studies of the articulation of working-class communities that were structured by race, gender, and ethnicity with a capitalist political economy that was being restructured by a new international division of labor, the deindustrialization of old industrial regions such as the Northeastern United States, and the shift away from the production of standardized, mass-produced commodities to customized goods (e.g. Nash 1983, 1989). Nash repeatedly pointed out that the political economic changes taking place in core industrial areas such as the United States had ramifications for peoples living on their peripheries. Cultural change and resistance were everyday features of societies on the margins that were experiencing economic development, structural adjustment, and human rights violations by repressive states (Nash 1976, 1993, 1995; Ong 1991).

While Gailey, Brodkin, Williams, and Nash to name only a few focused their attention on the dialectics of culture, class, gender, race, and ethnicity in state formative situations, others were influenced by Geertz's interpretive anthropology, by the hermeneutic turn in French phenomenology, by the rise of poststructuralism, by the ongoing relevance of the critical theory elaborated by the Frankfurt School, and by the growing prominence of literary critics such as Edward Said (b. 1935). In a nutshell, the proponents of these approaches believed that words were important. Words were how people perceived, thought, and talked about social life; people used words to construct social reality and to give meaning to cultural products such as a work of art or a piece of writing in contexts that were continually reconstituted with the help of words.

The linguistic turn in anglophone anthropology in the mid-1980s was simultaneously a postmodernist one which claimed that truth and morality among other things have no objective existence beyond how people think, talk, and write about them. There are no societies, no communities or objective realities waiting to be discovered. Social life, in this perspective, consists mainly of how people think about it, and they do this in diverse and changing ways from streams of ongoing conversation to abstract models, stories, and other representations.

The foundational texts of the genre were George E. Marcus (b. 1943) and Michael M. J. Fischer's (b. 1946) *Anthropology as Cultural Critique: An Experimental Moment in the Human Sciences*, James Clifford (b. 1945) and Marcus's *Writing Culture: The Poetics and Politics of Ethnography*, and Clifford's *The Predicament of Culture: Twentieth-Century Ethnography, Literature, and Art* (Marcus and Fischer 1986; Clifford and Marcus 1986; Clifford 1988). They asserted that what anthropologists wrote about others – i.e., how they represented the objects of their inquiries – often fueled dominant perceptions of non-Western peoples that maintained the uneven power relations existing between the industrial capitalist countries of the West and the rest of the world in the current "process of apparent global Westernization" (Marcus and Fischer 1986:1).

Marcus and Fischer (1986:3–4) argued that some of the new experimental strategies for writing ethnographies – e.g. the self-reflexive accounts of fieldworkers as actors in ethnographic encounters, descriptions of intersubjective interactions, or efforts to use non-traditional rhetorical forms – expressed "a new sensitivity to the difficulty of representing cultural differences, given current, almost overriding perceptions of the global homogenization of cultures." In their view, the distinctive method of anthropology and the core of the discipline itself was ethnography, which brought together the previously separate processes of data collecting and of analysis. Ethnography was

> a research process in which the anthropologist closely observes, records, and engages in the daily life of another culture – an experience labeled as the fieldwork method – and then writes accounts of this culture, emphasizing descriptive detail (Marcus and Fischer 1986:18).

Such an approach is underpinned by cultural relativism and by collapsing theory with the practice of writing and producing particular textual forms. In other words,

> [T]he hermeneutic or semiological form of the ethnographic text becomes an implicit theory of the social process described. ... Or, to put the problem from the point of view of postmodernism, writing practice is no longer estranged from theory; it is theory (Webster 1990:268).

Clifford's (1988) approach was different. He was concerned with the various literary forms that anthropologists used to establish their authority. He noted that ethnographers established their authority with two moves: initially asserting their first-hand experience with a culture – the "I was there" move – and then describing that culture without reference to the effects their presence might have had on the people in question or on themselves. Thus, ethnographers were "always caught up with the invention, not the representation, of cultures" (Clifford 1986:10). As a result, when Clifford (1988:277–346) described a legal case in which the Mashpee Wampanoag Tribal Council sued in federal court for possession of 16,000 acres on Cape Cod, he claimed that the identity of the Mashpee was constituted – i.e. invented – by the commentaries contained in trial transcripts and interviews with witnesses for the defense. This must have come as a surprise to the Mashpee who brought the suit in the first place! An additional problem with his approach was that Clifford did not distinguish testimony given for the Mashpee from that given for the defendant. As anyone who has watched an episode of "Judge Judy" on television knows, plaintiffs and defendants always have different points of view and interests.

By equating theory with the practice of writing, Marcus and Fischer, on the one hand, and Clifford, on the other, avoid coming to grips in serious ways with the insights of feminist anthropologists. While they questioned the power relations that traditionally existed between anthropologists and the "other," they did not deal adequately with feminists and anthropologists who wrote from gender and class positions or subjectivities that were different from their own. As a result, many feminist anthropologists were critical of the postmodern turn in anthropology, especially of Clifford's (1986:20–1) claim that "feminist ethnography has focused either on setting the record straight about women or revising anthropological categories . . . [and] has not produced either unconventional forms of writing or a developed reflection on ethnographic textuality as such." Besides being factually incorrect, Clifford's statement also blurred the distinctions that existed between feminists who had adopted different theoretical perspectives (Mascia-Lees, Sharpe, and Cohen 1989).

Marcus and Fischer (1986:82) argued that theoretical perspectives such as Marxism "must be translated by ethnographic inquiry into cultural terms and grounded in everyday life." This, of course, echoed the concerns of the Frankfurt School from the 1930s onward as well as the writings of a number of anthropologists who eschewed neither foundational theories such as Marxism nor culture; they tended to view modes of production as the skeleton of everyday life, and culture as its flesh and blood (e.g. Diamond 1974; Levine 1979).

One issue brought to the fore by the postmodern anthropologists was the conceptual difference between the individual and the subject. One commentator described the difference in the following way:

> Essentially, the term individual has the ideological weight of an entity that has a coherence, a stability, and a consciousness that transcends – gives meaning to – its cultural environment as a primary active force. . . . By its very nomenclature, the term subject denotes an entity that is less in charge of its destiny, but that is constituted by various cultural determinations rather than being constitutive of them. The subject in this sense is constructed, not only by these "outside" cultural forces or discourses, but

also by forces within itself that it cannot control. I have in mind here the Freudian idea of the unconscious and Lacan's linguistic revision, wherein the individual is subject to the "other's" discourse (Sullivan 1990:243).

The constitution of the subject and of subjectivities was, of course, the problem that occupied French philosopher and social critic Michel Foucault (1927–84) at different moments in his career (e.g. Foucault 1966/1973:xiv, 387). It should come as no surprise that Paul Rabinow (b. 1944) – an early commentator on the postmodern trend in American anthropology – was also a leading exponent and interpreter of Foucauldian social thought in the United States (e.g. Dreyfus and Rabinow 1982; Foucault 1994/1997; Rabinow 1989). Studies of subjectivity – the cultural construction of self and other – became increasingly frequent from the late 1980s onward (Lock 1993).

In sum, postmodern anthropology was rooted in a curious mixture of romantic and neoliberal thought. Its proponents displayed the sentimental edge of Romanticism rather than its critical capacity when they lamented the subordinated positions of Third World peoples in global power relations. They adopted the ahistorical central tenet of neoliberalism when they argued that identities were created not in social relations but rather in the exchange of words and ideas between peoples occupying different places in the hierarchy of power. Its proponents stressed cultural differences at the expense of underlining structural and cultural similarities. At the same time, they also accepted uncritically the idea that the world was becoming homogenized by the global Westernization resulting from computers and telecommunications, from the expansion of the global market in which social relations and identities were forged, and from the increased mobility of people who moved from one country to another and brought pieces of their cultures with them. The postmodernists dismissed the possibility of knowing past societies, because the past does not exist independently of historians and their rhetorical use of language as they construct narratives to represent it.

Furthermore, the postmodern anthropologists' claim that ethnography was the core of the discipline was divisive and had the potential to undermine the partnership between cultural or social anthropologists on the one hand, and their colleagues in archaeology, linguistics, and biological anthropology on the other. It was rooted in the ultimately flawed ideas that also underpinned the formation of Harvard's Department of Social Relations after the Second World War. In the mid-1990s, such views underwrote the balkanization of anthropology departments at Berkeley and Stanford and fueled acrimonious debates within the American Anthropological Association as the organization sought to reassert the unity of the profession.[3] Thus, the fields of reference for critique and politics mentioned in the titles of the postmodernists' books were not imperialism, colonialism, or capitalism but rather what was happening in university departments and in the profession (e.g. Rabinow

1985:10–12). By viewing identities as texts that were created by intersubjective communication, the postmodernists decanted concerns about class politics and struggle
from anthropology at a time when states around the world were becoming increasingly repressive and their neoliberal policies allowed transnational corporations
to suck the life out of workers, peasants, and tribal peoples.

Anthropology and Globalization after 1994

By the mid-1990s, globalization had become not only a fashionable term, a substitute
for the word "imperialism," but also a central issue for American anthropologists.
Today, globalization is used in three different ways to refer to: (1) "a state of international economic integration and interdependence"; (2) the expansion since the
1970s of the international flows of goods, factors of production, and finance; and
(3) the integration of economic interdependence and economic flows through
market-based intercourse (DeMartino 2000:2). In the first sense, globalization is
synonymous with colonialism and imperialism – processes that were already in
evidence by the end of the seventeenth century. The second meaning recognizes the
greater financial and trade integration that existed during the middle third of the
twentieth century and tacitly acknowledges that similar levels existed from the 1890s
through the 1920s. The third meaning focuses on the novelty of the current situation
but does not necessarily posit the emergence of a new stage of international capitalism associated with the cultural logic of postmodernity (Patterson 1999b:151–84).

Since globalization has a number of different meanings, let us briefly consider
what it is not. Most neoliberal boosters of globalism have argued that a free market
enveloping the whole world began to emerge in the 1970s and 1980s as a result of
the spread of the modern technologies of industrial production and of communication. They also presumed that the "economic life of every nation . . . [could] be
refashioned in the image of the American free market" (Gray 1998:4). They further
presumed that, as these nations modernized, they would adopt Western liberal democracy and values and would consume increasing quantities and varieties of Western
goods. As the world's nations were enmeshed and increasingly integrated into the
global economy, their cultures would converge toward that of the United States, and
the world's cultural diversity would be diminished by capitalist modernization and
the homogenization of consumption.

Conservative commentators on the idea of global capitalism, such as John Gray
(b. 1948), have pointed out that globalization was not the end-product of free market
forces and that it did not imply convergence, the homogenization of the world's
cultures, or even the adoption of American-style liberal democracy. They have
recognized, like the Marxists, that capital flowed across boundaries precisely
because of the differences that existed between localities, nations, and regions,
and that the process of globalization has accentuated rather than diminished uneven

development. They have also recognized that nations were integrated in varying degrees and in different ways into an increasingly internationalized capitalist economy dominated by Japan, the United States, and Western Europe. As a result, the free market was spawning new types of capitalism at the same time as it was propagating new types of political regimes (Gray 1998).

Radical commentators on the concept of globalization – such as economists Paul Sweezy (b. 1910) or Samir Amin (b. 1931) – have argued that it masks imperialism and the uneven development of capitalism, and that the processes involved in globalization were not new to the late twentieth century. This shield makes it difficult to study the historically specific processes that have produced and are producing that unevenness, and obscures the ways in which the inhabitants of localities and regions have responded to those circumstances (Sweezy 1997). Amin (1997:67) has pointed out that globalization has involved the crystallization of capitalist production around regional growth poles. As a result, nations on the periphery – i.e., the Third World reconceptualized as the South – have different possibilities for change and development from those in the industrial core areas. Globalization creates difficulties for countries on the periphery, because these states have different capacities to isolate capital and their citizens from the effects of being integrated into a world capitalist system. Like their conservative contemporaries, the radical commentators also recognized that alternatives to neoliberal policies were possible and desirable.

From the mid-1990s onward, George Marcus, Michael Fischer, and Michael Kearney (b. 1937) among others published synthetic articles dealing with the processes of globalization (Fischer 1999; Kearney 1995; Marcus 1995). Their essays dealt in different ways with the fact that people are very mobile; each year, millions of them cross national boundaries in search of work, to sample culture in museums, or to find pleasure in theme parks. They were concerned with how to comprehend people who have one set of social relations in their local communities and another set of relations and understandings after they have moved to a different locality in the capitalist world system.

Marcus (1995:95) described the problem in methodological terms:

> Ethnography moves from the conventional single-site location, contextualized by macro-constructions of a larger social order, such as the capitalist world system, to multiple sites of observation and participation that cross-cut dichotomies such as the "local" and the "global," the "lifeworld" and the "system."

He contrasted two modes of ethnographic inquiry. The first was the traditional method that involved observations at a single site and developed by other means its context in the world system. The second, which self-consciously built on "the intellectual capital of postmodernism," arose in part from interdisciplinary investigations – such as feminist, media, or cultural studies. Its practitioners believed that the world system is not the theoretically constituted holistic frame that gives context to the contemporary study of peoples or local subjects closely observed by ethnographers, but becomes, in a piecemeal way, integral to and embedded in discontinuous, multi-sited objects of study. Cultural logics so much sought . . . are always multiply produced, and any ethnographic account of these logics finds that they are at least partly constituted within sites of the so-called system (i.e. modern interlocking institutions of media, markets, states, industries, universities – the world of elites, experts, and middle classes). Strategies of quite literally following connections, associations, and putative relationships are thus at the very heart of designing multi-sited ethnographic research (Marcus 1995:97).

An important implication of multi-sited ethnography, according to Marcus (1995:101), is that anthropologists will have to give up their exclusive focus on "subaltern subjects positioned by systemic domination" and to consider in addition other sites of cultural production in which questions of resistance and accommodation would be "subordinated to different sorts of questions about the shape of systemic processes themselves and complicities with these processes among variously positioned subjects." Such a perspective would allow ethnographers, for example, to see how migrants became members of diasporic communities or how things shifted from resources to gifts to commodities within the world system.

Fischer (1999) indicated that anthropologists had to confront a number of challenges in the era of the capitalist world system glossed variously as late modernity, postmodernity, postindustrial society, knowledge society, or information society. At a methodological level, these challenges included the techniques of multi-sited ethnography for assessing different points in widespread processes; the ways in which multivocal texts map the situatedness of knowledge; and "acknowledging that anthropological representations are interventions within a stream of representations, mediations, and unequally inflected discourses competing for hegemonic control" (Fischer 1999:455). It was important for anthropologists to confront the challenges in a milieu shaped by the importance of science and technology, the effects of decolonization and the reconstruction of societies after trauma, and the new role played by electronic and visual media. Like Marcus, Fischer advocated making use of the insights gained in new fields such as cultural studies or social studies of science. Part of his reasoning was an effort to connect with the theory and methods of American anthropologists who worked either in other fields or outside the academy altogether.

Marcus and Fischer were concerned with the activities of anthropologists who – along with experts, elites and middle classes – were active agents in the world system and constructed representations of that system. Their representations were constituted in light of their own experiences, position, and understandings of the system; their representations interwove with those of individuals who had the same or different subjectivities. Knowledge of the system as a whole was constituted on the basis of ongoing debates among individuals with different situated knowledges and different positions in a hierarchy of power relations.

Marcus and Fischer also pointed out correctly that ethnogenesis occurred when the members of communities, including American anthropologists, had to confront new circumstances. What they failed to stress sufficiently was that the ethnogenetic processes and circumstances encountered by one community might be quite different from those encountered by others. For example, the members of the rising and declining fractions of the American middle class have had quite different experiences in the 1990s from those of their contemporaries in Rwanda or Kosovo. Thus it is essential, I believe, to distinguish the experiences of an upper-class woman from Japan who was touring New York from those of a poor, teenage girl from a Thai village who was sold into the sex trade in the Middle East.

Marcus and Fischer acknowledge the importance of class structures and then turn away from them, opting instead to analyze identity politics rather than class struggle. In another context, Leith Mullings (b. 1945) has written that the postmodernist concern with culture, identity politics, and new social movements

> is in part a reaction to the failures of liberal integration; in part a consequence of the state-sponsored destruction of the left; and in part a challenge to apologists for inequality who attribute the cause of increasing poverty to the culture [and biology] of African Americans [and other peoples of color] (Mullings 1994/1997:189).

If the goal of anthropology is to examine the various socio-economic and political factors that have shaped the practice of anthropology in the United States, then adopting the theoretical pluralism advocated by some feminist writers becomes useful in this regard (e.g. Harding 1986:136–62, 1991). Sandra Harding and others have argued that constructivist critiques, opposed to other viewpoints, provide space for developing new understandings of the discipline, its often unstated premises, and its socio-economic and political foundations. The common thread of their critical analyses

> is a concern to articulate an account of knowledge production that recognizes its own contingency and standpoint specificity, that repudiates any quest for a unitary ("master") narrative and any faith in context-transcendent "foundations," and that yet resists the implication that any comparison or judgment of credibility is irreducibly arbitrary, that "anything goes" (Wylie 1996:270).

The advantage of such constructivist critiques is that they do not conflate issues or problems emerging from the analysis of the global system with those that arise from particular theoretical foundations or with the practice of anthropology in a particular national context. At the same time, they afford opportunities to examine the interplay between theory and practice on the one hand and analyses of the capitalist world system on the other. Such critiques do not have to separate contemporary practices and interpretations from historical development. They do not have to treat the interpretations of anthropologists as a literary genre. They do not have to accept claims about the assets and/or liabilities of certain transcendental analytical categories. They do not have to accept claims that assert that, since meaning is culturally constructed, different cultures, even those in the same society, are incommensurate, and certainly cannot be understood by a Western observer, even one skilled in the art of interpretation. They do not have to accept the claim that, since all knowledge is subjective, all efforts to discover objective knowledge about the current capitalist system are doomed to fail.

Kearney was also concerned with the movement of people, capital, commodities, information, and symbols in global and transnational spaces. However, he eschewed the relativist standpoint adopted by Marcus and Fischer, and argued instead that it was necessary to pay attention to the relations and processes that take place within and transcend nation-states, because studies that were exclusively "limited to local processes, identities and units of analysis yield[ed] an incomplete understanding of the local" (Kearney 1995:548). He advocated focusing on the political economic underpinnings of the movement of people and things. In doing so, he pointed out the importance of distinguishing between the global and the transnational aspects of the processes involved. In his view, global processes were decentered from particular national spaces, whereas transnational processes occurred in and emanated from particular nation-states. Globalization implies "more abstract, less institutionalized, and less intentional processes occurring without reference to nations," whereas the term "transnational" focuses attention on "the cultural and political projects of nation-states as they vie for hegemony in relations with other nation-states, with their citizens and 'aliens'." Globalization concentrates on the "universal and impersonal" whereas transnationalism draws attention to the "political and ideological dimensions" of the processes (Kearney 1995:548–9). Kearney recognized that different states – e.g. the United States and Mexico – have different positions and play different roles in the global political economy.

Kearney's perspective also recognizes that agency is not restricted to experts, elites, and middle classes. In his view, members of the lower classes are also active agents who strive to shape their own destinies and to overcome the structural limitations imposed by local manifestations of global capitalism. This is an important distinction between his work and that of others on the one hand, and on the other that of Marcus and Fischer, who locate the motors of social and cultural change in the thoughts, understandings, and actions of the experts, elites, and middle classes.

The "political economic" perspective advocated by Kearney and other anthropologists opens up possibilities for examining the myriad processes that accompany transnationalism and globalization and that occur variously and differently at local, national, and transnational levels. A number of anthropologists have considered the relationship between nationalist projects of subject making and capitalist political economy. Karen Brodkin (Sacks) (2000), for example, points to the articulation in the United States of the capitalists' project of creating a labor force and various ethnoracial projects in which workers are simultaneously constituted as national subjects, men and women, native and foreign, and white or colored.

Aihwa Ong and Donald Nonini take a slightly different tack and look at the activities of relations of Chinese transnational capitalists in the Asia Pacific. They suggest that two variants of capitalism are associated with Chinese transnationalism:

> In one, Chinese transnational capitalists act out flexible strategies of accumulation in networks that cut across political borders and are linked through second-tier global cities. . . . These overlapping business, social, and kinship networks stitch together dynamic productive, financial, and marketing regions that are not contained by a single nation-state or subject to its influence.
>
> In the other, Chinese transnational capitalists flourish not only outside "the striated space of the nation-state" . . . but also within it, aligned closely to non-Chinese (and to a lesser extent, Chinese) state bureaucratic elites in joint ventures with state capital. . . . [M]uch of the new capitalism of the Asia Pacific is state-driven and state-sponsored, and Chinese trans]national capitalists, like those in other parts of the world, represent forces that nation-states can deploy and discipline to strengthen themselves (Ong and Nonini 1997:323–4).

Lynn Stephen (b. 1956) takes a third tack in her analyses of the interplay of class, local forms of exploitation, and the reconstruction of ethnic and national identity in Chiapas and Oaxaca in southern Mexico during the 1990s (Stephen 1997a, 1997b). The privatization of land fomented by NAFTA and the Zapatista rebellion form the backdrop of her discussions. Her focus is on the ways that peasants and rural proletarians are making their own history and recasting ethnic and national identities in contexts shaped by heightened state repression and armed resistance to its interventions. Peasants and rural proletarians from ethnic groups whose relations were sometimes antagonistic as recently as a decade or so ago, because they were pitted against one another by the ruling classes of the region and the state, now find themselves having similar experiences and common cause against their oppressors.

Anthropologists employing broadly political-economic perspectives have also begun to criticize conventional theories of the state which stress legitimacy and political power and see it as a set of institutions that can make and enforce laws. Carole Nagengast (b. 1942), for instance, has raised questions about the interrelations of violence, terrorism, the crisis of the state, and human rights (Nagengast 1994). She rightly pointed to the fragility of states. She wrote that

> The ideal state is one in which the illusion of a single nation-state is created and maintained and in which resistance is managed so that profound social upheaval, separatist activity, revolution, and *coups d'état* are unthinkable for most people most of the time. The state

thus attempts to ensure conformity to encompassing unitary images through diverse cultural forms and an array of institutions and activities that, taken together, help to determine the range of available social, political, ethnic, and national identities. . . .

The crisis of the contemporary state springs from its differentially successful monopolization of power and the contradiction between it and the demands of peripheralized people(s) who through resistance have created new subject positions that challenge fundamentally the definitions of who and what ought to be repressed. . . . When consensus fails, ethnic or political opposition, which is otherwise suppressed or subtle, becomes overt. The state, of course, cannot allow this to happen (Nagengast 1994:109–10).

Nagengast proceeds to point out that there was a veritable explosion of violence in the 1990s and a concomitant rise in human-rights abuses, as nation-states disintegrated or as states lent their force of arms to one side or another in these conflicts. Violence, in this perspective, is not a characteristic that is present or absent in some social group but rather is situated within the practices, discourses and ideologies that states deploy differentially within social and political relations to buttress themselves and maintain power (Nagengast 1994:111).

A political-economic perspective sensitive to culture both as an integral aspect of ethnogenesis and as an arena of class struggle has also underpinned studies concerned with a variety of issues. These include, for example, the formation of ethnic and national identities (Verdery 1991), revolutionary movements (Collier 1999), the state repression of indigenous peoples (Lee 1993), the position of indigenous peoples at the end of the millennium (Lee 2000), and the formation of transnational border communities (Vélez-Ibáñez 1996).

Discussion

The anthropological profession was feminized from the late 1960s onward. According to the American Anthropological Association's *Guide to Graduate Departments in Anthropology* which has been published annually since 1965, both the percentage and absolute number of women receiving doctorates have increased steadily. In the mid-1960s, less than a third of the 120 or so recipients of the Ph.D. degrees awarded each year in anthropology were women. By the early 1970s, roughly a third of the 300 or so individuals who received doctorates each year were women. By the late 1980s, women received about 45 percent of the 380 doctorates awarded each year. By the late 1990s, women were receiving about 55 percent of the 480 or so doctorates awarded annually. Furthermore, the number of women elected to the presidency of the AAA increased dramatically during the last three decades of the twentieth century, and the Association's policy is now for the presidency to alternate between men and women.[4]

The employment patterns of anthropologists during the last quarter of the twentieth century were more similar to those of the period from 1930 to 1945 than to the ones that prevailed from *c.* 1950 to 1975 when the profession's center of gravity was situated solidly in the academy. Today, anthropologists are employed in a variety of positions in the public sector, and their activities are potentially less sheltered from the problems of everyday life than are those of their contemporaries who toil in colleges and universities. Their jobs require that these applied anthropologists deal with issues ranging from curricular reform in elementary schools to participation in a national initiative sponsored by the Congressional Black Caucus and the Surgeon General's Office of HIV/AIDS Policy "to develop a rapid response to the AIDs crisis in ethnic minority communities" and in community-based health, advocacy, education, and service groups concerned with improving the health and well-being of urban and rural poor folks (Singer 2000).

One consequence of anthropology's growing involvement in the everyday life of communities at home and abroad is that announcements of its imminent demise are probably premature. Moreover, the idea that anthropologists study exotic peoples – a view promoted by the media and by some practitioners – must also be called into question. For more than a century, American anthropologists have addressed the pressing issues of the day. As you will recall, James Mooney provided congressional testimony supporting the rights of American Indians; Franz Boas's publications on the issues of immigration, race, and racism from *c.* 1890 to 1930 were probably more numerous than those dealing with the Northwest Coast; and Margaret Mead's reputation as a public intellectual rested as much on her monthly articles in *Redbook* which addressed the concerns of its readers (and were ridiculed by some of her contemporaries) as it did on her research in Samoa and New Guinea.

The discipline's longstanding concern with the activities that shape social life in groups, with how people communicate, and with the material evidence for the social and biological history of communities will undoubtedly persist as well. It is less certain, however, that the organizational structure of anthropology training programs will continue in their current form. The idea that anthropology was divided into four subfields – cultural anthropology, linguistics, archaeology, and biology anthropology – gained currency from the mid-1950s onward. In the process, discussions of the interconnections of the subfields became less frequent or more superficial, and the holistic perspective of the discipline became steadily more tenuous. At the same time, the amount of technical knowledge required in each of the subfields increased so that both students and professionals had less time or inclination to relate this information to what was happening elsewhere in the discipline or in related fields of inquiry.

In many training programs today, both students and teachers pay lip service to or have only dim recollections of the unity of the discipline. Students take a minimal number of courses outside their field of specialization, and professors rarely teach anything beyond their speciality. Such programs resemble the missile launch sites of the 1980s: Students enter one of four thoroughly insulated, self-sufficient silos and leave at some later time with little or no knowledge of and contact with what is happening in the other silos. As a consequence, the universities are training specialists who know more and more about less and less. This is unfortunate, particularly at a time when the public clamors less for technically specialized information and more for new perspectives and syntheses of information that address both ethical concerns and the pressing issues confronting the human community in this time of crisis.

Notes

1. The new archaeology which crystallized in the mid-1960s argued that it was necessary to move beyond the empiricism of the traditional aims and practices of American archaeologists. It was essential from the perspective of its proponents to examine the theoretical concepts and methodological underpinnings of the discipline. The rise of the new archaeology coincided with the rise of cultural resource management archaeology and the appearance of federal, state, and local regulations requiring easily understood, comparable, and hence relatively standardized statements about the significance of archaeological resources (Patterson 1995:106–19).
2. In a related way, Patterson (1988) discussed the creation of culture in prestate or nonstate societies.
3. By the mid-1990s, many AAA members were dissatisfied with the organization and were skeptical about its ability to represent "anthropology as the discipline that studies humankind in all its aspects, through archaeological, biological, ethnological and linguistic research; and to foster the use of anthropological knowledge in addressing human problems" (American Anthropological Association 1998:1). The structure of governance, the proliferation of sections composed mainly of sociocultural anthropologists, a perceived lack of representation, and the fact that a majority of the new Ph.D.s were employed outside the academy were four concerns expressed in a membership survey (Moses 1997). This coincided with widespread dissatisfaction, especially among the members of the Archaeology and General Anthropology Divisions, over the editorial policies and content of the *American Anthropologist* in the mid-1990s during the editorship of Dennis and Barbara Tedlock (Tedlock and Tedlock 1994).
4. This policy was initiated in the late 1980s to acknowledge the overwhelmingly high probability that an election in which the candidates were a man and a woman would yield a woman president.

Bibliography

Aarseff, Hans 1982. *From Locke to Saussure: Essays on the Study of Language and Intellectual History*. Minneapolis, MN: University of Minnesota Press.

Aarseff, Hans 1983. *The Study of Language in England, 1780–1860*. Minneapolis, MN: University of Minnesota Press.

Aberle, David F. 1960. The Influence of Linguistics on Early Culture and Personality Theory. In *Essays in the Science of Culture in Honor of Leslie A. White*, edited by Gertrude E. Dole and Robert L. Carneiro. New York: Thomas Y. Crowell, pp. 1–29.

Adams, Robert McC. 1956. Some Hypotheses on the Development of Early Civilization. *American Antiquity*, vol. XXI, no. 3, pp. 227–32. Salt Lake City.

Adams, Robert McC. 1960. Early Civilizations, Subsistence, and Environment. In *City Invincible: A Symposium on Urbanization and Cultural Development in the Ancient Near East*, edited by Carl H. Kraeling and Robert M. Adams. Chicago, IL: University of Chicago Press, pp. 269–95.

Adams, Robert McC. 1966. *The Evolution of Urban Society: Early Mesopotamia and Prehispanic Mexico*. Chicago, IL: Aldine.

Agassiz, Louis 1850. The Diversity of Origin of the Human Races. *Christian Examiner*, vol. 99, pp. 110–45. Boston.

Agassiz, Louis 1854. Sketch of the Natural Provinces of the Animal World and Their Relation to the Different Types of Man. In *Types of Mankind: Or Ethnological Researches, Based upon the Ancient Monuments, Paintings, Sculptures, and Crania of the Races, and upon Their Natural, Geographical, Philological, and Biblical History*, by Josiah C. Nott and George R. Gliddon, pp. lviii–lxxvii. Philadelphia, PA: Lippincott, Grambo.

Allen, Garland E. 1976. Genetics, Eugenics and Society: Internalists and Externalists in Contemporary History of Science. *Social Studies of Science*, vol. 6, no. 1, pp. 105–22. London.

Allen, Garland E. 1983. The Misuse of Biological Hierarchies: The American Eugenics Movement, 1900–1940. *History and Philosophy of the Life Sciences*, vol. 5, no. 2, pp. 105–28. Naples.

Allen, Garland E. 1986. The Eugenics Record Office at Cold Spring Harbor, 1910–1940: An Essay in Institutional History. *Osiris*, vol. 2, pp. 225–64. Philadelphia.

Allen, Garland E. 1987. The Role of Expert in Scientific Controversy. *In Scientific Controversies: Case Studies in the Resolution and Closure of Disputes in Science and Technology*, edited by H. Tristram Engelhardt, Jr. and Arthur L. Caplan, pp. 169–202. Cambridge, UK: Cambridge University Press.

American Anthropological Association 1942. Proceedings of the American Anthropological Association for the Year Ending December, 1941. *American Anthropologist*, vol. 44, no. 2, pp. 281–9. Menasha.

American Anthropological Association 1947. Proceedings of the American Anthropological Association for the Year Ending December 1946. *American Anthropologist*, vol. 49, no. 2, pp. 346–71. Menasha.

American Anthropological Association 1982. Adapting to Survive: A Proposal for the Reorganization of the American Anthropological Association. *Anthropology Newsletter*, vol. 23, no. 7, October, pp. 4–6. Washington.

American Anthropological Association 1983. Draft By-Laws of the American Anthropological Association. *Anthropology Newsletter*, vol. 24, no. 2, pp. 5–7. Washington.

American Anthropological Association 1998. Reorganization Plan Provides Framework for the Future. *Anthropology Newsletter*, vol. 39, no. 4, pp. 1, 6–7. Arlington.

Amin, Samir 1997. *Capitalism in the Age of Globalization: The Management of Contemporary Society*. London, UK: Zed Books.

Andresen, Julie T. 1990. *Linguistics in America, 1769–1924: A Critical History*. London, UK: Routledge.

Asad, Talal, editor 1973. *Anthropology and the Colonial Encounter*. Atlantic Highlands, NJ: Humanities Press.

Atwater, Caleb 1820. *Description of the Antiquities Discovered in the State of Ohio and Other Western States*. Archaeologia Americana: Transactions and Collections of the American Antiquarian Society, vol. 1, pp. 105–267. Worcester.

Babb, Florence E. 1976. *The Development of Sexual Inequality in Vicos, Peru*. Special Studies Series, Council on International Studies, State University of New York at Buffalo. Buffalo.

Baber, Willie 1999. St. Clair Drake: Scholar and Activist. In *African-American Pioneers in Anthropology*, edited by Ira E. Harrison and Faye V. Harrison, pp. 191–212. Urbana, IL: University of Illinois Press.

Baker, Lee D. 1998. *From Savage to Negro: Anthropology and the Construction of Race, 1896–1954*. Berkeley, CA: University of California Press.

Baritz, Loren 1960. *The Servants of Power: A History of the Use of Social Science in America*. Westport, CT: Greenwood Publishers.

Barkan, Elazar 1992. *The Retreat of Scientific Racism: Changing Concepts of Race in Britain and the United States between the World Wars*. Cambridge, UK: Cambridge University Press.

Barkan, Elazar 1996. The Politics of the Science of Race: Ashley Montagu and UNESCO's "Anti-Racist Declarations." In *Race and Other Misadventurers: Essays in Honor of Ashley Montagu in His Ninetieth Year*, edited by Larry T.

Reynolds and Leonard Lieberman, pp. 96–105. Dix Hills, NY: General Hall, Publishers.

Baron, Dennis E. 1982. *Grammar and Good Taste: Reforming the American Language*. New Haven, CT: Yale University Press.

Barton, Benjamin Smith 1798/1976. *New Views of the Origin of the Tribes and Nations of America*. Millwood, NY: Kraus Reprint.

Barton, Benjamin Smith 1803/1959. Ethnological Information Desired. In *Original Journals of the Lewis and Clark Expedition, 1804–1806*, edited by Reuben G. Thwaites, vol. 7, pp. 283–87. New York: Antiquarian Press.

Bashkow, Ira 1991. The Dynamics of Rapport in a Colonial Situation: David Schneider's Fieldwork on the Islands of Yap. In *Colonial Situations: Essays on the Contextualization of Ethnographic Knowledge*, edited by George W. Stocking, Jr. History of Anthropology, vol. 7, pp. 170–242. Madison, WI: University of Wisconsin Press.

Bauer, Raymond A., Alex Inkeles, and Clyde Kluckhohn 1956. *How the Soviet System Works*. Cambridge, MA: Harvard University Press.

Beardsley, Edward H. 1973. The American Social Scientist as Social Activist: Franz Boas, Burt G. Wilder, and the Cause of Racial Justice, 1900–1915. *Isis*, vol. 64, no. 221, pp. 50–66. Philadelphia.

Beardsley, Richard, Betty J. Meggers, Preston Holder, Alex D. Krieger, John B. Rinaldo, and Paul Kutsche 1956. Functional and Evolutionary Implications of Community Patterning. In *Seminars in Archaeology: 1955*, edited by Robert Wauchope. Society for American Archaeology Memoir, no. 11, pp. 129–57. Salt Lake City.

Bell, Daniel 1960/1988. *The End of Ideology*. Cambridge, MA: Harvard University Press.

Benedict, Ruth 1930. Psychological Types in the Cultures of the Southwest. *Proceedings of the Twenty-Third International Congress of Americanists Held at New York, September 17–22, 1928*, pp. 572–81. Lancaster, PA: Science Press Printing Company.

Benedict, Ruth 1932. Configurations of Culture in North America. *American Anthropologist*, vol. 34, no. 1, pp. 1–27. Lancaster.

Benedict, Ruth 1934/1989. *Patterns of Culture*. Boston, MA: Houghton Mifflin Company.

Benedict, Ruth 1940. *Race: Science and Politics*. New York: Modern Age Books.

Benedict, Ruth 1946. *The Chrysanthemum and the Sword: Patterns of Japanese Culture*. New York: Houghton Mifflin.

Benedict, Ruth and Mildred Ellis 1942 *Race and Cultural Relations: America's Answer to the Myth of the Master Race*. New York: National Association of Secondary School Principals and National Council for Social Sciences.

Benedict, Ruth and Gene Weltfish 1943. *The Races of Mankind*. New York: Public Affairs Committee.

Bennett, Wendell C. 1947. *The Ethnogeographic Board*. Smithonsian Miscellaneous Collection, vol. 107, no. 1. Washington.

Bennett, Wendell C., editor 1948. *A Reappraisal of Peruvian Archaeology*. Society for American Archaeology Memoir, no. 4. Salt Lake City.

Berman, Edward H. 1983. *The Influence of the Carnegie, Ford, and Rockefeller Foundations on American Foreign Policy: The Ideology of Philanthropy*. Albany, NY: State University of New York Press.

Bernstein, Henry 1972. Breakdowns of Modernization. *Journal of Development Studies*, vol. 8, no. 4, pp. 309–18. London.

Berreman, Gerald D. 1991. Ethics versus "Realism" in Anthropology. In *Ethics and the Profession of Anthropology: Dialogue for a New Era*, edited by Carolyn Fluehr-Lobban, pp. 36–71. Philadelphia, PA: University of Pennsylvania Press.

Bidney, David 1968. Cultural Relativism. In *International Encyclopedia of the Social Sciences*, edited by David L. Sills, vol. 3, pp. 543–7. New York: The Macmillan Company and the Free Press.

Bieder, Robert E. 1980. Scientific Attitudes toward Indian Mixed-Bloods in Early Nineteenth Century America. *Journal of Ethnic Studies*, vol. 8, no. 2, pp. 17–30. Bellingham.

Bieder, Robert E. 1986. *Science Encounters the Indian, 1820–1880: The Early Years of American Ethnology*. Norman OK: University of Oklahoma Press.

Bieder, Robert E. and Thomas G. Tax 1976. From Ethnologists to Anthropologists: A Brief History of the American Ethnological Society. In *American Anthropology: The Early Years*, edited by John V. Murra. 1974 Proceedings of the American Ethnological Society, pp. 11–22. St. Paul, MN: West Publishing Company.

Blackburn, Robin 1972. *Ideology in Social Science: Readings in Critical Social Theory*. Glasgow, UK: Fontana/Collins.

Blanchard, David 1979. Beyond Empathy: The Emergence of an Action Anthropology in the Life and Career of Sol Tax. In *Currents in Anthropology: Essays in Honor of Sol Tax*, edited by Robert Hinshaw, pp. 419–44. The Hague: Mouton Publishers.

Blom, Franz 1936. Introduction. In A Visit to Quirigua, by Carl Scherzer. *Maya Research*, vol. III, no. 1, pp. 1–2. New Orleans.

Bloomfield, Leonard 1925. Why a Linguistics Society? *Language*, vol. 1, no. 1, pp. 1–5. Menasha.

Bloomfield, Leonard 1926. A Set of Postulates for the Science of Language. *Language*, vol. 2, no. 2, pp. 153–64. Menasha.

Blumenbach, Johann F. 1795/1865. De Generis Humani Varietate Nativa, 3rd edn. In *Treatises of Johann Friedrich Blumenbach*, edited by T. Bendyshe, pp. 65–276. London, UK: Longmans, Green.

Boas, Franz 1887a. The Study of Geography. *Science*, vol. 9, no. 210, pp. 137–41. Washington.

Boas, Franz 1887b. The Occurrence of Similar Inventions in Areas Widely Apart. *Science*, vol. 9, no. 228, pp. 485–6. Washington.

Boas, Franz 1887c. Museums of Ethnology and Their Classification. *Science*, vol. 9, no. 229, pp. 587–9, 614. Washington.

Boas, Franz 1887/1974. Letter to Major J. W. Powell, June 12, 1887. In *A Franz Boas Reader: The Shaping of American Anthropology, 1883–1911*, edited by George W. Stocking, Jr., pp. 59–60. Chicago, IL: University of Chicago Press.

Boas, Franz 1888/1964. *The Central Eskimo*, with an introduction by Henry B. Collins. Lincoln, NB: University of Nebraska Press.

Boas, Franz 1894/1974. Human Faculty as Determined by Race. In *A Franz Boas Reader: The Shaping of American Anthropology, 1883–1911*, edited by George W. Stocking, Jr., pp. 221–42. Chicago, IL: University of Chicago Press.

Boas, Franz 1895. On Dr. William Townsend Porter's Investigation of the Growth of School Children in St. Louis. *Science*, vol. 1, no. 9, pp. 225–30. Washington.

Boas, Franz 1896/1940. The Limitations of the Comparative Method in Anthropology. *In Race, Language, and Culture* by Franz Boas, pp. 270–80. New York: Macmillan.

Boas, Franz 1899/1974. Fieldwork for the British Association, 1888–1897. In *A Franz Boas Reader: The Shaping of American Anthropology, 1883–1911*, edited by George W. Stocking, Jr., pp. 88–106. Chicago, IL: University of Chicago Press.

Boas, Franz 1901. The Mind of Primitive Man. *Journal of American Folk-Lore*, vol. XIV, no. 1, pp. 1–11. Boston.

Boas, Franz 1902. The Ethnological Significance of Esoteric Doctrines. *Science*, vol. XVI, no. 413, pp. 872–4. Cambridge.

Boas, Franz 1904. The History of Anthropology. *Science*, vol. XX, no. 512, pp. 513–24. Cambridge.

Boas, Franz 1904/1940. The Folk-Lore of the Eskimo. In *Race, Language, and Culture*, by Franz Boas, pp. 503–16. New York: Macmillan.

Boas, Franz 1910. The Real Race Problem. *The Crisis*, vol. 1, no. 1, pp. 22–5. New York.

Boas, Franz 1911. *Handbook of American Indian Languages*, Part I. Bureau of American Ethnology Bulletin 40. Washington.

Boas, Franz 1911/1912. *Change in Bodily Form of Descendants of Immigrants*. New York: Columbia University Press.

Boas, Franz 1916. *Tsimshian Mythology*. Thirty-First Annual Report of the Bureau of American Ethnology, 1910–11, pp. 1–1037. Washington.

Boas, Franz 1919 Nationalism. *The Dial*, March 8, pp. 232–7. New York.

Boas, Franz 1919/1974. Scientists as Spies. In *A Franz Boas Reader: The Shaping of American Anthropology, 1883–1911*, edited by George W. Stocking, Jr., pp. 336–7. Chicago, IL: The University of Chicago Press.

Boas, Franz 1920/1940 The Social Organization of the Kwakiut. In Race, Language, and Culture, by Franz Boas, pp. 350–69. New York: Macmillan.

Boas, Franz 1925. This Nordic Nonsense. *The Forum*, vol. 74, no. 4, pp. 502–11. New York.

Boas, Franz 1930. Some Problems of Methodology in the Social Sciences. In *The New Social Science*, edited by Leonard D. White, pp. 99–111. Chicago, IL: University of Chicago Press.

Boas, Franz 1936/1940. History and Science in Anthropology: A Reply. In *Race, Language, and Culture*, by Franz Boas, pp. 305–15. New York: Macmillan.

Boas, Franz 1938. An Anthropologist's Credo. *The Nation*, vol. 147, no. 9, 27 August, pp. 201–4. New York.

Braidwood, Robert J. 1952. *The Near East and the Foundations of Civilization: An Essay in Appraisal of the General Evidence*. Eugene, OR: Oregon State System of Higher Education.

Braidwood, Robert J. 1960. Levels in Prehistory: A Model for the Consideration of the Evidence. In *Evolution After Darwin: The University of Chicago Centennial*, edited by Sol Tax, vol. II, *The Evolution of Man*, pp. 143–52. Chicago, IL: University of Chicago Press.

Braidwood, Robert J. and Gordon R. Willey 1963. Conclusions and Afterthoughts. In *Courses Toward Urban Life: Archeological Considerations of Some Cultural Alternates*, edited by Robert J. Braidwood and Gordon R. Willey. Viking Fund Publications in Anthropology, no. 32, pp. 330–59. New York.

Brinton, Daniel G. 1890. *Races and Peoples: Lectures on the Science of Ethnography*. New York: N. D. C. Hodges.

Brinton, Daniel G. 1896. The Aims of Anthropology. *Popular Science Monthly*, vol. 48, no. 1, pp. 59–72. New York.

Brodkin, Karen 2000. Global Capitalism: What's Race Got to Do With It? *American Ethnologist*, vol. 27, no. 2, pp. 237–56. Arlington.

Brodkin Sacks, Karen 1989. Toward a Unified Theory of Class, Race, and Gender. *American Ethnologist*, vol. 16, no. 3, pp. 534–50. Washington.

Browne, Dallas L. 1999. Across Class and Culture: Allison Davis and His Works. In *African-American Pioneers in Anthropology*, edited by Ira E. Harrison and Faye V. Harrison, pp. 168–90. Urbana, IL: University of Illinois Press.

Brunhouse, Robert L. 1973. *In Search of the Maya: The First Archaeologists*. New York: Ballantine Books.

Bunzl, Matti 1996. Franz Boas and the Humboldtian Tradition: From Volkgeist and Nationalcharakter to an Anthropological Concept of Culture. In *Volkgeist as Method and Ethic: Essays on Boasian Ethnography and the German Anthropological Tradition*, edited by George W. Stocking, Jr. *History of Anthropology*, vol. 8, pp. 17–78. Madison, WI: University of Wisconsin Press.

Caffrey, Margaret M. 1989. *Ruth Benedict: Stranger in This Land*. Austin, TX: University of Texas Press.

Caldwell, Charles 1830. *Thoughts on the Original Unity of the Human Race*. New York: E. Bliss.

Bibliography

Capshew, James J. 1999 . The Yale Connection in American Psychology: Philanthropy, War and the Emergence of an Elite Academic. In *The Development of the Social Sciences in the United States and Canada: The Role of Philanthropy*, edited by Theresa Richardson and Donald Fisher, pp. 143–57. Stamford, CT: Ablex Publishing.

Carpenter, Carole H. 1999. Arthur Huff Fauset, Campaigner for Social Justice. In *African-American Pioneers in Anthropology*, edited by Ira E. Harrison and Faye V. Harrison, pp. 213–43. Urbana, IL: University of Illinois Press.

Cass, Lewis 1827. Review: Indian Treaties, and Laws and Regulations Relating to Indian Affairs: To Which is Added an Appendix, Containing the Proceedings of the Old Congress and Other Important State Papers in Relation to Indian Affairs. *The North American Review*, vol. XXIV, no. LV, pp. 365–442. Boston.

Cass, Lewis 1840. Review: Antiquités mexicaines. Relation de trois expéditions du Capitaine Dupaix. *The North American Review*, vol. LI, no. CIX, pp. 396–443. Boston.

Castañeda, Quetzil E. 1996. *In the Museum of Maya Culture: Touring Chichén Itzá*. Minneapolis, MN: University of Minnesota Press.

Chapple, Eliot D. 1953. Applied Anthropology in Industry. In *Anthropology Today: An Encyclopedic Inventory*, edited by Alfred L. Kroeber, pp. 819–31. Chicago, IL: The University of Chicago Press.

Chinard, Gilbert 1947. Eighteenth Century Theories on America as a Human Habitat. *Proceedings of the American Philosophical Society*, vol. 91, no. 1, pp. 27–57. Philadelphia.

Clifford, James 1986. Introduction: Partial Truths. In *Writing Culture: The Poetics and Politics of Ethnography*, edited by James Clifford and George E. Marcus, pp. 1–26. Berkeley, CA: University of California Press.

Clifford, James 1988. *The Predicament of Culture: Twentieth-Century Ethnography, Literature, and Art*. Cambridge, MA: Harvard University Press.

Clifford, James and George E. Marcus, editors 1986. *Writing Culture: The Poetics and Politics of Ethnography*. Berkeley, CA: University of California Press.

Cohen, Mark N. 1977. *The Food Crisis in Prehistory: Overpopulation and the Origins of Agriculture*. New Haven, CT: Yale University Press.

Colby, William M. 1977. *Routes to Rainy Mountain: A Biography of James Mooney, Ethnologist*. Ph.D. Dissertation in History, University of Wisconsin, Madison. Ann Arbor, MI: University Microfilms 78–4851.

Collier, George A. 1999. *Basta! Land and the Zapatista Rebellion in Chiapas*. Chicago, IL: Institute for Food and Development Policy.

Comas, Juan 1961. "Scientific" Racism Again? *Current Anthropology*, vol. 2, no. 4, pp. 303–40. Chicago.

Conn, Steven 1998. *Museums and American Intellectual Life, 1876–1926*. Chicago, IL: University of Chicago Press.

Coon, Carleton 1962. *The Origin of Races.* New York: Alfred A. Knopf.

Cove, John J. 1999. Cultural Relativism in the Americanist Tradition: From Anthropological Method to Indigenous Emancipation. *In Theorizing the Americanist Tradition,* edited by Lisa P. Valentine and Regna Darnell, pp. 108–20. Toronto, ON: University of Toronto Press.

Crèvecoeur, Hector St. John de 1782/1904. *Letters from an American Farmer, Describing Certain Provincial Situations, Manners, and Customs and Conveying Some Idea of the Late and Present Interior Circumstances of the British Colonies in North America.* New York: Fox, Duffield and Company.

Cumings, Bruce 1998. Boundary Displacement: Area Studies and International Studies During and After the Cold War. In *Universities and Empire: Money and Politics in the Social Sciences during the Cold War,* edited by Christopher Simpson, pp. 159–88. New York: New Press.

Curti, Merle 1980. *Human Nature in American Thought: A History.* Madison, WI: The University of Wisconsin Press.

d'Andrade, Roy G., Eugene A. Hammel, Douglas L. Adkins, and C. K. McDaniel 1975. Academic Opportunity in Anthropology, 1974–1990. *American Anthropologist,* vol. 77, no. 4, pp. 752–73. Washington.

Darnell, Regna D. 1969. *The Development of American Anthropology, 1879–1920: From the Bureau of American Ethnology to Franz Boas.* Ph.D. Dissertation in Anthropology, University of Pennsylvania, Philadelphia. Ann Arbor, MI: University Microfilms 70–7794.

Darnell, Regna D. 1970. The Emergence of Academic Anthropology at the University of Pennsylvania. *Journal of the History of the Behavioral Sciences,* vol. 6, no. 1, pp. 80–92. Brandon.

Darnell, Regna D. 1976. Daniel Brinton and the Professionalization of American Anthropology. In *American Anthropology: The Early Years,* edited by John V. Murra. 1974 Proceedings of the American Ethnological Society, pp. 69–98. St. Paul, MN: West Publishing Company.

Darnell, Regna D. 1982. Franz Boas and the Development of Physical Anthropology in North America. *Canadian Journal of Anthropology,* vol. 3, no. 1, pp. 101–12. Edmonton.

Darnell, Regna D. 1986. Personality and Culture: The Fate of the Sapirian Alternative. In *Malinowski, Rivers, Benedict and Others: Essays on Culture and Personality,* edited by George W. Stocking, Jr. *History of Anthropology,* vol. 2, pp. 156–83. Madison, WI: University of Wisconsin Press.

Darnell, Regna D. 1988. *Daniel Garrison Brinton: The "Fearless Critic" of Philadelphia.* University of Pennsylvania Publications in Anthropology, no. 3. Philadelphia.

Darnell, Regna D. 1990. *Edward Sapir: Linguist, Anthropologist, Humanist.* Berkeley, CA: University of California Press.

Darnell, Regna D. 1998. And Along Came Boas: Continuity and Revolution in Americanist Anthropology. *Amsterdam Studies in the Theory and History of Linguistic Science*, vol. 86. Amsterdam: John Benjamins Publishing Company.

Darrah, William C. 1951. *Powell of the Colorado*. Princeton, NJ: Princeton University Press.

Davenport, William 1985. The Thailand Controversy in Retrospect. *In Social Contexts of American Ethnology, 1840–1984*, edited by June Helm. 1984 Proceedings of the American Ethnological Society, pp. 65–72. Washington.

Davis, Allison 1948. *Social Class Influences upon Learning*. Cambridge, MA: Harvard University Press.

Davis, Allison and John Dollard 1940. *Children of Bondage: The Personality Development of Negro Youth in the Urban South*. Washington, DC: American Council on Education.

Davis, Allison, Burleigh B. Gardner, and Mary R. Gardner 1941. *Deep South: A Social Anthropological Study of Caste and Class*. Chicago, IL: University of Chicago Press.

Day, Carolyn Bond 1930. Race-Crossings in the United States. *The Crisis*, vol. 37, no. 1, pp. 81–2, 103. New York.

Day, Carolyn Bond 1932. *A Study of Some Negro-White Families in the United States*, with a forward and notes on anthropometric data by Earnest A. Hooton. Cambridge, MA: Peabody Museum of Harvard University.

Deitchman, Seymour J. 1976. *The Best-Laid Schemes: A Tale of Social Research and Bureauracy*. Cambridge, MA: MIT Press.

DeMartino, George F. 2000. *Global Economy, Global Justice: Theoretical Objections and Policy Alternatives to Neoliberalism*. New York: Routledge.

Dexter, Ralph W. 1966. Putnam's Problems in Popularizing Anthropology. *American Scientist*, vol. 54, no. 3, pp. 315–32. New Haven.

Dexter, Ralph W. 1970. The Role of F. W. Putnam in Founding the Field Museum. *Curator*, vol. XIII, no. 1, pp. 21–6. New York.

Dexter, Ralph W. 1976. The Role of F. W. Putnam in Developing Anthropology at the American Museum of Natural History. *Curator*, vol, no. 19, no. 4, pp. 303–10. New York.

Dexter, Ralph W. 1980. F. W. Putnam's Role in Developing the Peabody Museum of American Archaeology and Ethnology. *Curator*, vol. 23, no. 2, pp. 183–94. New York.

Diamond, Sigmund 1992. *Compromised Campus: The Collaboration of Universities with the Intelligence Community, 1945–1955*. New York: Oxford University Press.

Diamond, Stanley 1969. Anthropology in Question. In *Reinventing Anthropology*, edited by Dell Hymes, pp. 401–29. New York: Vintage Books.

Diamond, Stanley 1974. *In Search of the Primitive: A Critique of Civilization*. New Brunswick, NJ: Transaction Books.

Dinnerstein, Leonard 1994. *Antisemitism in America*. New York: Oxford University Press.

Dolgin, Janet L., David S. Kemnitizer, and David M. Schneider 1977. "As People Express Their Lives, So They Are . . .". In *Symbolic Anthropology: A Reader in the Study of Symbols and and Meanings*, edited by Janet L. Dolgin, David S. Kemnitzer, and David M. Schneider, pp. 3–44. New York: Columbia University Press.

Dollard, John 1937. *Caste and Class in a Southern Town*. New Haven, CT: Yale University Press.

Douglass, Frederick 1854/1950. The Claims of the Negro Ethnologically Considered. In *The Life and Writings of Frederick Douglass*, edited by Philip S. Foner, pp. 289–309. New York: International Publishers.

Dower, John W. 1986. *War Without Mercy: Race and Power in the Pacific War*. New York: Pantheon Books.

Drake, St. Clair 1980. Anthropology and the Black Experience. *The Black Scholar*, vol. 11, no. 7, pp. 2–31. Amherst.

Drake, St. Clair and Horace Cayton 1945. *Black Metropolis: A Study of Negro Life in a Northern City*, 2 vols. New York: Harcourt Brace and Company.

Dreyfus, Hubert L. and Paul Rabinow, editors 1982. *Michel Foucault: Beyond Structuralism and Hermeneutics*. Chicago, IL: University of Chicago Press.

Drinnon, Richard 1980 *Facing West: The Metaphysics of Indian-Hating and Empire-Building*. New York: New American Library.

Drinnon, Richard 1987. *Keeper of the Concentration Camps: Dillon S. Myer and American Racism*. Berkeley, CA: University of California Press.

DuBois, Cora A. 1944/1960. *The People of Alor: A Social-Pscyhological Study of An East Indian Island*. Cambridge, MA: Harvard University Press.

Du Bois, W. E. B. 1899/1967. *The Philadelphia Negro: A Social Study*. New York: Schocken Books.

Du Ponceau, Peter S. 1819. Report of the Historical and Literary Committee of the American Philosophical Society. – Read 9th January, 1818. *Transactions of the Historical and Literary Committee of the American Philosophical Society*, vol. I, pp. xi-xvi. Philadelphia.

Du Ponceau, Peter S. 1838. *Mémoire sur le système grammaticale des langues des quelques nations indiennes de l'Amérique du Nord*. Paris: A. Pihan de la Forest.

Durkheim, Émile 1886. Les études de science sociale. *Revue Philosophique*, tome XXII, pp. 61–80. Paris.

Durkheim, Émile 1887. La science positive de la morale en Allemagne. *Revue Philosophique*, tome XXIV, pp. 33–58, 113–43, 275–84. Paris.

Eames, Edwin and Judith Goode 1977. *Anthropology of the City: An Introduction to Urban Anthropology*. Englewood Cliffs, NJ: Prentice-Hall.

Edgerton, Franklin 1943. Notes on Early American Work in Linguistics. *Proceedings of the American Philosophical Society*, vol. 87, no. 1, pp. 25–34. Philadelphia.

Eggan, Fred, editor 1937. *Social Organization of North American Tribes: Essays in Social Organization, Law, and Religion Presented to Professor A. R. Radcliffe-Brown*. Chicago, IL: University of Chicago Press.

Ekirch, Arthur A., Jr. 1969. *Ideologies and Utopias: The Impact of the New Deal on American Thought*. Chicago, IL: Quadrangle Books.

Embree, John F. 1944. Community Analysis – An Example of Anthropology in Government. *American Anthropologist*, vol. 46, no. 3, pp. 277–91. Menasha.

Engels, Frederick 1884/1972. *The Origin of the Family, Private Property and the State: In Light of the Researches of Lewis H. Morgan*, with an introduction and notes by Eleanor B. Leacock. New York: International Publishers.

Epperson, Terrence W. 1994. The Politics of Empiricism and the Construction of Race as an Analytical Category. *Transforming Anthropology*, vol. 5, no. 1–2, pp. 15–19. Washington.

Erb, Claude C. 1982 *Nelson Rockefeller and United States – Latin American Relations, 1940–1945*. Ph.D. Dissertation in History, Clark University, Worcester (University Microfilms Order no. 8300730).

Erickson, Paul A. 1997a. Caldwell, Charles (1772–1853). In *History of Physical Anthropology: An Encyclopedia*, edited by Frank Spencer, vol. 1, pp. 241–2. New York: Garland Publishing.

Erickson, Paul A. 1997b. Phrenology. In *History of Physical Anthropology: An Encyclopedia*, edited by Frank Spencer, vol. 2, pp. 817–20. New York: Garland Publishing.

Erickson, Paul A. 1997c. Nott, Josiah Clark (1804–1873). In *History of Physical Anthropology: An Encyclopedia*, edited by Frank Spencer, vol. 2, pp. 757–9. New York: Garland Publishing.

Etienne, Mona and Eleanor Leacock, editors 1980. *Women and Colonization: Anthropological Perspectives*. Brooklyn NY: J. F. Bergin Publishers.

Faguette, Paul H., Jr. 1985 *Digging for Dollars: The Impact of the New Deal on the Professionalization of American Archaeology*. Ph.D. Dissertation in Anthropology, University of California, Riverside.

Feeley, Francis M. 1999. *America's Concentration Camps during World War II*. New Orleans, LA: University Press of the South.

Fenton, William N. 1947. *Area Studies in American Universities*. Washington, DC: Commission on Implications of Armed Services Education Programs, American Council on Education.

Fischer, Michael M. J. 1999. Emergent Forms of Life: Anthropologies of Late or Postmodernities. *Annual Review of Anthropology*, vol. 28, pp. 455–78. Palo Alto.

Fisher, Donald 1983. The Role of Philanthropic Foundations in the Reproduction and Production of Hegemony: Rockefeller Foundations and the Social Sciences. *Sociology*, vol. 17, no. 2, pp. 206–33. Cardiff.

Fisher, Donald 1986. Rockefeller Philanthropy and British Social Anthropology? *Anthropology Today*, vol. 2, no. 1, pp. 5–8. London.

Fisher, Donald 1993. *Fundamental Development of the Social Sciences: Rockefeller Philanthropy and the United States Social Science Research Council*. Ann Arbor, MI: University of Michigan Press.

Flannery, Kent V. 1968. Archeological Systems Theory and Early Mesoamerica. In *Anthropological Archeology in the Americas*, edited by Betty J. Meggers, pp. 67–87. Washington, DC: Anthropological Society of Washington.

Flannery, Kent V. 1972. The Cultural Evolution of Civilizations. *Annual Review of Ecology and Systematics*, vol. 3, pp. 399–426. Palo Alto.

Foner, Eric 1988. *Reconstruction, 1863–1877: America's Unfinished Revolution*. New York: Harper and Row, Publishers.

Ford, James A. 1938. *Report of the Conference on Southeastern Pottery Typology*. Ceramic Repository, Museum of Anthropology, University of Michigan. Ann Arbor.

Ford, James A. and Gordon R. Willey 1941. An Interpretation of the Prehistory of the Eastern United States. *American Anthropologist*, vol. 43, no. 3, pp. 325–63. Menasha.

Foucault, Michel 1966/1973. *The Order of Things: An Archaeology of the Human Sciences*. New York: Vintage Books.

Foucault, Michel 1994/1997. *The Essential Works of Michel Foucault*, edited by Paul Rabinow, vol. 1, *Michel Foucault: Ethics, Subjectivity and Truth*. New York: The New Press.

Fowler, Don D. 1999. Harvard vs. Hewett: The Contest for Control of Southwestern Archaeology, 1904–1930. In *Assembling the Past: Studies in the Professionalization of Archaeology*, edited by Alice B. Kehoe and Mary Beth Emmerichs, pp. 165–212. Albuquerque, NM: University of New Mexico Press.

Frank, André G. 1966/1969. The Development of Underdevelopment. In *Latin America: Underdevelopment or Revolution*, by André G. Frank, pp. 3–17. New York: Monthly Review Press.

Frank, André G. 1967. *Capitalism and Underdevelopment in Latin America: Historical Studies of Chile and Brazil*. New York: Monthly Review Press.

Frank, Gelya 1997. Jews, Multiculturalism, and Boasian Anthropology. *American Anthropologist*, vol. 99, no. 4, pp. 731–45. Washington.

Franklin, Benjamin 1789/1848. *The Works of Dr. Benjamin Franklin: Consisting of Essays, Humorous, Moral, and Literary: With his Life, Written by Himself*. Hartford, CT: S. Andrus and Son.

Fredrickson, George M. 1965. *The Inner Civil War: Northern Intellectuals and the Crisis of the Union*. New York: Harper and Row.

Freeman, John F. 1967. The American Philosophical Society in American Anthropology. In *The Philadelphia Anthropological Society: Papers Presented on its Golden Anniversary*, edited by Jacob W. Gruber, pp. 32–46. Philadelphia, PA: Temple University Press.

Fried, Morton H. 1967. *The Evolution of Political Society: An Essay in Political Anthropology*. New York: Random House.

Friedman, Jonathan 1974. Marxism, Structuralism and Vulgar Materialism. *Man*, vol. 9, no. 3, pp. 444–69. London.

Gailey, Christine W. 1983. Categories without Culture: Structuralism, Ethnohistory and Ethnocide. *Dialectical Anthropology*, vol. 8, no. 3, pp. 241–50. Amsterdam.

Gailey, Christine W. 1987a. Culture Wars: Resistance to State Formation. In *Power Relations and State Formation*, edited by Thomas C. Patterson and Christine W. Gailey, pp. 35–56. Washington, DC: Archeology Section/American Anthropological Association.

Gailey, Christine W. 1987b. *Kinship to Kingship: Gender Hierarchy and State Formation in the Tongan Islands*. Austin, TX: University of Texas Press.

Gailey, Christine W. 1992. Introduction: Civilization and Culture in the Work of Stanley Diamond. In *Dialectical Anthropology*, Vol. 1, *Civilization in Crisis: Anthropological Perspectives*, edited by Christine W. Gailey, pp. 1–25. Gainesville, FL: University Press of Florida.

Gailey, Christine W. 1994. Politics, Colonialism, and the Mutable Color of Southern Pacific Peoples. *Transforming Anthropology*, vol. 5, no. 1–2, pp. 34–40. Washington.

Gailey, Christine W. 1998. Feminist Methods. In *Handbook of Methods in Cultural Anthropology*, edited by H. Russell Bernard, pp. 203–33. Walnut Creek, CA: Altamira Press.

Gallatin, Albert 1836/1973. A Synopsis of the Indian Tribes within the United States East of the Rocky Mountains and in the British and Russian Possessions in North America. *Archaeologia Americana, Transactions and Collections of the American Antiquarian Society*, vol. 2, pp. 1–422. New York: AMS Press.

Gallatin, Albert 1845. Notes on the Semi-civilized Nations of Mexico, Yucatan, and Central America. *Transactions of the American Ethnological Society*, vol. 1, pp. 1–352. New York.

Gallatin, Albert 1848. Introduction to Hale's Indians of North-west America, and Vocabularies of North America. *Transactions of the American Ethnological Society*, vol. 2, pp. xxiii–clxxxviii. New York.

Gearing, Fred, Robert McC. Netting, and Lisa R. Peattie 1960. *Documentary History of the Fox Project, 1948–1959: A Program in Action Anthropology*. Chicago, IL: University of Chicago Press.

Geertz, Clifford 1956. *The Development of the Javanese Economy: A Socio-Cultural Approach*. Economic Development Program C/56–18. Center for International Studies, Massachusetts Institute of Technology. Cambridge.

Geertz, Clifford 1963a. *Agricultural Involution: The Processes of Ecological Change in Indonesia*. Berkeley, CA: University of California Press.

Geertz, Clifford 1963b. The Integrative Revolution: Primordial Sentiments and Civic Politics in the New States. In *Old Societies and New States: The Quest for Modernity in Asia and Africa*, edited by Clifford Geertz, pp. 105–57. Glencoe, IL: The Free Press.

Geertz, Clifford 1971. After the Revolution: The Fate of Nationalism in New States. In *Stability and Social Change*, edited by Bernard Barber and Alex Inkeles, pp. 357–76. Boston, MA: Little, Brown and Company.

Geertz, Clifford 1973. Thick Description: Toward an Interpretive Theory of Culture. In *The Interpretation of Cultures*, by Clifford Geertz, pp. 3–30. New York: Basic Books.

Gendzier, Irene L. 1998. Play It Again Sam: The Practice and Apology of Development. In *Universities and Empire: Money and Politics in the Social Sciences during the Cold War*, edited by Christopher Simpson, pp. 57–96. New York: New Press.

Gerbi, Antonello 1973. *The Dispute of the New World: The History of a Polemic, 1750–1900*. Pittsburgh, PA: University of Pittsburgh Press.

Gerstein, Dean R. 1986. The Social Sciences as a National Resource: 1948 and 1982. In *The Nationalization of the Social Sciences*, edited by Samuel Z. Klausner and Victor M. Lidz, pp. 247–64. Philadelphia, PA: University of Pennsylvania Press.

Givens, Douglas R. 1992. *Alfred Vincent Kidder and the Development of Americanist Archaeology*. Albuquerque, NM: University of New Mexico Press.

Godoy, Ricardo 1970. Franz Boas and his Plans for an International School of American Archaeology and Ethnology in Mexico. *Journal of the History of the Behavioral Sciences*, vol. 13, no. 1, pp. 228–42. Brandon.

Goetzmann, William H. 1959. *Army Exploration in the American West, 1803–1863*. New Haven, CT: Yale University Press.

Goetzmann, William H. 1966. *Exploration and Empire: The Explorer and the Scientist in the Winning of the American West*. New York: W. W. Norton.

Goldenweiser, Alexander 1913. The Principle of Limited Possibilities in the Development of Culture. *Journal of American Folk-Lore*, vol. 26, no. 3, pp. 259–90. Boston.

Goldfield, Michael 1997. *The Color of Politics: Race and the Mainsprings of American Politics*. New York: The New Press.

Goldschmidt, Walter 1947. *As You Sow*. New York: Harcourt, Brace and Company.

Golla, Victor 1986. Sapir, Kroeber, and North American Linguistic Classification. In *New Perspectives in Language, Culture, and Personality (Proceedings of the Edward Sapir Centenary Conference (Ottawa, 1–3 Oct. 1984)*, edited by William Cowan, Michael K. Foster, and Konrad Koerner. Studies in the History of the

Language Sciences 41, pp. 17–38. Amsterdam: John Benjamins Publishing Company.

Gorer, Geoffrey 1942. Themes in Japanese Culture. *Transactions of the New York Academy of Sciences*, ser. 2, vol. 5, no. 5, pp. 106–24. New York.

Gorer, Geoffrey and John Rickman 1949/1962. *The People of Great Russia: A Psychological Study*. New York: W. W. Norton and Company.

Gough, Kathleen 1968a . Anthropology: Child of Imperialism. *Monthly Review*, vol. 19, no. 11, pp. 12–27. New York.

Gough, Kathleen 1968b. New Proposals for Anthropologists. *Current Anthropology*, vol. 9, no. 5, pp. 405–35. Chicago.

Gould, Stephen J. 1981. American Polygeny and Craniometry before Darwin: Blacks and Indians as Separate, Inferior Species. In *The Mismeasure of Man* by Stephen J. Gould, pp. 30–72. New York: W. W. Norton and Company.

Grant, Madison 1916. *The Passing of the Great Race*. New York: Scribner.

Gray, Edward G. 1999. *New World Babel: Languages and Nations in Early America*. Princeton, NJ: Princeton University Press.

Gray, John 1998. *False Dawn: The Delusions of Global Capitalism*. London, UK: Granta Books.

Greene, John C. 1954. The American Debate on the Negro's Place in Nature, 1780–1815. *Journal of the History of Ideas*, vol. XV, no. 3, pp. 384–96. Lancaster.

Greene, John C. 1984. *American Science in the Age of Jefferson*. Ames, IO: The Iowa State University Press.

Griffen, Joyce 1989. Ruth Murray Underhill. *In Women Anthropologists: Selected Biographies*, edited by Ute Gacs, Aisha Khan, Jerrie McIntyre, and Ruth Weinberg, pp. 355–60. Urbana, IL: University of Illinois Press.

Grinde, Donald A., Jr. and Bruce E. Johansen 1991. *Exemplars of Liberty: Native America and the Evolution of Democracy*. Los Angeles, CA: American Indian Studies Center, University of California.

Grozdins, Morton 1949. *American Betrayed: Politics and the Japanese Evacuation*. Chicago, IL: University of Chicago Press.

Haas, Mary R. 1953. The Application of Linguistics to Language Teaching. In *Anthropology Today: An Encyclopedic Inventory*, edited by Alfred L. Kroeber, pp. 807–18. Chicago, IL: University of Chicago Press.

Haas, Mary R. 1969. Grammar or Lexicon? The American Indian Side of the Question from Duponceau to Powell. *International Journal of American Linguistics*, vol. 35, no. 3, pp. 239–55. Baltimore.

Haddon, Alfred C., editor 1901. *Report of the Cambridge Anthropological Expedition to the Torres Straits*, vol. II, *Physiology and Psychology*. Cambridge, UK: Cambridge University Press.

Haller, John S., Jr. 1971. *Outcasts from Evolution: Scientific Attitudes of Racial Inferiority, 1859–1900*. Urbana, IL: University of Illinois Press.

Hallowell, A. Irving 1960. The Beginnings of Anthropology in America. *In Selected Papers from the American Anthropologist*, edited by Frederica de la Laguna, pp. 1–90. Evanston, IL: Row, Peterson and Company.

Handler, Richard 1986. Vigorous Male and Aspiring Female: Poetry, Personality, and Culture in Edward Sapir and Ruth Benedict. In *Malinowski, Rivers, Benedict and Others: Essays on Culture and Personality*, edited by George W. Stocking, Jr. *History of Anthropology*, vol. 4, pp. 127–55. Madison, WI: University of Wisconsin Press.

Hansen, Asael T. 1934. The Ecology of a Latin American City. In *Race and Culture Contacts*, edited by E. Reuter, pp. 124–42. New York: McGraw-Hill.

Hansen, Asael T. 1976. Robert Redfield, The Yucatán Project, and I. In *American Anthropology: The Early Years*, edited by John V. Murra. 1974 Proceedings of the American Ethnological Society, pp. 167–86. St. Paul.

Haraway, Donna J. 1989. Remodeling the Human Way of Life: Sherwood Washburn and the New Physical Anthropology, 1950–1980. In *Primate Visions: Gender, Race, and Nature in the World of Modern Science*, by Donna Haraway, pp. 186–230. New York: Routledge.

Harding, Sandra 1986. *The Science Question in Feminism*. Ithaca, NY: Cornell University Press.

Harding, Sandra 1991. *Whose Science? Whose Knowledge? Thinking from Women's Lives*. Ithaca, NY: Cornell University Press.

Harris, Marvin 1968. *The Rise of Anthropological Theory: A History of Theories of Culture*. New York: Thomas Y. Crowell Company.

Harris, Marvin 1979 *Cultural Materialism: The Struggle for a Science of Culture*. New York: Random House.

Harrison, Faye V. 1992. The Du Boisian Legacy in Anthropology. *Critique of Anthropology*, vol. 12, no. 3, pp. 239–60. London.

Harrison, Faye V. and Ira E. Harrison 1999. Introduction: Anthropology, African Americans, and the Emancipation of a Subjugated Knowledge. In *African-American Pioneers in Anthropology*, edited by Ira E. Harrison and Faye V. Harrison, pp. 1–36. Urbana, IL: University of Illinois Press.

Harrison, Ira E. 1999. Louis Eugene King, the Anthropologist Who Never Was. In *African-American Pioneers in Anthropology*, edited by Ira E. Harrison and Faye V. Harrison, pp. 70–84. Urbana, IL: University of Illinois Press.

Harvey, David 1982. *The Limits to Capital*. Chicago, IL: University of Chicago Press.

Haven, Samuel 1855. *Archaeology of the United States. Or Sketches, Historical and Bibliographical, of the Progress of Information and Opinion Respecting Vestiges of Antiquity in the United States*. Smithsonian Contributions to Knowledge. Philadelphia, PA: T. K. and P. G. Collins, Printers.

Hawes, Joseph M. 1968. Social Scientists and Immigration Restriction: Highlights of a Debate, 1890–1924. *Journal of World History*, vol. XI, no. 3, pp. 467–82. Paris.

Heath, Shirley B. 1977. A National Language Academy? Debate in the New Nation. *Linguistics. An International Review*, no. 189, pp. 9–43. Paris.

Henshaw, Henry W. 1883. Animal Carvings from the Mounds of the Mississippi Valley. *Second Annual Report of the Bureau of Ethnology, 1880-'81*, pp. 4–35. Washington.

Henshaw, Henry W. and James A. Mooney 1885. *Linguistic Families of the Indian Tribes North of Mexico*. Washington, DC: Bureau of American Ethnology.

Herskovits, Melville J. 1926. On the Relation between Negro-White Mixture and Standing in Intelligence Tests. *The Pedagogical Seminary and Journal of Genetic Psychology*, vol. XXXIII, no. 1, pp. 30–42. Worcester.

Herskovits, Melville J. 1928. *The American Negro: A Study in Race Crossing*. New York: Alfred A. Knopf.

Herskovits, Melville J. 1930. *The Anthropometry of the American Negro*. Columbia University Contributions to Anthropology, vol. XI. New York: Columbia University Press.

Herskovits, Melville J. 1941/1958. *The Myth of the Negro Past*. Boston, MA: Beacon Press.

Herskovits, Melville J. 1943. Franz Boas as Physical Anthropologist. *In Franz Boas, 1858–1942*, by A. L. Kroeber, Ruth Benedict, Murray B. Emeneau, Melville J. Herskovits, Gladys A. Reichard, and J. Alden Mason. Memoir of the American Anthropological Association, no. 61, pp. 39–51. Menasha.

Hewitt de Alcántara, Cynthia 1984. *Anthropological Perspectives on Rural Mexico*. London, UK: Routledge and Kegan Paul

Higgs, Robert 1987. *Crisis and Leviathan: Critical Episodes in the Growth of American Government*. New York: Oxford University Press.

Hinsley, Curtis M., Jr. 1976. Amateurs and Professionals in Washington Anthropology, 1879 to 1903. In *American Anthropology: The Early Years*, edited by John V. Murra. 1974 Proceedings of the American Ethnological Society, pp. 36–68. St. Paul, MN: West Publishing Company.

Hinsley, Curtis M., Jr. 1981. *Savages and Scientists: The Smithsonian Institution and the Development of American Anthropology, 1846–1910*. Washington, DC: Smithsonian Institution Press.

Hinsley, Curtis M., Jr. 1985a. Hemispheric Hegemony in Early American Anthropology, 1841–1851: Reflections on John Lloyd Stephens and Lewis Henry Morgan. In *Social Contexts of American Ethnology, 1840–1984*, edited by June Helm. 1984 Proceedings of the American Ethnological Society, pp. 28–40. Washington, DC: American Ethnological Society.

Hinsley, Curtis M., Jr. 1985b. From Shell-Heaps to Stelae: Early Anthropology at the Peabody Museum. In *Objects and Others: Essays on Museums and Material Culture*, edited by George W. Stocking, Jr. *History of Anthropology*, vol. 3, pp. 49–74. Madison, WI: University of Wisconsin Press.

Hinsley, Curtis M., Jr. 1986. Edgar Lee Hewett and the School of American Research in Santa Fe, 1906–1912. In *American Archaeology Past and Future: A Celebration of the Society for American Archaeology, 1935–1985*, edited by David J. Meltzer, Don D. Fowler, and Jeremy A. Sabloff, pp. 217–33. Washington, DC: Smithsonian Institution Press.

Hinsley, Curtis M., Jr. 1991. The World as Marketplace: Commodification of the Exotic at the World's Columbian Exposition, Chicago, 1893. In *Exhibiting Cultures: The Poetics and Politics of Museum Display*, edited by Ivan Karp and Steven D. Lavine, pp. 344–65. Washington, DC: Smithsonian Institution Press.

Hinsley, Curtis M., Jr. and Bill Holm 1976 A Cannibal in the National Museum: The Early Career of Franz Boas in America. *American Anthropologist*, vol. 78, no. 2, pp. 306–16. Washington.

Hirabayashi, Lane R. and James Hirabayashi 1989. The 'Credible' Witness: The Central Role of Richard S. Nishimoto in JERS. In *Views from Within: The Japanese American Evacuation and Resettlement Study*, edited by Yuji Ichioka, pp. 31–63. Los Angeles, CA: UCLA Asian American Studies Center.

Hodge, Frederick W., editor 1907–10. *Handbook of American Indians North of Mexico*, 2 vols. Bureau of American Ethnology Bulletin 30. Washington.

Hofstatter, Richard 1955. *Social Darwinism in American Thought*. Boston, MA: Beacon Press.

Hoijer, Harry 1973. History of American Indian Linguistics. In *Linguistics in North America. Current Trends in Linguistics*, edited by Thomas A. Sebeok, vol. 10, pp. 657–76. The Hague: Mouton Publishers.

Holmberg, Allan R. 1955/1964. Experimental Intervention in the Field. *In Peasants, Power, and Applied Social Change: Vicos as a Model*, edited by Henry F. Dobyns, Paul L. Doughty and Harold D. Lasswell, pp. 21–32. Beverly Hills, CA: Sage Publications.

Holmberg, Allan R. 1964. The Role of Power in Changing Values and Institutions of Vicos. In *Peasants, Power, and Applied Social Change: Vicos as a Model*, edited by Henry F. Dobyns, Paul L. Doughty and Harold D. Lasswell, pp. 33–64. Beverly Hills, CA: Sage Publications.

Holmes, William H. 1878. Report on the Ancient Ruins of Southwestern Colorado, Examined during the Summer of 1875 and 1876. *Tenth Annual Report, U.S. Geological and Geographical Survey of the Territories, 1876*, pp. 383–408. Washington.

Holmes, William H. 1884. Prehistoric Textile Fabrics from the United States, Derived from Impressions on Pottery. *Third Annual Report of the Bureau of Ethnology, 1881-'82*, pp. 393–425. Washington.

Holmes, William H. 1885. Evidence of the Antiquity of Man on the Site of the City of Mexico. *Transactions of the Anthropological Society of Washington*, vol. III, pp. 68–81. Washington.

Holmes, William H. 1892. Evolution of the Aesthetic. *Proceedings of the Forty-first Meeting, American Association for the Advancement of Science, Rochester, 1892*, pp. 239–55. Washington.

Hooton, Earnest A. 1931. *Up from the Ape*. New York: Macmillan.

Horowitz, Irving L. 1967. The Rise and Fall of Project Camelot. In *The Rise and Fall of Project Camelot: Studies in the Relationship Between Social Science and Practical Politics*, edited by Irving L. Horowitz, pp. 3–44. Cambridge, MA: The MIT Press.

Horsman, Reginald 1967. *Expansion and American Indian Policy, 1783–1812*. Lansing, MI: Michigan State University Press.

Horsman, Reginald 1981. *Race and Manifest Destiny: The Origins of American Racial Anglo-Saxonism*. Cambridge, MA: Harvard University Press.

Hrdlička, Aleš 1917. The Old White Americans. *Proceedings of the Nineteenth International Congress of Americanists, Held at Washington, December 27–31, 1915*, edited by F. W. Hodge, pp. 582–601. Washington.

Hrdlička, Aleš, in collaboration with W. H. Holmes, B. Willis, F. Wright, and C. Fenner 1912. *Early Man in South America*. Bureau of American Ethnology Bulletin, no. 52. Washington.

Hyatt, Marshall 1990. *Franz Boas, Social Activist: The Dynamics of Ethnicity*. Contributions to the Study of Anthropology, no. 6. Westport, CT: Greenwood Press.

Hymes, Dell H. 1963. Notes Toward a History of Linguistic Anthropology. *Anthropological Linguistics*, vol. V, no. 1, pp. 59–103. Bloomington.

Hymes, Dell H. 1971. Morris Swadesh: From the First Yale School to World Prehistory. In *The Origin and Diversification of Language*, edited by Joel Scherzer, pp. 228–70. Chicago, IL: Aldine Atherton.

Hymes, Dell H. 1983. A Message from the President. *Anthropology Newsletter*, September, special issue, pp. 1–2. Washington.

Hymes, Dell H. 1999. Introduction to the Ann Arbor Paperbacks Edition. In *Reinventing Anthropology*, edited by Dell Hymes, pp. v-xlix. Ann Arbor, MI: University of Michigan Press.

Hymes, Dell, editor 1969. *Reinventing Anthropology*. New York: Random House.

Hymes, Dell and John Fought 1975. *American Structuralism*. The Hague: Mouton Publishers.

Ichioka, Yuji 1989. JERS Revisited: Introduction. In *Views from Within: The Japanese American Evacuation and Resettlement Study*, edited by Yuji Ichioka, pp. 3–27. Los Angeles, CA: UCLA Asian American Studies Center.

Inkeles, Alex 1973. Clyde Kluckhohn's Contributions to Studies of Russia and the Soviet Union. In *Culture and Life: Essays in Memory of Clyde Kluckhohn*, edited by Walter W. Taylor, John L. Fischer, and Evon Z. Vogt, pp. 58–70. Carbondale, IL: Southern Illinois Press.

Inkeles, Alex, Eugenia Hanfmann, and Helen Beier 1961. Modal Personality and Adjustment to the Soviet Socio-Political System. In *Studying Personality Cross-Culturally*, edited by Bert Kaplan, pp. 201–24. New York: Harper and Row, Publishers.

Jackson, Walter 1986. Melville Herskovits and the Search for Afro-American Culture. In *Malinowski, Rivers, Benedict and Others: Essays on Culture and Personality*, edited by George W. Stocking, Jr. *History of Anthropology*, vol. 4, pp. 95–126. Madison, WI: The University of Wisconsin Press.

Jackson, Walter 1990. *Gunnar Myrdal and America's Conscience: Social Engineering and Racial Liberalism, 1938–1987*. Chapel Hill, NC: University of North Carolina Press.

Janssens, Rudolf V. A. 1999. Toilet Training, Shame, and the Influence of Alien Cultures: Cultural Anthropologists and American Policy Making for Postwar Japan, 1944–1945. In *Anthropology and Colonialism in Asia and Oceania*, edited by Jan van Bremen and Akitoshi Shimizu, pp. 285–304. Richmond, Surrey, UK: Curzon Press.

Jarvis, Edward 1842. Statistics on Insanity in the United States. *Boston Medical and Surgical Journal*, vol. 27, pp. 116–21, 181–2. Boston.

Jefferson, Thomas 1785/1982. *Notes on the State of Virginia*, edited by William Peden. Chapel Hill, NC: University of North Carolina Press.

Jefferson, Thomas 1803a/1962. Letter to Benjamin Smith Barton, 27 February 1803. In *Letters of the Lewis and Clark Expedition with Related Documents, 1783–1854*, edited by Donald Jackson, editor, pp. 16–17. Urbana, IL: University of Illinois Press.

Jefferson, Thomas 1803b/1962. Instructions to Meriwether Lewis, 20 June 1803. In *Letters of the Lewis and Clark Expedition with Related Documents, 1783–1854*, edited by Donald Jackson, editor, pp. 61–7. Urbana, IL: University of Illinois Press.

Jordan, Winthrop D. 1968. *White over Black: American Attitudes toward the Negro, 1550–1812*. Chapel Hill, NC: University of North Carolina Press.

Jorgensen, Joseph G. 1971. Indians and the Metropolis. In *The American Indian in Urban Society*, edited by Jack O. Wadell and O. Michael Watson, pp. 67–113. Boston, MA: Little, Brown and Company.

Jorgensen, Joseph G. 1978. Energy, Agriculture, and Social Science in the American West. In *Native Americans and Energy Development*, by Joseph G. Jorgensen, Richard O. Clemmer, Ronald L. Little, Nancy J. Owens, and Lynn A. Robbins, pp. 3–16. Cambridge, MA: Anthropology Resource Center.

Jorgensen, Joseph G. 1993. Kathleen Gough's Fight Against the Consequences of Class and Imperialism on Campus. *Anthropologica*, vol. XXXV, no. 2, pp. 227–34. Waterloo, Ontario, Canada.

Joyce, Barry A. 2001. *The Shaping of American Ethnography: The Wilkes Exploring Expedition, 1838–1842*. Lincoln, NB: University of Nebraska Press.

Judd, Neil M. 1967. *The Bureau of American Ethnology*. Norman, OK: University of Oklahoma Press.

Kardiner, Abram 1939/1974. *The Individual and His Society: The Psychodynamics of Primitive Social Organization*. Westport, CT: Greenwood Press.

Kearney, Michael 1995. The Local and the Global: The Anthroplogy of Globalization and Transnationalism, *Annual Review of Anthropology,* vol. 24, pp. 547–65. Palo Alto.

Kejariwal, O. P. 1995. William Jones: The Copernicus of History. In *Objects of Enquiry: The Life, Contributions, and Influences of Sir William Jones (1746–1794)*, edited by Garland Cannon and Kevin R. Brine, pp. 102–15. New York: New York University Press.

Kelly, Lawrence C. 1975. The Indian Reorganization Act: The Dream and the Reality. *Pacific Historical Review*, vol. XLVI, no. 3, pp. 291–313. Berkeley.

Kelly, Lawrence C. 1980. Anthropology and Anthropologists in the Indian New Deal. *Journal of the History of the Behavioral Sciences*, vol. 16, no. 1, pp. 6–24. Brandon.

Kelly, Lawrence C. 1985a. Why Applied Anthropology Developed When It Did: A Commentary on People, Money, and Changing Times, 1930–1945. In *Social Context of American Ethnology, 1840–1984*, edited by June Helm. 1984 Proceedings of the American Ethnological Society, pp. 122–38. Washington.

Kelly, Lawrence C. 1985b. Anthropology in the Soil Conservation Service. *Agricultural History*, vol. 59, no. 2, pp. 136–47. Berkeley.

Kennard, Edward A. and Gordon Macgregor 1953. Applied Anthropology in Government: United States. In *Anthropology Today: An Encyclopedic Survey*, edited by Alfred L. Kroeber, pp. 832–40. Chicago, IL: University of Chicago Press.

Kennedy, Raymond 1945. The Colonial Crisis and the Future. In *The Science of Man in the World Crisis*, edited by Ralph Linton, pp. 306–47. New York: Columbia University Press.

Kerber, Linda K. 1975. The Abolitionist Perception of the Indian. *The Journal of American History,* vol. LXII, no. 2, pp. 271–95. Menasha.

Kidder, Alfred V. 1924. *An Introduction to the Study of Southwestern Archaeology, with a Preliminary Account of the Excavations at Pecos*. Papers of the Southwestern Expedition, Peabody Academy, no. 1. New Haven, CT: Yale University Press.

Kimball, Solon T. and John H. Provinse 1942. Navajo Social Organization in Land Use Planning. *Applied Anthropology*, vol. 1, pp. 20–5. Washington.

King, Louis E. 1951. *Negro Life in a Rural Community*. Ph.D. Dissertation in Anthropology, Columbia University. New York.

Kiste, Robert C. and Mac Marshall, editors 1999. *American Anthropology in Micronesia: An Assessment*. Honolulu, HI: University of Hawai'i Press.

Klausner, Samuel Z. 1986. The Bid to Nationalize American Social Science. In *The Nationalization of the Social Sciences*, edited by Samuel Z. Klausner and Victor M. Lidz, pp. 3–40. Philadelphia, PA: University of Pennsylvania Press.

Kluckhohn, Clyde 1943. Covert Culture and Administrative Problems. *American Anthropologist*, vol. 45, no. 2, pp. 213–27. Menasha.

Kluckhohn, Clyde 1955/1961. Studies of Russian National Character. In *Soviet Society: A Book of Readings*, edited by Alex Inkeles and Kent Geiger, pp. 607–19. Boston, MA: Houghton Mifflin.

Kohl, Phillip L. 1981. Materialist Approaches in Prehistory. *Annual Review of Anthropology*, vol. 10, pp. 89–118. Palo Alto.

Köhnke, Klaus C. 1991. *The Rise of Neo-Kantianism: German Academic Philosophy between Idealism and Positivism.* Cambridge, UK: Cambridge University Press.

Kolko, Joyce 1988 *Restructuring the World Economy*. New York: Pantheon Books.

Krader, Lawrence 1974. Introduction. In *The Ethnological Notebooks of Karl Marx*, pp. 1–93. Assen: Van Gorcum and Company.

Kroeber, Alfred L. 1917/1952. The Superorganic. In *The Nature of Culture*, by Alfred L. Kroeber, pp. 22–51. Chicago, IL: University of Chicago Press.

Kroeber, Alfred L. 1948. *Anthropology*. New York: Harcourt Brace.

Kroeber, Alfred L., editor 1953. *Anthropology Today: An Encyclopedic Inventory*. Chicago, IL: University of Chicago Press.

Kroeber, Alfred L. and Talcott Parsons 1958. The Concepts of Culture and of Social System. *American Sociological Review*, vol. 23, no. 5, pp. 582–3. New York.

Krook, Susan P. 1993. *An Analysis of Franz Boas's Achievements and Work Emphasis during the Last Five Years of His Life, Based on Documentation and Interpretation of the Federal Bureau of Investigation File Maintained on Him from 1936 to 1950.* Ph.D. Dissertation in Anthropology, University of Colorado, Boulder (University Microfilms no. 9423513).

Kuper, Adam 1985. The Development of Lewis Henry Morgan's Evolutionism. *Journal of the History of the Behavioral Sciences*, vol. 21, no. 1, pp. 3–22. Brandon, VT.

Lagemann, Ellen C. 1989. *The Politics of Knowledge: The Carnegie Corporation, Philanthropy, and Public Policy.* Chicago, IL: The University of Chicago Press.

Lauria-Perricelli, Antonio 1989. *A Study in Historical and Cultural Anthropology: The Making of "The People of Puerto Rico."* Ph.D. Dissertation in Anthropology, New School for Social Research. Ann Arbor, MI: University Microfilms no. 9121295.

Leacock, Eleanor B. 1963. Introduction. In *Ancient Society, Or Researches in the Lines of Human Progress from Savagery through Barbarism to Civilization*, by Lewis Henry Morgan. New York: World Publishing Company.

Leacock, Eleanor B. 1971. Introduction. In *The Culture of Poverty: A Critique*, edited by Eleanor B. Leacock, pp. 9–37. New York: Simon and Schuster.

Leacock, Eleanor B. 1972. Introduction. In *The Origin of the Family, Private Property and the State: In Light of the Researches of Lewis H. Morgan,* by Frederick Engels, pp. 7–67. New York: International Publishers.

Leacock, Eleanor B. 1982a. Marxism and Anthropology. In *The Left Academy: Marxist Scholarship on American Campuses,* edited by Bertell Ollman and Edward Vernoff, pp. 242–76. New York: McGraw-Hill Book Company.

Leacock, Eleanor B. 1982b. Relations of Production in Band Society. *In Politics and History in Band Societies,* edited by Eleanor Leacock and Richard Lee, pp. 159–70. Cambridge, UK: Cambridge University Press.

Leacock, Eleanor B. 1993. Being an Anthropologist. In *From Labrador to Samoa: The Theory and Practice of Eleanor Burke Leacock,* edited by Constance R. Sutton, pp. 1–32. Washington, DC: Association for Feminist Anthropology, American Anthropological Association.

Leacock, Eleanor and Helen I. Safa, editors 1986. *Women's Work: Development and the Division of Labor by Gender.* South Hadley, MA: Bergin and Garvey Publishers.

Lee, Richard B. 1993. *The Dobe Ju/'hoansi.* Ft. Worth, TX: Harcourt Brace College Publishers.

Lee, Richard B. 2000. Indigenism and its Discontents: Anthropology and the Small Peoples at the Millennium. Keynote Address, Annual Meeting of the American Ethnological Society, 25 March, Tampa.

Lee, Richard B. and Irven DeVore, editors 1968. *Man the Hunter.* Chicago, IL: Aldine Publishing Company.

Lee, Richard B. and Karen Brodkin Sacks 1993. Anthropology, Imperialism and Resistance: The Work of Kathleen Gough. *Anthropologica,* vol. XXXV, no. 2, pp. 181–93. Waterloo, Ontario, Canada.

Leeds-Hurwitz, Wendy 1983. *Jaime de Angulo: An Intellectual Biography.* Ph.D. Dissertation in Folklore and Folklife, University of Pennsylvania. Philadelphia.

Leeds-Hurwitz, Wendy 1985. The Committee on Research in Native American Languages. *Proceedings of the American Philosophical Society,* vol. 129, no. 2, pp. 129–60. Philadelphia.

Leighton, Alexander 1949. *Human Relations in a Changing World: Observations on the Use of the Social Sciences.* New York: E. P. Dutton and Company.

Lesser, Alexander 1933. *The Pawnee Ghost Dance Hand Game: A Study of Cultural Change.* Columbia University Contributions to Anthropology, vol. XVI. New York: Columbia University Press.

Lesser, Alexander 1968. Boas, Franz. In *International Encyclopedia of the Social Sciences,* edited by David L. Sills, vol. 2, pp. 99–110. New York: The Macmillan Company and The Free Press.

Lesser, Alexander 1981. Franz Boas. In *Totems and Teachers: Perspectives on the History of Anthropology,* edited by Sydel Silverman, pp. 1–33. New York: Columbia University Press.

Levine, Stephen K. 1979. Marxist Anthropology and the Critique of Everyday Life. In *Toward a Marxist Anthropology: Problems and Perspectives*, edited by Stanley Diamond, pp. 13–29. The Hague: Mouton Publishers.

Lewis, Oscar 1951. *Life in a Mexican Village: Tepotztlán Restudied*. Urbana, IL: University of Illinois Press.

Lewis, Oscar 1966. *La Vida: A Puerto Rican Family in the Culture of Poverty – San Juan and New York*. New York: Random House.

Lewontin, Richard C. 1997. The Cold War and the Transformation of the Academy. In *The Cold War and the University: Toward an Intellectual History of the Postwar Years*, edited by André Schiffrin, pp. 1–34. New York: New Press.

Linton, Ralph 1924. An Anthropological View of Race Mixture. *Publications of the American Sociological Society*, vol. XXI, pp. 69–76. Chicago.

Linton, Ralph 1940. Introduction. In *Acculturation in Seven American Indian Tribes*, edited by Ralph Linton, pp. vii–xi. New York: D. Appleton-Century Company.

Linton, Ralph 1945. *The Cultural Background of Personality*. New York. D. Appleton-Century Company.

Lock, Margaret 1993. Cultivating the Body: Anthropology and the Epistemologies of Bodily Practice and Knowledge. *Annual Review of Anthropology*, vol. 22, pp. 133–55. Palo Alto.

Locke, John 1690/1980. *Second Treatise of Government*, edited by Crawford B. Macpherson. Indianapolis, IN: Hackett Publishing Company.

Lowie, Robert H. 1917/1966. *Primitive Society*, edited by Stanley Diamond. New York: Basic Books.

Lynd, Robert S. and Helen M. Lynd 1929. *Middletown: A Study of Contemporary American Culture*. New York: Harcourt, Brace and Company.

Lyon, Edwin A. 1996. *A New Deal for Southeastern Archaeology*. Tuscaloosa, AL: University of Alabama Press.

McCaughey, Robert A. 1984. *International Studies and Academic Enterprise: A Chapter in the Enclosure of American Learning*. New York: Columbia University Press.

McCulloh, James H., Jr. 1829. *Researches Philosophical and Antiquarian Concerning the Aboriginal History of America*. Baltimore, MD: Fielding Lucas.

McGuire, Randall H. and Robert Paynter, editors 1991. *The Archaeology of Inequality*. Oxford, UK: Basil Blackwell.

McVicker, Donald 1990. Putnam, Boas, and Holmes – Establishing Anthropology at the Field Columbian Museum. *History of Anthropology Newsletter*, vol. XVII, no. 2, pp. 3–8. Chicago.

McVicker, Donald 1999. Buying a Curator: Establishing Anthropology at the Field Columbian Museum. In *Assembling the Past: Studies in the Professionalization of Archaeology,* edited by Alice B. Kehoe and Mary Beth Emmerichs, pp. 37–52. Albuquerque, NM: University of New Mexico Press.

Malinowski, Bronislaw 1938. Introductory Essay: The Anthropology of Changing African Cultures. In *Methods of Study of Culture Contact in Africa*, edited by Lucy P. Mair, pp. vii–xxxviii. Oxford, UK: Oxford University Press.

Manson, William C. 1986. Abram Kardiner and the Neo-Freudian Alternative in Culture and Personality. In *Malinowski, Rivers, Benedict and Others: Essays on Culture and Personality*, edited by George W. Stocking, Jr. History of Anthropology, vol. 2, pp. 72–94. Madison, WI: University of Wisconsin Press.

Marcus, George E. 1995. Ethnography in/of the World System: The Emergence of Multi-Sited Ethnography. *Annual Review of Anthropology,* vol. 24, pp. 95–114. Palo Alto.

Marcus, George E. and Michael M. J. Fischer 1986. *Anthropology as Cultural Critique: An Experimental Moment in the Human Sciences*. Chicago, IL: University of Chicago Press.

Mark, Joan 1980. *Four Anthropologists: An American Science in its Early Years*. New York: Science History Publications.

Marx, Karl 1880–2/1974. *The Ethnological Notebooks of Karl Marx*, transcribed and edited with an introduction by Lawrence Krader. Assen: Van Gorcum and Company.

Mascia-Lees, Frances E., Patricia Sharpe, and Colleen Ballerino Cohen 1989 The Postmodernist Turn in Anthropology: Cautions from a Feminist Perspective. *Signs*, vol. 15, no. 1, pp. 7–33. Chicago.

Mead, Margaret 1926. The Methodology of Racial Testing: Its Significance for Sociology. *American Journal of Sociology*, vol. 31, no. 5, pp. 657–67. Chicago.

Mead, Margaret 1928. *Coming of Age in Samoa: A Psychological Study of Primitive Youth for Western Civilization*. New York: William Morrow.

Mead, Margaret 1930. *Growing Up in New Guinea: A Comparative Study of Primitive Education*. New York: William Morrow.

Mead, Margaret 1935. *Sex and Temperament in Three Primitive Societies*. New York: William Morrow.

Mead, Margaret 1953. Introduction. In *The Study of Culture at a Distance*, edited by Margaret Mead and Rhoda Métraux, pp. 3–53. Chicago, IL: University of Chicago Press.

Mead, Margaret 1979. Anthropological Contributions to National Policies During and Immediately After World War II. In *The Use of Anthropology*, edited by Walter Goldschmidt. Special Publication of the American Anthropological Association, no. 11, pp. 124–44. Washington.

Mead, Margaret and Rhoda Métraux, editors 1953 *The Study of Culture at a Distance*. Chicago, IL: University of Chicago Press.

Medicine, Beatrice 1989. Ella Cara Deloria (1888–1971). In *Women Anthropologists: Selected Biographies*, edited by Ute Gacs, Aisha Khan, Jerrie McIntyre, and Ruth Weinberg, pp. 45–50. Urbana, IL: University of Illinois Press.

Meek, Ronald L. 1976. *Social Science and the Ignoble Savage*. Cambridge, UK: Cambridge University Press.

Meggers, Betty 1960. The Law of Cultural Evolution as a Practical Research Tool. In *Essays in the Science of Culture*, edited by Gertrude Dole and Robert Carneiro, pp. 302–16. New York: Thomas Crowell.

Meltzer, David J. and Robert C. Dunnell 1992. Introduction. In *The Archaeology of William Henry Holmes*, edited by David J. Meltzer and Robert C. Dunnell, pp. vii–l. Washington, DC: Smithsonian Institution Press.

Mikell, Gwendolyn 1989. Zora Neale Hurston (1903–1960). In *Women Anthropologists: Selected Biographies*, edited by Ute Gacs, Aisha Khan, Jerrie McIntyre, and Ruth Weinberg, pp. 160–6. Urbana, IL: University of Illinois Press.

Miller, Charles A. 1988. *Jefferson and Nature: An Interpretation*. Baltimore, MD: The Johns Hopkins University Press.

Miller, John C. 1991. *The Wolf by the Ears: Thomas Jefferson and Slavery*. Charlottesville, VA: University of Virginia Press.

Miller, R. Berkeley 1975. Anthropology and Institutionalization: Frederick Starr at the University of Chicago, 1892–1923. *The Kroeber Anthropological Society Papers*, nos. 51–52, pp. 49–60. Berkeley.

Millikan, Marx F. and Walt W. Rostow 1954/1998. Notes on Foreign Economic Policy. In *Universities and Empire: Money and Politics in the Social Sciences during the Cold War*, edited by Christopher Simpson, pp. 39–56. New York: New Press.

Mintz, Sidney 1953. The Folk-Urban Continuum and the Rural Proletarian Community. *American Journal of Sociology*, vol. 59, no. 1, pp. 136–43. Chicago.

Montagu, M. F. Ashley 1942/1997. *Man's Most Dangerous Myth: The Fallacy of Race*, 6th edn. Walnut Creek, CA: Altamira Press.

Montagu, M. F. Ashley 1951. *Statement on Race*. New York: Henry Schuman.

Montgomery, David 1997. Introduction. In *The Cold War and the University: Toward an Intellectual History of the Postwar Years*, edited by André Schiffrin, pp. xi–xxxvii. New York: New Press.

Montgomery, Edward and John W. Bennett 1979. Anthropological Studies of Food and Nutrition: The 1940s and the 1970s. In *The Uses of Anthropology*, edited by Walter Goldschmidt. Special Publication of the American Anthropological Association, no. 11, pp. 124–44. Washington.

Mooney, James E. 1896. The Ghost-Dance Religion and the Sioux Outbreak of 1890. *Fourteenth Annual Report of the Bureau of Ethnology, 1892-'93*, pp. 653–1136. Washington.

Morgan, Lewis H. 1851. *League of the Ho-de-no-sau-nee, or Iroquois*. Rochester, NY: Sage and Brothers.

Morgan, Lewis H. 1871. *Systems of Consanguinity and Affinity of the Human Family*. Smithsonian Contributions to Knowledge, vol. XVII. Washington, DC: Smithsonian Institution.

Morgan, Lewis H. 1876. The Hue and Cry Against the Indians. *The Nation*, vol. XXIII, no. 577, pp. 40–1. New York.

Morgan, Lewis H. 1877/1963. *Ancient Society, Or Researches in the Lines of Human Progress from Savagery through Barbarism to Civilization*, edited by Eleanor B. Leacock. New York: World Publishing Company.

Morgan, Lewis H. 1880a. On the Ruins of a Stone Pueblo on the Animas River in New Mexico. *Twelfth Annual Report of the Peabody Museum of American Archaeology and Ethnology, Harvard University*, pp. 536–56. Cambridge.

Morgan, Lewis H. 1880b. Study of the Houses of the American Aborigines with Suggestions for the Exploration of the Ruins of New Mexico, Arizona, the Valley of the San Juan and in Yucatan and Central America. *First Annual Report of the Executive Committee, Archaeological Institute of America, 1879–1880*, pp. 27–80. Cambridge.

Morgan, Lewis H. 1881. *Houses and House Life of the American Aborigines*. U.S. Geological Survey, Contributions to North American Ethnology, vol. IV. Washington.

Morton, Samuel G. 1839. *Crania Americana, or a Comparative View of the Skulls of Various Aboriginal Nations of North and South America*. Philadelphia, PA: Dobson.

Morton, Samuel G. 1844. *Crania Aegyptica: Observations on Egyptian Ethnography, Derived from Anatomy, History, and the Monuments*. Philadelphia, PA: John Pennington.

Moses, Lester G. 1984. *The Indian Man: A Biography of James Mooney*. Urbana, IL: The University of Illinois Press.

Moses, Yolanda T. 1997. Are Four Fields in Our Future? *Anthropology Newsletter*, vol. 38, no. 9, pp. 8–11. Arlington.

Moynihan, Daniel P. 1965. *The Negro Family: The Case for National Action*. Washington, DC: U.S. Department of Labor.

Mullings, Leith 1993. Eleanor Leacock and Urban Anthropology in the United States. In *From Labrador to Samoa: The Theory and Practice of Eleanor Burke Leacock*, edited by Constance R. Sutton, pp. 67–76. Washington, DC: Association for Feminist Anthropology/American Anthropological Association.

Mullings, Leith 1994/1997. Reclaiming Culture: The Dialectics of Identity. In *In Our Own Terms: Race, Class, and Gender in the Lives of African American Women*, by Leith Mullings, pp. 189–94. New York: Routledge.

Murray, Stephen O. 1994. *Theory Groups and the Study of Language in North America: A Social History*. Studies in the History of the Language Sciences, 69. Amsterdam: John Benjamins Publishing Company.

Myrdal, Gunnar 1944/1962 *An American Dilemma: The Negro Problem and Modern Democracy*. New York: Harper and Row Publishers.

Nagengast, Carole 1994. Violence, Terror, and the Crisis of the State. *Annual Review of Anthropology*, vol. 23, pp. 109–36. Palo Alto.

Nash, Gary 1986. *Race, Class, and Politics: Essays on American Colonial and Revolutionary Society*. Urbana, IL: University of Illinois Press.

Nash, June 1976. Ethnology in a Revolutionary Setting. In *Ethics and Anthropology: Dilemmas in Fieldwork*, edited by R. Rynklewich and James P. Spradley, pp. 148–66. Toronto, ON: Wiley and Sons.

Nash, June 1983. The Impact of the Changing International Division of Labor on Different Sectors of the Work Force. In *Women, Men, and the International Division of Labor*, edited by June Nash and María Fernández-Kelly, pp. 3–38. Albany, NY: State University of New York Press.

Nash, June 1989. From Tank Town to High Tech. Albany, NY: State University of New York Press.

Nash, June 1993. Maya Household Production in the World Market: The Potters of Amatenango del Valle, Chiapas, Mexico. In *Crafts in the World Market: The Impact of Global Exchange on Middle American Artisans*, edited by June Nash, pp. 127–53. Albany, NY: State University of New York Press.

Nash, June 1995. The Reassertion of Indigenous Identity: Mayan Responses to State Intervention in Chiapas. *Journal of Latin American Research*, vol. 30, no. 3, pp. 7–41. Austin.

Needell, Allan A. 1998. Project Troy and the Cold War Annexation of the Social Sciences. In *Universities and Empire: Money and Politics in the Social Sciences during the Cold War*, edited by Christopher Simpson, pp. 3–38. New York: New Press.

Nelson, Nels C. 1916 Chronology of the Tano Ruins, New Mexico. *American Anthropologist*, vol. 18, no. 2, pp. 150–80. New York.

Nishimoto, Richard S. 1995. *Inside an American Concentration Camp: Japanese American Resistance at Postan, Arizona*, edited by Lane R. Hirabayashi. Tucson, AZ: University of Arizona Press.

Noelke, Virginia H. M. 1974. *The Origin and Early History of the Bureau of American Ethnology, 1879–1910*. Ph.D. Dissertation in History, University of Texas, Austin. Ann Arbor, MI: University Microfilms 75–24,994.

Nonini, Donald M. 1985. Varieties of Materialism. *Dialectical Anthropology*, vol. 9, nos. 1–4, pp. 7–64. Amsterdam.

Nott, Josiah Clark 1843. The Mulatto a Hybrid – Probable Extermination of the Two Races if the White and Blacks Are Allowed to Intermarry. *American Journal of Medical Sciences*, vol. 6, pp. 252–256. Philadelphia.

O'Brien, Donal Cruise 1972. Modernization, Order, and the Erosion of a Democratic Ideal: American Political Science, 1960–1970. *Journal of Development Studies*, vol. 8, no. 4, pp. 351–78. London.

O'Laughlin, Bridget 1975. Marxist Approaches in Anthropology. *Annual Review of Anthropology*, vol. 4, pp. 341–70. Palo Alto.

Olien, Michael D. 1985. E. G. Squier and the Moskito: Anthropological Scholarship and Political Propaganda. *Ethnohistory*, vol. 32, no. 2, pp. 111–33. Tucson.

Ong, Aihwa 1991. The Gender and Labor Politics of Postmodernity. *Annual Review of Anthropology*, vol. 20, pp. 279–309. Palo Alto.

Ong, Aihwa and Donald Nonini 1997. Toward a Cultural Politics of Diaspora and Transnationalism. In *Underground Empire: The Cultural Politics of Modern Chinese Transnationalism*, edited by Aihwa Ong and Donald Nonini, pp. 323–32. New York: Routledge.

Opler, Morris E. 1952. The Creek "Town" and Problem of Creek Political Reorganization. In *Human Problems in Technological Change*, edited by Edward H. Spicer, pp. 165–80. New York: Russell Sage Foundation.

Opler, Morris E. 1961. Cultural Evolution, Southern Athapaskans, and Chronology in Theory. *Southwestern Journal of Anthropology*, vol. 17, no. 1, pp. 1–20. Albuquerque.

Orlove, Benjamin S. 1980. Ecological Anthropology. *Annual Review of Anthropology*, vol. 9, pp. 235–73. Palo Alto.

Ortner, Sherry B. 1984/1994. Theory in Anthropology since the 1960s. In *Culture/Power/History: A Reader in Contemporary Social Theory*, edited by Nicholas B. Dirks, Geoff Eley and Sherry B. Ortner, pp. 372–411. Princeton, NJ: Princeton University Press.

Parsons, Talcott 1973 Clyde Kluckhohn and the Integration of Social Science. In *Culture and Life: Essays in Memory of Clyde Kluckhohn*, edited by Walter W. Taylor, John L. Fischer, and Evon Z. Vogt, pp. 30–57. Carbondale, IL: Southern Illinois University Press.

Partridge, William L. and Elizabeth M. Eddy 1987. The Development of Applied Anthropology in America. In *Applied Anthropology in America*, 2nd edn, edited by Elizabeth M. Eddy and William L. Partridge, pp. 33–55. New York: Columbia University Press.

Pathé, Ruth E. 1979. Gene Weltfish. In *Women Anthropologists: Selected Biographies*, edited by Ute Gacs, Aisha Khan, Jerrie McIntyre, and Ruth Weinberg, pp. 372–82. Urbana, IL: University of Illinois Press.

Patterson, Thomas C. 1986. The Last Sixty Years: Toward a Social History of Americanist Archaeology in the United States. *American Anthropologist*, vol. 88, no. 1, pp. 7–26. Washington.

Patterson, Thomas C. 1988. La creación de cultura en las formaciones sociales pre-estatales y no estatales. *Boletín de Antropología Americana*, no. 14, pp. 53–61. Mexico.

Patterson, Thomas C. 1995. *Toward a Social History of Archaeology in the United States*. Ft. Worth, TX: Harcourt, Brace and Company.

Patterson, Thomas C. 1999a. The Political Economy of Archaeology in the United States. *Annual Review of Anthropology*, vol. 28, pp. 155–74. Palo Alto.

Patterson, Thomas C. 1999b. *Change and Development in the Twentieth Century*. Oxford, UK: Berg Publishers.

Patterson, Thomas C. and Antonio Lauria-Perricelli 1999. Julian Steward and the Construction of Area-Studies Research in the United States. In *Julian Steward and the Great Basin: The Making of an Anthroplogist*, edited by Richard O. Clemmer, L. Daniel Myers, and Mary E. Rudden, pp. 219–40. Salt Lake City, UT: University of Utah Press.

Patterson, Thomas C. and Frank Spencer 1994. Racial Hierarchies and Buffer Races. In *Race, Racism, and the History of U.S. Anthropology*, edited by Lee D. Baker and Thomas C. Patterson. Transforming Anthropology, vol. 5, no. 1–2, pp. 20–8. Washington.

Paynter, Robert 1989. The Archaeology of Equality and Inequality. *Annual Review of Anthropology*, vol. 18, pp. 369–99. Palo Alto.

Peace, William J. 1993 Leslie White and Evolutionary Theory. *Dialectical Anthropology*, vol. 18, no. 2, pp. 123–52. Dordrecht.

Pels, Richard H. 1973. *Radical Visions and American Dreams: Culture and Social Thought in the Depression Years*. New York: Harper and Row.

Perry, Helen S. 1982. *Psychiatrist of America: The Life of Harry Stack Sullivan*. Cambridge, MA: Harvard University Press.

Petersen, Glenn 1999. Politics in Postwar Micronesia. In *American Anthropology in Micronesia: An Assessment*, edited by Robert C. Kiste and Mac Marshall, pp. 145–96. Honolulu, HI: University of Hawai'i Press.

Phillips, Kevin P. 1993. *Boiling Point: Democrats, Republicans, and the Decline of Middle Class Prosperity*. New York: Random House.

Pickering, John 1849. Presidential Address. *Journal of the American Oriental Society*, vol. 1, pp. 1–60. New Haven.

Powdermaker, Hortense 1939. *After Freedom: A Cultural Study in the Deep South*. New York: Viking.

Powell, John W. 1877. *Introduction to the Study of Indian Languages, with Words, Phrases, and Sentences to be Collected*. Washington, DC: U.S. Government Printing Office.

Powell, John W. 1878. *Report on the Methods of Surveying the Public Domain to the Secretary of the Interior at the Request of the National Academy of Sciences*. Washington, DC: U.S. Government Printing Office.

Powell, John W. 1882. Darwin's Contribution to Philosophy. *Proceedings of the Biological Society of Washington*, vol. I, pp. 60–70. Washington.

Powell, John W. 1883. Human Evolution. *Transactions of the Anthropological Society of Washington*, vol. I, pp. 176–208. Washington.

Powell, John W. 1885. From Savagery to Barbarism. *Transactions of the Anthropological Society of Washington*, vol. II, pp. 173–96. Washington.

Powell, John W. 1888. From Barbarism to Civilization. *American Anthropologist*, o.s., vol. I, no. 2, pp. 97–123. Washington.

Powell, John W. 1891. Indian Linguistic Families North of Mexico. *Seventh Annual Report of the Bureau of Ethnology, 1885–'86*, pp. 7–139. Washington.

Powell, John W. 1894. *Twelfth Annual Report of the Bureau of Ethnology. Twelfth Annual Report of the Bureau of Ethnology, 1890–'91*, pp. xxi–xlviii. Washington.

Powell, John W. 1896. The Director's Report. *Fourteenth Annual Report of the Bureau of Ethnology, 1892–'93*, pp. xxvii–lx. Washington.

Powell, John W. and George W. Ingalls 1874. *Report on the Conditions of the Ute Indians of Utah; the Pai-Utes of Utah, Northern Arizona, Southern Nevada, and Southeastern California; the Go-Si-Utes of Utah and Nevada; the Northwestern Shoshones of Idaho and Utah; and the Western Shoshones of Nevada. (43rd Cong., 1st Sess; Report of the Secretary of the Interior, I)*. Washington, DC: Government Printing Office.

Price, David H. 1998 Cold War Anthropology: Collaborators and Victims of the National Security State. *Identities*, vol. 4, nos. 3–4, pp. 389–430. Amsterdam.

Price, David H. 2000. Anthropologists as Spies. *The Nation*, vol. 271, no. 16, November 20, pp. 24–7. New York.

Prucha, Francis P. 1967. *Lewis Cass and American Indian Policy*. Detroit, MI: Wayne State University Press.

Quimby, George I., Jr. 1979. A Brief History of WPA Archaeology. *In The Uses of Anthropology*, edited by Walter Goldschmidt. Special Publication of the American Anthropological Association, no. 11, pp. 110–23. Washington, DC.

Rabinow, Paul 1985. Discourse and Power: On the Limits of Ethnographic Texts. *Dialectical Anthropology*, vol. 10, nos. 1–2, pp. 1–14. Amsterdam.

Rabinow, Paul 1989. *French Modern: Norms and Forms of the Social Environment*. Cambridge, MA: The MIT Press.

Radcliffe-Brown, A. R. 1924/1986. Science and Native Problems: How to Understand the Bantu. *Anthropology Today*, vol. 2, no. 4, pp. 17–21. London.

Radcliffe-Brown, A. R. 1937/1957. *A Natural Science of Society*. Chicago, IL: University of Chicago Press.

Ransom, David 1974. Ford Country: Building an Elite for Indonesia. *In The Trojan Horse: A Radical Look at Foreign Aid*, edited by Steve Weisman, pp. 93–116. San Francisco, CA: Ramparts Press.

Rappaport, Roy A. 1971. Nature, Culture, and Ecological Anthropology. In *Man, Culture, and Society*, edited by Harry L. Shapiro, pp. 237–67. Oxford, UK: Oxford University Press.

Rappaport, Roy A. 1977. Ecology, Adaptation and the Ills of Functionalism (Being, Among Other Things, A Response to Jonathan Friedman). *Michigan Discussions in Anthropology*, no. 2, pp. 138–90. Ann Arbor.

Redfield, Robert 1930. *Tepoztlan: A Mexican Village: A Study of Folk Life*. Chicago, IL: University of Chicago Press.

Redfield, Robert 1934. Culture Changes in Yucatan. *American Anthropologist*, vol. 36, no. 1, pp. 57–69. Menasha.

Redfield, Robert 1941. *The Folk Culture of Yucatan*. Chicago, IL: University of Chicago Press.

Redfield, Robert 1957/1960. Comments on Papers Read on the Program "Values in Action." In *Documentary History of the Fox Project, 1948–1959: A Program in Action Anthropology*, edited by Fred Gearing, Robert McC. Netting and Lisa R. Peattie, pp. 418–22. Chicago, IL: University of Chicago Press.

Redfield, Robert and Alfonso Villa Rojas 1934. *Chan Kom, A Maya Village*. Carnegie Institution of Washington Publication 448. Washington.

Redfield, Robert, Ralph Linton, and Melville J. Herskovits 1936. Memorandum for the Study of Acculturation. *American Anthropologist*, vol. 38, no. 1, pp. 149–52. Menasha.

Reed, Adolph, Jr. 1999. *Stirrings in the Jug: Black Politics in the Post-Segregation Era*. Minneapolis, MN: University of Minnesota Press.

Reingold, Nathan 1979. National Science Policy in a Private Foundation: The Carnegie Institution of Washington. In *The Organization of Knowledge in Modern America, 1860–1920*, edited by Alexandra Oleson and John Voss, pp. 313–41. Baltimore, MD: The Johns Hopkins University Press.

Reiter, Rayna Rapp, editor 1975. *Toward an Anthropology of Women*. New York: Monthly Review Press.

Resek, Carl P. 1960. *Lewis Henry Morgan: American Scholar*. Chicago, IL: University of Chicago Press.

Richardson, F. L. W. 1979. Social Interaction and Industrial Productivity. *In The Uses of Anthropology*, edited by Walter R. Goldschmidt. American Anthropological Association Special Publication, no. 11, pp. 79–99. Washington.

Richardson, Theresa and Donald Fisher 1999. Introduction: The Social Sciences and Their Philanthropic Mentors. In *The Development of the Social Sciences in the United States and Canada: The Role of Philanthropy*, edited by Theresa Richardson and Donald Fisher, pp. 3–21. Stamford, CT: Ablex Publishing Corporation.

Rigdon, Susan M. 1988. *The Culture Facade: Art, Science, and Politics in the Work of Oscar Lewis*. Urbana, IL: University of Illinois Press.

Rosaldo, Michelle Z. and Louise Lamphere, editors 1974. *Women, Culture and Society*. Stanford, CA: Stanford University Press.

Ross, Hubert B., Amelia M. Adams, and Lynne M. Williams 1999. Carolyn Bond Day: Pioneer Black Physical Anthropologist. In *African-American Pioneers in Anthropology*, edited by Ira E. Harrison and Faye V. Harrison, pp. 37–50. Urbana, IL: University of Illinois Press.

Rostow, Walt W. 1960. *The Stages of Economic Growth: A Non-Communist Manifesto*. Cambridge, UK: Cambridge University Press.

Rubenstein, Robert A. 1991. Introduction: Reflection and Reflexivity. In *Fieldwork: The Correspondence of Robert Redfield and Sol Tax*, edited by Robert A. Rubenstein, pp. 1–36. Boulder, CO: Westview Press.

Rumbaut, Rubén G. 1991. Passages to America: Perspectives on the New Immigration. In *America at Century's End*, edited by Alan Wolfe, pp. 208–44. Berkeley, CA: University of California Press.

Rydell, Robert W. 1984. *All the World's a Fair: Visions of Empire at American International Expositions, 1876–1916*. Chicago, IL: University of Chicago Press.

Sahlins, Marshall D. 1960. Evolution: Specific and General. In *Evolution and Culture*, edited by Marshall D. Sahlins and Elman R. Service, pp. 12–44. Ann Arbor, MI: University of Michigan Press.

Sahlins, Marshall D. 1976. *Culture and Practical Reason*. Chicago, IL: University of Chicago Press.

Sahlins, Marshall D. 1981. *Historical Metaphors and Mythical Realities: Structure in the Early History of the Sandwich Islands Kingdom*. Association for Social Anthropology in Oceania Special Publications no. 1. Ann Arbor, MI: University of Michigan Press.

Sahlins, Marshall D. 1989. Cosmologies of Capitalism: The Trans-Pacific Sector of "The World System." *Proceedings of the British Academy*, vol. LXXIV, pp. 1–51. London.

Sapir, Edward 1917. Do We Need a "Superorganic"? *American Anthropologist*, vol. 19, no. 3, pp. 441–7. Washington.

Sapir, Edward 1921/1984. A Bird's-Eye View of American Languages North of Mexico. In *Edward Sapir: Appraisals of his Life and Work*, edited by Konrad Koerner. Studies in the History of the Language Sciences, vol. 36, p. 140. Amsterdam: John Benjamins Publishing Company.

Sapir, Edward 1924/1949. Culture: Genuine and Spurious. In *Selected Writings of Edward Sapir in Language, Culture and Personality*, edited by David G. Mandelbaum, pp. 308–31. Berkeley, CA: University of California Press.

Sapir, Edward 1925/1949. Sound Patterns in Language. In *Selected Writings of Edward Sapir in Language, Culture and Personality*, edited by David G. Mandelbaum, pp. 33–45. Berkeley, CA: University of California Press.

Saxton, Alexander 1990. *The Rise and Fall of the White Republic: Class Politics and Mass Culture in Nineteenth-Century America*. London, UK: Verso.

Schneider, David M. 1969/1977. Kinship, Nationality, and Religion in American Culture: Toward a Definition of Kinship. In *Symbolic Anthropology: A Reader in the Study of Symbols and Meanings*, edited by Janet L. Dolgin, David S. Kemnitzer, and David M. Schneider, pp. 63–71. New York: Columbia University Press.

Schneider, David M. 1976. Notes toward a Theory of Culture. In *Meaning in Anthropology*, edited by Keith H. Basso and Henry A. Selby, pp. 197–220. Albuquerque, NM: University of New Mexico Press.

Schoolcraft, Henry R. 1851–7. *Historical and Statistical Information Respecting the History, Condition, and Prospects of the Indian Tribes of the United States,* 6 vols. Philadelphia, PA: Lippincott, Grambo and Company.

Schrecker, Ellen W. 1986. *No Ivory Tower: McCarthyism and the Universities.* New York: Oxford University Press.

Service, Elman R. 1960. The Law of Evolutionary Potential. In *Evolution and Culture,* edited by Marshall D. Sahlins and Elman R. Service, pp. 93–122. Ann Arbor, MI: University of Michigan Press.

Service, Elman R. 1962. *Primitive Social Organization: An Evolutionary Perspective.* New York: Random House.

Sheehan, Bernard W. 1973. *Seeds of Extinction: Jeffersonian Philanthropy and the American Indian.* New York: W. W. Norton.

Silverberg, Robert 1968. *Mound Builders of Ancient America; The Archaeology of a Myth.* Athens, OH: Ohio University Press.

Simpson, Christopher 1994. *Science of Coercion: Communication Research and Psychological Warfare, 1945–1960.* New York: Oxford University Press.

Simpson, Christopher 1998. Universities, Empire, and the Production of Knowledge: An Introduction. In *Universities and Empire: Money and Politics in the Social Sciences during the Cold War,* edited by Christopher Simpson, pp. xi–xxxiv. New York: New Press.

Simpson, George E. 1973. *Melville Herskovits.* New York: Columbia University Press.

Singer, Merrill 2000. Why I am not a Public Anthropologist. *Anthropology News,* vol. 41, no. 6, pp. 6–7. Arlington.

Singham, Archie W. and Shirley Hune 1986. *Non-Alignment in an Age of Alignments.* Westport, CT: Lawrence and Hill.

Siskind, Janet 1978. Kinship and Mode of Production. *American Anthropologist,* vol. 80, no. 4, pp. 860–72. Washington.

Smith, Dennis 1988. *The Chicago School: A Liberal Critique of Capitalism.* New York: St. Martin's Press.

Smith, Henry N. 1950. *Virgin Land: The American West as Symbol and Myth.* Cambridge, MA: Harvard University Press.

Smith, Henry N. 1967. *Popular Culture and Industrialism, 1865–1890.* New York: New York University Press.

Smith, Murphy D. 1983. Peter Stephen Du Ponceau and his Study of Languages. *Proceedings of the American Philosophical Society,* vol. 127, no. 3, pp. 143–79. Philadelphia.

Smith, Raoul N. 1979. The Interest in Language and Linguistics in Colonial and Federal America. *Proceedings of the American Philosophical Society,* vol. 123, no. 1, pp. 29–46. Philadelphia.

Smith, Samuel Stanhope 1810/1965. *An Essay on the Causes of the Variety of Complexion and Figure in the Human Species,* edited by Winthrop D. Jordan. Cambridge, MA: Harvard University Press.

Solomon, Barbara J. 1985. *In the Company of Educated Women: A History of Women in Higher Education in America*. New Haven, CT: Yale University Press.

Southern, David W. 1987. *Gunnar Myrdal and Black-White Relations: The Use and Abuse of An American Dilemma, 1944–1969*. Baton Rouge, LA: Louisiana State University Press.

Spencer, Frank 1979. *Aleš Hrdlička, M.D., 1869–1943; A Chronicle of the Life and Work of an American Physical Anthropologist*. Ph.D. Dissertation in Anthropology, University of Michigan. Ann Arbor, MI: University Microfilms 8007842.

Spencer, Frank 1997. American Association of Physical Anthropologists. In *History of Physical Anthropology: An Encyclopedia*, edited by Frank Spencer, vol. 1, pp. 60–3. New York: Garland Publishing.

Spicer, Edward A. 1977. Early Applications of Anthropology in North America. In *Perspectives on Anthropology 1976*, edited by Anthony F. C. Wallace, J. Lawrence Angel, Richard Fox, Sally McLendon, Rachel Sady, and Robert Sharer, pp. 116–41. Washington.

Spiller, Robert E., editor 1967. *The American Literary Revolution, 1783–1837*. New York: New York University Press.

Squier, Ephraim G. and Edwin H. Davis 1848. *Ancient Monuments of the Mississippi Valley*. Smithsonian Contributions to Knowledge, vol. 1. Washington.

Stanton, William 1960. *The Leopard's Spots: Scientific Attitudes toward Race in America, 1815–59*. Chicago, IL: University of Chicago Press.

Stephen, Lynn 1997a. The Zapatista Opening: The Movement for Indigenous Autonomy and State Discourses on Indigenous Rights in Mexico, 1970–1996. *Journal of Latin American Anthropology*, vol. 2, no. 2, pp. 2–41. Arlington.

Stephen, Lynn 1997b. Redefined Nationalism in Building a Movement for Indigenous Autonomy in Southern Mexico. *Journal of Latin American Anthropology*, vol. 3, no. 1, pp. 72–101. Arlington.

Stephens, John Lloyd 1841. *Incidents of Travel in Central America, Chiapas, and Yucatan*, 2 vols. New York: Harper and Brothers.

Steward, Julian H. 1941/1977. Determinism in Primitive Society? In *Evolution and Ecology: Essays in Social Transformation*, edited by Jane C. Steward and Robert F. Murphy, pp. 180–7. Urbana, IL: The University of Illinois Press.

Steward, Julian H. 1949. Cultural Causality and Law: A Trial Formulation of the Development of Early Civilizations. *American Anthropologist*, vol. 51, no. 1, pp. 1–27. Menasha.

Steward, Julian H. 1950. *Area Research: Theory and Practice*. Social Science Research Council Bulletin, no 63. New York.

Steward, Julian H. 1955 Theory of Culture Change. Urbana, IL: University of Illinois Press.

Steward, Julian H., editor 1956/1972 *The People of Puerto Rico: A Study in Social Anthropology*. Urbana, IL: University of Illinois Press.

Stocking, George W., Jr. 1968. *Race, Culture, and Evolution: Essays in the History of Anthropology*. Chicago, IL: The University of Chicago Press.

Stocking, George W., Jr. 1976. Ideas and Institutions in American Anthropology: Thoughts Toward a History of the Interwar Years. In *Selected Papers from the American Anthropologist*, edited by George W. Stocking, Jr., pp. 1–53. Washington.

Stocking, George W., Jr. 1979. *Anthropology at Chicago: Tradition, Discipline, Department*. Chicago, IL: The Joseph Regenstein Library, University of Chicago.

Stocking, George W., Jr. 1982. The Santa Fe Style in American Anthropology: Regional Interest, Academic Initiative, and Philanthropic Policy in the First Two Decades of the Laboratory of Anthropology. *Journal of the History of the Behavioral Sciences*, vol. XVIII, no. 1, pp. 3–19. Brandon.

Stocking, George W., Jr. 1985. Philanthropoids and Vanishing Cultures: Rockefeller Funding and the End of the Museum Era in Anglo-American Anthropology. In *Objects and Others: Essays on Museums and Material Culture*, edited by George W. Stocking, Jr. *History of Anthropology*, vol. 3, pp. 112–45. Madison, WI: University of Wisconsin Press.

Stocking, George W., Jr. 1995. *After Tylor: British Social Anthropology, 1888–1951*. Madison, WI: University of Wisconsin Press.

Sullivan, Paul 1989. *Unfinished Conversations: Mayas and Foreigners between Two Wars*. Berkeley, CA: University of California Press.

Sullivan, Robert 1990. Marxism and the "Subject" of Anthropology. *In Modernist Anthropology from Fieldwork to Text*, edited by Marc Manganaro, pp. 243–65. Princeton, NJ: Princeton University Press.

Suzuki, Peter T. 1980. A Retrospective Analysis of a Wartime "National Character" Study. *Dialectical Anthropology*, vol. 5, no. 1, pp.33–46. Dordrecht.

Suzuki, Peter T. 1981. Anthropologists in the Wartime Camps for Japanese Americans: A Documentary Study. *Dialectical Anthropology*, vol. 6, no. 1, pp. 23–60. Dordrecht.

Suzuki, Peter T. 1989. For the Sake of Inter-University Comity: The Attempted Suppression by the University of California of Morton Grozdins' Americans Betrayed. In *Views from Within: The Japanese American Evacuation and Resettlement Study*, edited by Yuji Ichioka, pp. 95–123. Berkeley, CA: University of California Press.

Sweezy, Paul M. 1997. More (or Less) on Globalization. *Monthly Review*, vol. 49, no. 4, pp. 1–4. New York.

Szwed, John F. 1979. The Ethnography of Ethnic Groups in the United States. In *The Uses of Anthropology*, edited by Walter R. Goldschmidt. American Anthropological Association Special Publication, no. 11, pp. 100–9. Washington.

Takaki, Ronald 1990. *Iron Cage: Race and Culture in 19th-Century America*. New York: Oxford University Press.

Tanner, J. M. 1959. Boas' Contributions to Knowledge of Human Growth and Form. In *The Anthropology of Franz Boas*, edited by Walter Goldschmidt. Memoir of the American Anthropological Association, no. 89, pp. 76–111. Menasha.

Tax, Sol 1937. The Municipios of the Midwestern Highlands of Guatemala. *American Anthropologist*, vol. 39, no. 3, pp. 423–44. Menasha.

Tax, Sol 1939. Culture and Civilization in Guatemalan Societies. *Scientific Monthly*, vol. LXVIII, no. 5, pp. 463–7. Washington.

Tax, Sol 1952. Economics and Technology. In *Heritage of Conquest*, edited by Sol Tax, pp. 43–76. Glencoe, IL: The Free Press.

Tax, Sol 1955. The Integration of Anthropology. *In Yearbook of Anthropology – 1955*, edited by William L. Thomas, Jr., pp. 313–28. New York: Wenner-Gren Foundation for Anthropological Research.

Tax, Sol, editor 1951/1960. Action Anthropology. In *Documentary History of the Fox Project, 1948–1959: A Program in Action Anthropology*, edited by Fred Gearing, Robert McC. Netting, and Lisa R. Peattie, pp. 167–71. Chicago, IL: University of Chicago Press.

Tax, Sol, editor 1953. *An Appraisal of Anthropology Today*. Chicago, IL: University of Chicago Press.

Tax, Sol, editor 1964. *Horizons in Anthropology*. New York: Aldine Publishers.

Tax, Thomas G. 1973. *The Development of American Archaeology, 1800–1879*. Ph.D. Dissertation in History, University of Chicago. Ann Arbor, MI: University Microfilms.

Taylor, Charles 1992. *Multiculturalism and "the Politics of Recognition."* Princeton, NJ: Princeton University Press.

Taylor, Walter W. 1948. *A Study of Archeology*. American Anthropological Association Memoir, no. 69. Menasha.

Tedlock, Barbara and Dennis Tedlock 1994. From the Editors. *American Anthropologist*, vol. 96, no. 3, pp. 521–2. Arlington.

Thomas, William L., Jr. 1955. Dissertations in Anthropology. In *Yearbook of Anthropology – 1955*, edited by William L. Thomas, Jr., pp. 701–52. Baltimore, MD: Printed for the Wenner-Gren Foundation for Anthropological Research by the Lord Baltimore Press.

Thompson, Laura 1951. *Personality and Government: Findings and Recommendations of the Indian Administration Research*. Mexico, DF: Ediciones del Instituto Indigenista Inter-Americano.

Trahair, Richard C. S. 1984. *The Humanist Temper: The Life and Work of Elton Mayo*. New Brunswick, NJ: Transaction Books.

Trautmann, Thomas R. 1987. *Lewis Henry Morgan and the Invention of Kinship*. Berkeley, CA: University of California Press.

Trigger, Bruce G. 1989. *A History of Archaeological Thought*. Cambridge, UK: Cambridge University Press.

Turner, Victor 1969. *The Ritual Process: Structure and Anti-Structure*. Chicago, IL: Aldine Publishing Company.

Turner, Victor 1974. *Dramas, Fields, and Metaphors: Symbolic Action in Human Society*. Ithaca, NY: Cornell University Press.

Turner, Victor 1975. Symbolic Studies. *Annual Review of Anthropology*, vol. 4, pp. 145–61. Palo Alto.

Tylor, Edward B. 1871/1958. *The Origins of Culture and Religion in Primitive Culture*, 2 vols. New York: Harper and Brothers.

van der Pilj, Kees 1984. *The Making of an Atlantic Ruling Class*. London, UK: Verso.

van Doren, Carl 1943. The Beginnings of the American Philosophical Society. *Proceedings of the American Philosophical Society*, vol. 87, no. 3, pp. 277–89. Philadelphia.

van Willigen, John 1993. *Applied Anthropology: An Introduction*, rev. edn. Westport, CT: Bergin and Garvey.

Vayda, Andrew P. and Bonied J. McCay 1975. New Directions in Ecology and Ecological Anthropology. *Annual Review of Anthropology*, vol. 4, pp. 293–306. Palo Alto.

Vélez-Ibáñez, Carlos G. 1996. *Border Visions: Mexican Cultures of the Southwest*. Tucson, AZ: University of Arizona Press.

Verdery, Katherine 1991. *Nationalist Ideology under Socialism: Identity and Cultural Politics in Ceausescu's Romania*. Berkeley, CA: University of California Press.

Villa Rojas, Alfonso 1945. *The Maya of East Central Quintana Roo*. Carnegie Institution of Washington Publication 559. Washington.

Vincent, Joan 1974. The Structuring of Ethnicity. *Human Organization*, vol. 33, no. 4, pp. 375–9. Washington.

Vincent, Joan 1986. System and Process, 1974–1985. *Annual Review of Anthropology*, vol. 15, pp. 99–119. Palo Alto.

Vogt, Evon Z. 1994. *Fieldwork among the Maya: Reflections on the Harvard Chiapas Project*. Albuquerque, NM: University of New Mexico Press.

Vogt, Evon Z. and Ethel Albert, editors 1966. *People of Rimrock: A Study of Values in Five Cultures*. Cambridge, MA: Harvard University Press.

Wakin, Eric 1992. *Anthropology Goes to War: Professional Ethics and Counterinsurgency in Thailand*. University of Wisconsin Center for Southeast Asian Studies Monograph no. 7. Madison.

Wallerstein, Immanuel 1974. *The Modern World-System*, Vol. 1, *Capitalist Agriculture and the Origins of the European World-Economy of the Sixteenth Century*. New York: Academic Press.

Wallerstein, Immanuel 1979. *The Capitalist World-Economy: Essays by Immanuel Wallerstein*. Cambridge, UK: Cambridge University Press.

Wallerstein, Immanuel 1997. The Unintended Consequences of Cold War Area Studies. In *The Cold War and the University: Toward an Intellectual History of the Postwar Years*, edited by André Schiffrin, pp. 195–233. New York: New Press.

Warner, W. Lloyd 1937. American Caste and Class. *American Journal of Sociology*, vol. XLII, no. 2, pp. 234–7. Chicago.

Warner, W. Lloyd 1940. Social Anthropology and the Modern Community. *American Journal of Sociology*, vol. XLVI, no. 6, pp. 785–96. Chicago.

Warner, W. Lloyd and Allison Davis 1939. A Comparative Study of American Caste. In *Race Relations and the Race Problem: A Definition and an Analysis*, edited by Edgar T. Thompson, pp. 219–45. Durham, NC: Duke University Press.

Washburn, Sherwood L. 1951a. The New Physical Anthropology. *Transactions of the New York Academy of Sciences*, ser. II, vol. 13, no. 7, pp. 298–304. New York.

Washburn, Sherwood L. 1951b. The Analysis of Primate Evolution with Particular Reference to the Origin of Man. In *Origin and Evolution of Man*. Cold Spring Harbor Symposia on Quantitative Biology, vol. XV, pp. 67–78. Cold Spring Harbor, NY: The Biological Laboratory

Washburn, Sherwood L. 1953. The Strategy of Physical Anthropology. In *Anthropology Today: An Encyclopedic Inventory*, edited by Alfred L. Kroeber, pp. 714–27. Chicago, IL: University of Chicago Press.

Washburn, Sherwood L. 1963. The Study of Race. *American Anthropologist*, vol. 65, no. 3, pp. 521–31. Menasha.

Washburn, Sherwood L. and Virginia Avis 1958. Evolution of Human Behavior. In *Behavior and Evolution*, edited by Anne Roe and George G. Simpson, pp. 421–36. New Haven, CT: Yale University Press.

Washburn, Wilcomb E. 1959. The Moral and Legal Justification for Dispossessing the Indians. In *Seventeenth-Century America: Essays in Colonial History*, edited by James. M. Smith, pp. 15–32. Chapel Hill, NC: The University of North Carolina Press.

Webster, Noah 1789. *Dissertations on the English Language, With Notes Historical and Critical*. Boston, MA: I. Thomas.

Webster, Steven 1990. The Historical Materialist Critique of Surrealism and Postmodernist Ethnography. In *Modernist Anthropology from Fieldwork to Text*, edited by Marc Manganaro, pp. 266–99. Princeton, NJ: Princeton University Press.

Weyant, Robert G. 1973. Helvétius and Jefferson: Studies of Human Nature and Government in the Eighteenth Century. *Journal of the History of the Behavioral Sciences*, vol. 9, no. 1, pp. 29–41. Brandon.

Whalen, Terence 1999. *Edgar Allan Poe and the Masses: The Political Economy of Literature in Antebellum America*. Princeton, NJ: Princeton University Press.

White, Leslie A. 1949 *The Science of Culture: A Study of Man and Civilization*. New York: Grove Press.

White, Leslie A. 1957 How Morgan Came to Write *Systems of Consanguinity and Affinity*. Papers of the Michigan Academy of Arts and Sciences, vol. XLII, pp. 257–68. Ann Arbor.

White, Leslie A. 1958 Introduction. In *Ancient Society*, by Lewis Henry Morgan, edited by Leslie A. White, pp. xiii–xlii. Cambridge, MA: Harvard University Press.

Whitney, William D. 1867/1971. Language and the Study of Language. In *Whitney on Language: Selected Writings of William Dwight Whitney*, edited by Michael Silverstein, pp. 7–110. Cambridge, MA: The MIT Press.

Whyte, William F. 1987. Organizational Behavior Research: Changing Styles of Research and Action. In *Applied Anthropology in America*, 2nd edn, edited by Elizabeth M. Eddy and William L. Partridge, pp. 159–83. New York: Columbia University Press.

Willey, Gordon R. 1953. *Prehistoric Settlement Patterns in the Virú Valley, Peru*. Bureau of American Ethnology Bulletin, no. 155. Washington.

Willey, Gordon R. 1960a. New World Prehistory. *Science*, vol. 131, no. 3393, pp. 73–86. Washington.

Willey, Gordon R. 1960b. Historical Patterns and Evolution in Native New World Cultures. In *Evolution After Darwin: The University of Chicago Centennial*, edited by Sol Tax, vol. II, *The Evolution of Man*, pp. 111–42. Chicago, IL: University of Chicago Press.

Willey, Gordon R. 1974. The Virú Valley Settlement Pattern Study. In *Archaeological Researches in Retrospect*, edited by Gordon R. Willey, pp. 149–78. Cambridge, MA: Winthrop Publishers.

Willey, Gordon R. and Philip Phillips 1958. *Method and Theory in American Archaeology*. Chicago, IL: The University of Chicago Press.

Willey, Gordon R. and Jeremy A. Sabloff 1993. *A History of American Archaeology*, 3rd edn. New York: W. H. Freeman and Company.

Willey, Thomas E. 1978. *Back to Kant: The Revival of Kantianism in German Social and Historical Thought, 1860–1914*. Detroit, MI: Wayne State University Press.

Williams, Brackette F. 1989. A Class Act: Anthropology and the Race to Nation across Ethnic Terrain. *Annual Review of Anthropology*, vol. 18, pp. 401–44. Palo Alto.

Williams, Vernon, J., Jr. 1989. *From a Caste to a Minority: Changing Attitudes of American Sociologists Toward Afro-Americans, 1896–1945*. Contributions in Afro-American and African Studies, no. 121. New York: Greenwood Press.

Williams, Vernon, J., Jr. 1996. *Rethinking Race: Franz Boas and his Contemporaries*. Lexington, KY: University Press of Kentucky.

Williams, William A. 1961. *The Contours of American History*. Cleveland, OH: World Publishing Company.

Williams, William A. 1972. *The Tragedy of American Diplomacy*, 2nd edn. New York: Dell Publishers.

Willis, William S., Jr. 1975. Franz Boas and the Study of Black Folklore. In *The New Ethnicity: Perspectives from Ethnology*, edited by John W. Bennett. 1973 Proceedings of the American Ethnological Society, pp. 307–34. St. Paul, MN: West Publishing Company.

Winkler, Allan M. 1978. *The Politics of Propaganda: The Office of War Information, 1942–1945*. New Haven, CT: Yale University Press.

Wolf, Eric R. 1955. Types of Latin American Peasantry: A Preliminary Discussion. *American Anthropologist*, vol. 57, no. 3, pp. 452–71. Menasha.

Wolf, Eric R. 1959. *Sons of the Shaking Earth*. Chicago, IL: University of Chicago Press.

Wolf, Eric R. 1969. *Peasant Wars of the Twentieth Century*. New York: Harper and Row.

Wolf, Eric R. 1980. They Divide and Subdivide, and Call It Anthropology. *The New York Times*, November 30, 1980, p. E9. New York.

Wolf, Eric R. 1982. *Europe and the People without History*. Berkeley, CA: University of California Press.

Woodbury, Richard B. 1973. *Alfred V. Kidder*. New York: Columbia University Press.

Woodbury, Richard B. 1993. *Sixty Years of Southwestern Archaeology: A History of the Pecos Conference*. Albuquerque, NM: University of New Mexico Press.

Wright, George F. 1892. *Man and The Glacial Period: With an Appendix on Tertiary Man by Prof. Henry W. Haynes*, 2nd edn. Akron, OH: Werner.

Wright, Robin M. 1988. Anthropological Presuppositions of Indigenous Advocacy. *Annual Review of Anthropology*, vol. 17, pp. 365–90. Palo Alto.

Wylie, Alison 1996. Alternative Histories: Epistemic Disunity and Political Integrity. In *Making Alternative Histories: The Practice of Archaeology in Non-Western Settings*, edited by Peter Schmidt and Thomas C. Patterson, pp. 255–72. Santa Fe, NM: SAR Press.

Index

Index

Index